THE EINSTEIN OF SEX

ALSO BY DANIEL BROOK

The Accident of Color:
A Story of Race in Reconstruction

A History of Future Cities

The Trap:
Selling Out to Stay Afloat in Winner-Take-All America

THE EINSTEIN OF SEX

Dr. Magnus Hirschfeld
Visionary of Weimar Berlin

DANIEL BROOK

W. W. NORTON & COMPANY
Independent Publishers Since 1923

Printed in the United States of America
First Edition

For information about permission to reproduce selections from this book, write to
Permissions, W. W. Norton & Company, Inc., 500 Fifth Avenue, New York, NY 10110

For information about special discounts for bulk purchases, please contact
W. W. Norton Special Sales at specialsales@wwnorton.com or 800-233-4830

Manufacturing by Sheridan
Book design by Chris Welch
Production manager: Anna Oler

ISBN 978-1-324-00724-1

W. W. Norton & Company, Inc.
500 Fifth Avenue, New York, NY 10110
www.wwnorton.com

W. W. Norton & Company Ltd.
15 Carlisle Street, London W1D 3BS

1 2 3 4 5 6 7 8 9 0

Für meine Nichte und ihre Generation

Fine specimens of humanity, those Germans, and to think I'm actually one of them!

—*Anne Frank,*
born 1929 in Frankfurt, Germany

Ain't nothing wrong with being a little gay. Everybody's a little gay.

—*Alana "Honey Boo Boo" Thompson,*
born 2005 in Georgia, USA

CONTENTS

A NOTE ON LANGUAGE

Language is evolving today, particularly the terms used to describe people's sexuality and gender identity. Certain terms that have been retired (e.g., "the third sex" or "transvestite") are included in this book when they are crucial to telling the story of events unfolding in an earlier era when such language was used. Otherwise, the author has used current language even as he knows it too may eventually come to seem dated and possibly, in unforeseen ways, insensitive.

Introduction

O Magnus Mysterium

Bust of Magnus Hirschfeld paraded at the book burning in Berlin, 1933.

IN 1896, PENNING his first gay-rights pamphlet, German-Jewish physician Magnus Hirschfeld staked a provocative claim: sexual orientation is a continuum. Between extremes of heterosexuality and homosexuality ranged innumerable shades in between.

A decade later, as a renowned Berlin psychotherapist, Hirschfeld theorized that each person is a mix of masculinity and femininity and opened the door to trans identity. "The sex of a person lies more in his mind than in his body," he wrote, "more in the brain than in the genitals."

In his final work, published posthumously in the Nazi years, Hirschfeld issued his last prophetic pronouncement. Writing in exile after a globe-spanning research trip, he declared that race is a social construction—a human invention, not a scientific discovery.

In his remarkable life, cut too short, Dr. Hirschfeld was more than a transformational thinker, he was a passionate activist as well. In World War I, he advocated for gay, lesbian, and trans individuals to serve openly in the German military. In the 1920s, he built his Institute for Sexual Science, which housed both the clinic where the world's first gender-affirming surgeries were performed and the sex museum that became Weimar Berlin's must-see tourist attraction. When the Nazis gained power and drove him abroad, he tried with his last breath to rally the allies he called "we anti-racists" against what he chillingly termed the "poison gas [of] racism."

He was world famous. As a celebrity sex therapist, Hirschfeld, with his trademark walrus moustache, made newsreel cameos. He gave interviews to newspapers everywhere from Seattle to Shanghai. As the intellectual impresario of Weimar Berlin, there was even a bawdy cabaret number about him, "Der Hirschfeld kommt!," that poked good-natured fun at the rumpled sexologist.

Above all, though, Hirschfeld was a visionary. He saw the natural world as one of seamless continua and endless variation, and we humans were part of it. For his theory of sexual relativity, he was dubbed the "Einstein of Sex." Flattered and humbled, a blushing Hirschfeld conceded that there was something to it. As he wrote in exile, "Though I have always protested against this comparison with the founder of the theory of relativity," there's an obvious parallel between Einstein's theory of relativity and "the view, sustained by me, that each human being [is] not absolutely but only relatively . . . male or female."

This theory could change your life. A Chinese journalist who interviewed Hirschfeld in Shanghai in 1931, told readers how it had changed his. "Whether you like it or not," wrote E. K. Moy of the *China Press*, "you bear certain characteristics of the opposite sex in more or less extent." In his own case, Moy confessed, he'd long been haunted by his "predilection for what is commonly recognized as a stereotypically feminine interest in flowers." But now, guided by Hirschfeld's theory of sexual relativity, he realized that such an interest "is natural and normal to me." From this seed of self-compassion, Moy explained, a wider compassion for everyone else blossomed. Making peace with one's own gender nonconformity—the inevitable queerness in oneself—led to an acceptance of the queerness in all others.

For those who think themselves "*normal*," Moy wrote, "a homosexual is regarded as a criminal; a person who cannot be happy unless he or she can wear the garments affected by the opposite sex, is a freak." But as Hirschfeld taught, "there is no *normal* male or female." Indeed, if each individual is composed of a unique assortment of qualities deemed masculine and those deemed feminine, the categories themselves collapse. What, after all, is so feminine about flower arranging? Or, for that matter, so masculine about journalism?

Traveling the globe, Hirschfeld discerned that race was relative too. He got welcomed into spaces in foreign-dominated Shanghai as a "European" and in America as a "white" person from which his native Germany now barred him as a "Semite." Yet he was the same Magnus Hirschfeld wherever he went. Racial categories, he now saw, were arbitrary creations conjured by those in power. Biologically, each person's race was a record of all the reproductive sex their far-flung ancestors had had, openly or in secret. Our race was as unique as our fingerprints.

Yet today the Einstein of Sex, once so famous and still so astonishingly ahead of his time, is little known. While Albert Einstein is justly renowned, his theories—even for those who can understand them—won't change your life. Try telling the gate agent that time is relative the next time you miss a flight. Meanwhile it is the Einstein of Sex whose transformative ideas focus on our everyday obsessions of identity and sexuality, the visionary who can help you understand who you are—from your complex ethnic background to your secret kinks—who has gone missing. Hirschfeld's 1907 pronouncement that "the sex of a person lies more in [the] mind than in [the] body" sounds like it was written last week. How do we not know him?

The Nazis, of course, with their fanatical insistence on strict gender roles and even stricter bloodlines, did plenty to destroy Hirschfeld. They nearly stoned him to death in the streets of Munich, chased him from Berlin, and raided his institute. On that infamous Berlin night in 1933, those were Hirschfeld's books they were burning. As they paraded a bust of Hirschfeld on a pike, illuminated by the flames of over ten thousand volumes seized from his institute's archive, one stormtrooper sneered that had Hirschfeld not already fled, they'd "string him up or beat him to death."

Yet even as they threatened Hirschfeld, the Nazis never disappeared him. Instead, they fulminated endlessly about their gay, Jewish, social democratic archenemy. Even as they shuttered his institute and destroyed documents from its archives—including some on which former patients, now prominent Nazis, had placed themselves on Hirschfeld's continuum of queerness—they continued to trot out Hirschfeld in their propaganda as "the most repulsive of all Jewish monsters."

Instead, it was Hirschfeld's ostensive allies, colleagues like Sigmund Freud and other well-meaning opponents of fascism who went silent on him, terrified that his gayness would discredit the cause of human freedom. This is why today we may know Hirschfeld's theory of sexual orientation as a continuum but call it the "Kinsey Scale" for Alfred Kinsey, the crew-cut Midwestern sex researcher who swiped Hirschfeld's concept decades later. And it is why we know the Nazi book burning so well that we can conjure the grainy newsreel footage in our minds, yet we were never taught whose books were being burned. For many historians and educators, Hirschfeld was until just recently too hot, too controversial, and, frankly, too queer to mention.

In fairness, it wasn't just Hirschfeld's liberal allies who didn't want to talk about his queerness; he himself didn't want to talk about it either. To be taken seriously as a theorist and advocate in his time and place, he had to present himself as a disinterested scientist whose personal life was beside the point. In his writings, he kept his gay identity studiously private, invariably writing about "the homosexuals" in the closest third person as "they," not "we." Playing the stodgy German man of science, for his theory of sexual relativity, he even came up with his own $e = mc^2$. Hirschfeld's complex factorial equation, when computed, shows that there are over forty-three million possible mixtures of masculinity and femininity in any given human, in effect, forty-three million possible genders.

Recovering Hirschfeld today requires reading like a sleuth. Luckily, he left quite a trail of breadcrumbs—tens of thousands of pages of books, pamphlets, articles, questionnaires, travel guides, and open letters. He also left the annual reports of the Scientific Humanitarian Committee, the queer-rights organization he founded and led, numerous photographs of the exhibits he mounted at his institute, and even footage from the 1919 gay-rights film he made, which miraculously survived the Nazis.

In his sprawling oeuvre, Hirschfeld's life, like his gayness, hides in plain sight. He writes, for example, of the "images and inscriptions by homosexuals [of] phalluses sketched with coal or pencil" that he "found scratched into [men's room] walls . . . all the way from Chicago to Tangier" to signal a cruising spot. From the chronology of his life, we know that he visited Chicago and Tangier as a gay man in his twenties during his first overseas trip. We can't know for sure what went down, but it was presumably something. In the gender-bending Weimar Berlin that he more than anyone created, he depicted trans nightlife spaces as if he were purely a researcher, not a participant. But from a colleague reminiscing long after his death we can infer that Magnus sometimes went in drag as "Auntie Magnesia" (*Tante Magnesia*), a dowdy feminine version of his buttoned-down self. Similarly, most of what we know about Hirschfeld's long-term partnerships with Berlin-born Karl Giese and Li Shiu Tong of Hong Kong, comes from gossipy descriptions by members of their circle. Among those dishing was Christopher Isherwood, the British writer behind *Goodbye to Berlin* (the novel that inspired the musical, *Cabaret*) who boarded at Hirschfeld's institute as a young gay expat in the 1920s. Hirschfeld feared that being known as a queer polyamorist would have discredited him. In his era, it surely would have. A century later, needing to read Hirschfeld between the lines can be frustrating. But it can also be fun.

It is an urgent task in our moment. Of late, Hirschfeld's intellectual project has been resurrected as every binary—gender, sexual orientation, race—is rightly interrogated anew. At the same time, the book bans are back and a resurgent fascist politics of "us" and "them" threatens us all. It's Hirschfeld's world we're living in, shouldn't we know the guy?

Yes. Now is the time to meet our Magnus.

Chapter 1

Born This Way

Magnus Hirschfeld's childhood home in Kolberg, Prussia.

IT WAS IDYLLIC, mostly. The baby came just in time for summer, on May 14, 1868. As the clouds cleared, the beach beckoned. The Baltic seashore in the tidy Prussian city of Kolberg was a mere stroll from the spacious family home, one of the ones by the park with a breezy second-floor verandah to take in the greenery.

To the rather unwieldy family name Hirschfeld—"deer field" in both German and Yiddish, a typical cognate in these kissing-cousin languages whose main difference is their alphabets—the proud parents appended the mellifluous moniker Magnus, Latin for "great."

Born in the right time and place, it seemed, Magnus was one lucky child. With an entourage of big sisters and a live-in maid, the baby boy of the family could count on a childhood of constant doting; two big brothers would be role models. While his sisters were groomed for good marriages, Magnus and his brothers were groomed for greatness.

And being born Prussian was a stroke of luck. Long lagging behind its neighbors to the west, Prussia had emerged from the Napoleonic Wars of the early 1800s as an economic and military powerhouse. It was now on the cusp of unifying all of Germany under it in a constitutional monarchy with universal male suffrage. It would achieve this goal in 1871 through the leadership of its indefatigable chancellor, Otto von Bismarck, with the King of Prussia, Wilhelm I, becoming the emperor (*kaiser*) of Germany. The nation's rise was so meteoric that political theorist Georg Wilhelm Friedrich Hegel proposed in all seriousness that modern Prussia was the culmination of world history, the very pinnacle of human civilization. His proposition was, of course, subject to debate. Some disagreed. But no one laughed.

Being born Jewish was, historically speaking, rather ominous. In Europe for the previous two millennia, it had often meant hard times or worse. But the Continent, it seemed, was changing. When Napoleon marched the egalitarian values of the French Revolution eastward to Kolberg in 1812, the port city was reopened to Jewish residents for the first time in over three centuries.

Soon Magnus's parents, Hermann and Friederike, gravitated to Kolberg's wider horizons. Both had been born in the sleepy inland villages of Pomerania, Prussia's easternmost province. The couple met in 1853 in Berlin, Prussia's capital, where Friederike was attending a girls' boarding school and Hermann was studying medicine. No one fretted over their decade-wide age gap. Conventional wisdom held that women should marry as soon as they reached adulthood—Friederike would be an eighteen-year-old bride—and men, when they had attained a stable profession, medicine being an ideal choice. That the pair were not too distantly related—Hermann's father was Friederike's great-uncle—was considered no bar to their union. The Jewish world of Pomerania had historically been tight-knit from a vicious cycle of bigotry and insularity, and the liberal opening after Napoleon now appeared to be over. In the words of one contemporary historian, in Germany, Jewish emancipation "had gone far [but] then stopped short." The most honored positions, like full professor in a university, were typically held just beyond the reach of even the most talented Jewish candidates; powerful public-sector jobs, like prosecutor, were entirely off-limits. Still, resentments rose as Prussian Jews took on more prominent roles in the newly integrated society and tribal nationalisms tempted those unmoved by the Enlightenment's bloodless universalism. Marrying in seemed to make everything simpler and safer.

Hermann and Friederike's generation—the first raised after the French-imposed emancipation—invented what it meant to be a secular Jew in the modern world. A diasporic people that at last had the freedom and wherewithal to visit far-flung relatives raised effortlessly worldly children. Habits of scholarship honed for centuries over Talmudic minutiae were now applied to every subject that could be studied. And no group defended the liberal creed of free inquiry, social equality, and equal opportunity more fiercely. For secular Jews, liberalism was worth dying for out of a clear-eyed estimation of the stakes. Without liberalism, their existence was impossible, their very lives were in danger. As one contemporary scholar has observed of the era, "in Berlin . . . liberalism and Judaism became almost indistinguishable."

As a medical student, Hermann had risked life and limb for liberalism. In 1848, liberals and radicals rose up in an ill-fated bid to secure the liberties the Enlightenment had promised—the right to vote, to assemble, to speak and publish freely. As urban protests swept Europe and were met with violent repression, Hermann triaged patients wounded on the barricades of Berlin. Even after settling down in Kolberg to raise a family and treat more mundane maladies—as a spa town acclaimed for its spring water and even its mud, it drew a steady stream of convalescing patients—Hermann continued to defend the liberal faith. Every Friday, his column appeared in the *Pomeranian News*, offering a summary of the week's events from a liberal-nationalist perspective, backing a powerful and unified Germany with equal rights for all. Living the Enlightenment faith that human reason could ameliorate social ills, Hermann served as a municipal public health official where he worked to build Kolberg's first drinking-water system and expand its sewers. Unobservant but public about his background, Hermann served as president of the city's Jewish community.

While the move to Kolberg had been a leap into the wider world for his parents, the locale felt constricting to Magnus and his siblings. Kolberg wasn't exactly provincial. His father had worked hard to modernize the city, and it was never quite as sheltered as it seemed. Sailing out from Kolberg, a ship could head through the straits between Denmark and Sweden and then, in theory, anywhere—Tangier, Cape Town, New York, even Rio. And for all its loud assertions of Germanness, Kolberg was more of a crossroads than it let on. Nestled at the convergence of Western Europe, Eastern Europe, and Scandinavia, the city had changed hands many times over for centuries. A mix of Catholic, Protestant, and Jewish, Germanic, Slavic, and Nordic, Kolberg was an odd fit in an age of rising nationalism. (What was, in Magnus's time, a proud part of Germany is now in Poland and called Kołobrzeg.) As a tourist town, it seemed to Magnus like the summertime vacationers all lived somewhere more interesting where more important things happened. Well-to-do Berliners flocked in annually on a newly built train line to stay at grand seaside hotels, but they left at the end of the season. Visitors went on and on about the freshness of the sea air in little Kolberg, but as an old German expression put it, it was city air that made you free. Young Magnus couldn't help but want out.

Magnus was captivated and confused by his first inklings of the wider world. His very first memory was of French POWs being marched through the streets of Kolberg during the Franco-Prussian War. These Frenchmen were the enemy and yet his father was giving them medical treatment. Why heal the enemy in a war, he wondered. Wasn't the whole point of a war to kill the enemy? Even stranger, the Hirschfeld home harbored an enemy. The family's maid was from France. Somehow the French were the enemy, but the maid was not.

And the maid raised other questions Magnus couldn't answer. Behind her back, the Hirschfeld children called her Madame Moustache, poking fun at her fuzzy upper lip. Young Magnus learned never to utter this to her face. Apparently, it was insulting since men had mustaches and women did not. Except that the maid was almost certainly a woman, and she most definitely had a mustache.

At age ten, Magnus resolved to explore the world. The stocky little boy with thick dark hair hatched a grand plan to run away from home. First, he would walk to Hamburg, Germany's greatest port city, and then onwards to Paris, "the capital of the nineteenth century," as German-Jewish polymath Walter Benjamin would dub it. Despite Europe's nationalistic fervor—every country a contrasting color on the map—the route had few natural boundaries. Europe needed its fearsome border guards precisely because the landscape has so few physical features—raging rivers, imposing mountain ranges, and the like—to separate one country from the next. Given enough time, walking from Kolberg to Paris was eminently doable. Just not for a ten-year-old. After three days, Magnus gave up and returned home, much to the relief of Hermann, Friederike, and Madame Moustache.

Even at age ten, Paris already asserted a magnetic pull for Magnus. It wasn't just the mysterious presence in his household of a maid from France. For German Jews, France—at once both their conqueror and their liberator—was captivating. The French revolutionaries of 1789 were the first to declare all citizens equal regardless of religion, striking down myriad regulations that had restricted Jews physically, to officially designated ghettos, and socially, to second-class status.

Magnus was also indebted to France in another way. As adolescence set in, he knew that he was sexually attracted to other boys. And just as the French Revolution had emancipated Europe's Jews, it had liberated Europe's gays. The new legal code safeguarded the rights of the individual: it specified that no sex act could be criminal as long as it was consensual. Just as the state would no longer dictate which body of religious or political ideas one subscribed to, it wouldn't regulate which human bodies one was attracted to. The French Revolution was also a sexual revolution. Under the Old Regime in France, men who had sex with men lived in terror of a barbaric three-strikes law. For the first offense, the testicles were surgically removed; on the second, the penis sliced off; on the third, the mutilated man was publicly burned alive. Gay men in Prussia did not even get these second chances; they were burned alive for the first offense.

Napoleon imposed France's revolutionary legal code on the territories he seized, opening up new life possibilities for gays and Jews (and gay Jews). But after Napoleon's defeat, there was backsliding on both fronts. Within the new secular outlook, old prejudices could find new rationales. Individual rights, especially the rights of minorities, would continue to be contested. They would still need defenders.

The day after Magnus turned three, in 1871, the just-unified German state recriminalized homosexuality for the first time since the Napoleonic Age. Paragraph 175 of the German Criminal Code made consensual sex between men a crime, punishable by up to five years in prison.

In 1880, when Magnus was thirteen, a conservative group petitioned Chancellor Bismarck urging him to revoke the religious freedom law that had enshrined the emancipation of Germany's Jews. The petitioners argued that Germany needed to be emancipated *from* its Jews, whom they viewed as an alien, parasitic community. Before the modern age, Judaism had been viewed by the Church as a religious rival to Christianity, and Jews were deemed heretics. In this view, a Jew was a person—like all people, created in the image of God—who, sadly, harbored misguided beliefs about said God. In this scheme, a Jew could cease to be a Jew by converting. But in the 1880 petitioners' conception, being Jewish was a permanent condition that could not be negated through conversion, secularization, or intermarriage. In their view, Judaism was not a religion but an incurable hereditary condition—a "race"—and the key social distinction was not between Jews and Christians but between Jews ("Semites") and Germans ("Aryans"). Many of the nearly three hundred thousand petition signers rallied to the League of Antisemites, which had been founded by Wilhelm Marr, in 1879, shortly after he divorced his half-Jewish wife. In the racial struggle for dominance, Marr fretted, the Jews had lapped the Germans and now, occupying formerly forbidden positions of authority, had all but taken over the country. He urged his racial brethren to wake up, fight back, and stop race-mixing, as he had done with his recent divorce.

Bismarck pointedly ignored the petition and Germany's religious freedom law remained in force. But this new "scientific" form of antisemitism would endure. In the elections the following year, right-wing parties ousted liberals to attain a majority in the unified Germany's parliament for the first time.

This new antisemitism dovetailed with a new "scientific" homophobia. In the Middle Ages, gays were considered sinners. Of course, in the teachings of the Church, all people were sinners, each yielding to a different cocktail of temptations. Some coveted thy neighbor's wife and became adulterers; others coveted thy neighbor's ass and became thieves; still others coveted thy neighbor—they became "sodomites." But in the new scheme, the homosexual became a medical subject—a person whose psychology had somehow gone awry, usually due to a traumatic event during childhood that had turned them gay. Through a sentence in a penitentiary, an individual could reflect on the roots of their homosexuality and hopefully overcome their urges. While the secular, scientific outlook saw homosexuality as a fixable condition and Judaism as an incurable state, it allowed both anti-Jewish and anti-gay prejudices to shape-shift and endure in a modern world that had initially promised liberation.

The appeal to impartial science made these claims hard to counter. German universities were ruled by a new and imperious figure: the erudite, bespectacled *Herr Doktor Professor.* Students would file into his class and dutifully scribble down every word of his lecture as if it were the gospel truth. Questions were only asked of him with the greatest deference. In place of the infallible Church, a new priestly caste had set itself up as the arbiters of reality. And to join their ranks, being a Christian was not much less of a qualification than it had been for becoming a priest; being straight was arguably even more a requirement for joining the faculty than it had ever been for joining the priesthood.

Around the time of the antisemitic petition, Hermann and Friederike enrolled their precocious son at the Kolberg Cathedral High School. The academy was nominally affiliated with the town's cathedral, a massive redbrick pile that dominated Kolberg as if it were still the Middle Ages. Founded as Catholic, it had been reconsecrated Lutheran following the Reformation. There was no way around it: the Cathedral School was the best academy in Kolberg, and it was not unusual for secular Jewish families to send their sons there. Each school day, young Magnus headed to school crossing Kolberg's central square, the Kaiserplatz.

The smattering of Christian theology that came with the pedagogy didn't faze Magnus. As was typical for secular German-Jewish families of their social stratum, the Hirschfelds blended a cultural Jewishness of Friday night gatherings at grandma's house for chicken schnitzel with fulsome celebrations of Christmas in their home as a nonreligious winter festival. Magnus always loved the holiday season, especially decorating the tree and singing the carols. What rattled young Magnus at school was the rampant homophobia of the student body. Of the roughly two hundred boys enrolled, it seemed that only two besides Magnus were gay, one of whom was mercilessly teased with a girl's first name. Magnus, presenting as notably unflamboyant, was spared the worst, but he smarted at his all-male academy's push to inculcate and police masculine norms.

Beyond the walls of the Cathedral School, Bismarck's Germany was a land of strict gender roles. Urban space itself was gendered. On the beachfront in Kolberg, men and women were directed to different sections for bathing despite their farcically full-coverage swimwear. Only in a small designated "family bathing area" could they intermingle under the alibi that they were doing it for the children. In a society projecting military strength and unification through what Bismarck called "blood and iron," an overperformance of masculinity was mandatory and taken to absurd lengths. The perpetually mustachioed Chancellor Bismarck was fond of appearing in full military regalia crowned by a *pickelhaube*, a hardhat topped by a shiny metal phallic symbol. But, of course, no one could publicly describe it as such. While the leader of the new Germany pranced around with what was, essentially, a dildo on his head, the people expressed their loyalty by remaining straight-faced. It was like living in a real-life version of the Hans Christian Andersen fairy tale "The Emperor's New Clothes."

For a queer teen like Magnus, German society felt like a straitjacket. Save for a fleeting liberal moment after the French Revolution, homosexuality had gone directly from a sin to a psychiatric disorder. This thinking was embedded in the German language itself: The German word for straight was *normalsexuell*. There was no vocabulary for expressing same-sex attraction as anything other than abnormal, deviant.

Yet as young Magnus learned as a student in the Cathedral School, in other times and places same-sex attraction had been considered normal. Embedded in the classical Greek and Latin curriculum Magnus studied was a deeply accepting take on homosexuality—one that went far beyond even that of revolutionary France. The modern French idea was that gays, like Jews, were minorities who deviated from the norm but were nonetheless entitled to tolerance; the ancient Greek idea was that same-sex attraction was to be expected. In ancient Greece, the notion that men would be attracted to handsome men was assumed with the same blitheness that men being attracted to beautiful women was in Magnus's Germany.

Implicit in an endless number of ancient texts, same-sex attraction was explicit in many. Even in the most bigoted corners of nineteenth-century Europe, there was no denying that the ancient poet Sappho of Lesbos, with her odes to female beauty, was a "sapphic" "lesbian." Even those uncomfortable with Greco-Roman sexual mores had to acknowledge them. Christian conservatives argued that queer tolerance had been the fatal flaw in these otherwise advanced civilizations which caused them to collapse in sodomite decadence.

Of all ancient texts, perhaps the clearest explication of same-sex attraction is Plato's *Symposium*, the classic Socratic dialogue on the nature of love. Set at an Athenian dinner party, a few drinks into the night, the handsome young Alcibiades confesses that he'd once tried and failed to seduce his fellow guest, Socrates the philosopher. For openly bisexual Socrates, it was only a steely commitment to the life of the mind that allowed him to resist Alcibiades's advances. Everyone at the table understood the temptation. Alcibiades looked like a god who'd wandered down off Mt. Olympus.

As the party progresses, each guest is asked to offer a theory of love. Since same-sex attraction was a fact of life, no more notable than opposite-sex attraction, every theory of love needed to account for it. Taking the floor, the comedic playwright Aristophanes presented his origin myth of love. "In the beginning," Aristophanes explains, human beings were eight-limbed creatures like conjoined twins. "The shape of each human being was completely round, with back and sides in a circle; they had four hands each, as many legs as hands, and two faces, exactly alike, on a rounded neck. Between the two faces, which were on opposite sides, was one head with four ears. There were two sets of sexual organs." As Aristophanes explains, some of these double humans were made of a male and a female, some of two males, and some of two females.

Zeus grew jealous of these powerful creatures, who could move very fast by turning cartwheels on all eight limbs, so he hatched a plan to cut them down to size. The king of the gods sliced each creature in half.

"Now," Aristophanes went on, "since their natural form had been cut in two, each one longed for its own other half, and so they would throw their arms about each other, weaving themselves together, wanting to grow together." Those whose origins were in the half-man/half-woman creatures became heterosexuals; those whose origins lay in the all-male duos became gay men who "love men and enjoy lying with men and being embraced by men"; and "women who are split from a woman," Aristophanes concludes, "are oriented more towards women, and lesbians come from this class."

One can only imagine the awkward jokes and uncomfortable silences that would ensue when a text like this was taught at Kolberg Cathedral High School—and how liberating the class still must have felt to Magnus. Reading ancient authors offered him hope. First, they revealed that human society had been structured differently in the past and thus could be structured differently in the future. And second, they offered a model of brave social critique. After all, the genius of Socrates's social criticism was why his words were still being read in Magnus's time, two millennia after his execution.

Smarting against the strict gender roles of his own society, young Magnus thrilled at watching Socrates challenge the gender roles of his native Athens and seeing the naysayers flail. In *The Republic*, a philosophical disquisition on the ideal state, Socrates, circa 375 BCE, draws a key distinction between biological sex and sociological gender. Fundamentally, as Socrates puts it, men and women "differ only in this respect, that the females bear children while the males beget them." This being the sole distinction, his acknowledgement that men tend to be physically stronger than women comes with the crucial caveat that there are, of course, many strong women (and many weak men). Logic dictates, Socrates argues, that in an ideal state, strong women would be enlisted in the military. Similarly, in a just state, equal education would be available to all, and the wisest women, like the wisest men, would be entrusted with political power. This proposition was at odds with the realities of ancient Athens just as it was with Bismarck's Germany. Both societies stifled educational opportunities for women no matter how intelligent. Magnus witnessed his brilliant big sister, the novelist and suffragist Franziska Mann (née Hirschfeld), in particular, bridling at such restrictions.

In Socrates, Magnus found a role model. A man with a beautiful mind who was hardly a looker was easy for Magnus, a young person already saddled with his first pair of clunky glasses, to identify with. Like Magnus, Socrates lived in an arrogant society. But Socrates could make arrogant Athenians talk themselves through their assumptions and leave them hog-tied in their own rhetorical knots. For all their differences, if you squinted, you could see ancient Athens and modern Germany as parallel societies whose outsized self-confidence masked myriad injustices and insanities. That Socrates was ultimately put to death by his fellow Athenians was perhaps not a fact to dwell on for too long.

Modernity, as conceived in Bismarck's Germany, was a devil's bargain. In theory, all could participate—but only at the price of assimilating, slicing off deviant parts of one's identity. The physical maiming of the Middle Ages was supplanted by a new modern maiming of the self that was in some ways more disturbing since it had to be self-inflicted. The unspoken assumption that the straight Aryan Christian male was the neutral arbiter of reality left little room for Magnus in the public square. Guided by the idea that no one can be a judge in his own case, few would take seriously a plea for gay rights from a gay author or an argument for Jewish equality penned by a Jew.

This struck Magnus as absurd and unfair. Was he really that different? Yes, he had a few more holidays on the calendar than his Christian peers. So what? And he was more into boys than into girls. What of it? Did this somehow make him so irredeemably different that he couldn't fully participate in his own society? Did these incidental, luck-of-the-draw qualities estrange him from the rest of humanity? At the very least, wasn't that *his* decision to make? How could someone else impose it on him? What gave them that frightening power?

In this formative phase, Magnus found fellowship with one of the few gay students at the Cathedral School, Richard Kantorowicz. The scion of a wealthy German-Jewish merchant family, Richard had spent his early childhood in his hometown of Posen, Prussia (now Poznan, Poland), but, beset by chronic sinus problems, he was sent to Kolberg for the fresh air. A worldly child with an intellectual bent, Richard gravitated to Magnus and the bookish Hirschfeld home. For the final years of high school, Richard moved in as a kind of foster child.

In their late high school years, the two spent innumerable hours together walking and talking along the seafront promenade. Their discussions ranged from literature and science to history and politics. As Magnus later reflected, his interest in history and politics really constituted a single interest: "My historical inclination . . . was transferred . . . to the historical currents of the present, which are usually called 'politics.' " But on their walks, the pair never spoke of sex—a rare conversational gap for two teenagers—perhaps out of mutual fear of the other's reaction. Their youthful relationship was a chaste one; Magnus maintained that he didn't even realize Richard was also gay until they were adults.

Both boys quietly struggled with what to do with their lives. Like many gay males born into late-nineteenth-century Germany, threatened by Paragraph 175, Richard saw no place for himself in his homeland. A few years later, he would expatriate to Africa as an explorer.

Envisioning a career, Magnus was torn between journalism and the family métier, medicine, between becoming a man of letters and a man of science. Long tasked with fetching the Cologne newspaper every evening for his father, Magnus would devour the paper on the way home. In adolescence, he'd begun submitting unsolicited articles by mail. Only after publication did the editor realize that his Kolberg contributor was a high school student.

Magnus's father had modelled a multifaceted career, serving as a physician, public health official, and newspaper columnist—and Magnus was inspired by his father's example that one could be both a thinker and a doer. But he would have to chart his future without Hermann's guidance. In the summer of 1885, while Magnus was still in high school, his father died of kidney failure. Along with the grief, with the sole breadwinner gone, the family finances grew precarious. Magnus's sisters made ends meet in Kolberg by turning the family house into a bed-and-breakfast for tourists.

In 1887, after several uncles and an aunt stepped up to support Magnus through higher education, he left for college. Taking a stab at independence, he initially rejected the family tradition of medicine, studying comparative language at the University of Breslau (now Wroclaw, Poland). The year before his arrival, the college had been rocked by a flareup of antisemitism. Christian students took to slandering their Jewish classmates with bigoted invective and then denying them the gentlemanly "satisfaction" (*Satisfaktionsfähigkeit*) of an avenging fencing duel, since a Jew, as they saw it, could never be a gentleman. On his official registration at the university, Magnus changed his religion from "Jewish" to "dissident." Was he was seeking to duck the tensions by not enlisting with a tribe? Or asserting that his deepest faith was in the right to think for himself? Or a bit of both? As antisemitism continued to stalk him—his dark curls, glasses, and last name gave him nowhere to hide—Magnus later found "satisfaction" in helping to found a Jewish dueling fraternity.

Practical concerns soon brought Magnus back to the family's traditions. In 1889, he transferred to study medicine at the University of Strasbourg. Now he was literally walking in his big brothers' footsteps, training to become a physician at the school where they both had graduated, one as a doctor and one as a pharmacist. But Strasbourg, a French-German border city that had been annexed by Germany after the Franco-Prussian War, still felt constricting.

Seeking a balance between meeting family expectations and realizing his own, Magnus decided to study medicine in a metropolis. He transferred to Berlin University, Hermann's alma mater, and hoped to study human sexuality. The classes were stultifying. Any deviations from the *normalsexuell* standard were addressed only in whispers as "perversions." As Magnus later recounted, "as many colleges as I attended, I hardly ever heard the expression 'sexual' from the mouth of a professor." Even in anatomy class, chalkboard diagrams of the reproductive system would be studiously erased at the end of class lest students for the next lecture catch a glimpse. Sex was undeniably a part of medicine, but the medical faculty did their best to avoid it.

Only once in his entire medical school career did Magnus hear homosexuality addressed in an academic setting. A doctor who viewed homosexuality and pedophilia as inseparable included same-sex attraction in his lecture series on mental disorders. Each week, this professor would lecture on a different type of "insanity," often presenting his views as he poked and prodded a "morality criminal" on loan from a local asylum or penitentiary. Being a proudly modern man of science, the expert debunked the conventional wisdom that "pederasts" were physically deformed—an earlier theory held that gay men had funnel-shaped anuses. Instead, he speculated, same-sex attraction was acquired through excessive masturbation during adolescence, possibly in response to trauma. The dread Magnus felt sitting through this lecture must have been unbearable. Three decades later he could still describe the lecture in detail.

Outside of class, life in Berlin was more stimulating. Magnus soon immersed himself in its wider cultural currents. He began a lifelong friendship with August Bebel, the chair of Germany's Social Democratic Party, who, like Magnus, was keenly interested in the relationship between gender and politics. Bebel's 1879 book, *Women and Socialism*, had been one of the first to challenge the rigid gender roles of modern Germany and argue that women's emancipation was integral to the emancipation of humanity. But Berlin was not yet the gay mecca or cultural hub it would become, and Magnus was drawn south to Munich, then a more vibrant city artistically and culturally. In the Bavarian capital, Magnus thrived, meeting expatriate Norwegian playwright Henrik Ibsen and becoming close to literary critic Leo Berg. Long sympathetic to queer rights, Berg would become a vocal defender of gay Irish writer Oscar Wilde during his 1895 trial.

An older and more confident Magnus returned to Berlin in 1890 to write his medical thesis. He was advised by a faculty committee that included Rudolf Virchow, a noted physician and anthropologist who had also taught his father. A political liberal, Virchow had bravely spoken out against Paragraph 175 when it was first proposed. The state board of medical advisors which he chaired put out a statement arguing that there were no "reasons why sex between men should be punished by law when other forms of illicit relations [such as adultery] are not." Given the overall climate in academia, Magnus decided against engaging a sexual topic and wrote his medical school thesis on the effects of influenza on the nervous system.

In 1892, Magnus graduated. Becoming licensed to practice medicine required passing the state medical examination. Likely buoyed by his uncles' and aunt's largesse, Magnus spent a stretch studying for the exams in Paris, the city he had long dreamed of running away to. There he found easy entrée to the city's German-Jewish expat scene but found even within it strains of homophobia. He was also put off by what he regarded as their insular, provincial responses to antisemitism—a Jewish-nationalist politics that tacitly accepted the idea that Jews could never truly be Germans or Frenchmen.

In 1893, Magnus passed the licensure exam and officially became the newest in a long line of Dr. Hirschfelds. Feeling himself a poor fit for the medical world, rather than open a medical practice, he bolted to take a job as an overqualified cub reporter for a newspaper in Hamburg.

"Inwardly," he later wrote, "I've [always] felt more closely and essentially connected to journalists, men of letters, writers, poets and artists than I have to doctors." Thinkers like Ibsen, Bebel, and Berg saw more deeply than the medical establishment even when engaging ostensibly scientific questions. Tellingly, the most important German gay rights advocate up to that point, Karl Heinrich Ulrichs, had been a lawyer, not a doctor. Ulrichs had bravely called for gay equality at an Association of German Jurists conference in 1867—and been heckled off the stage.

Ulrichs spent the 1860s and 1870s bravely publishing books and pamphlets advocating for gay rights, but worsening homophobia made selling them or even keeping copies of them a daring act. Ulrichs was never mentioned in any of Magnus's medical school classes. In fact, Magnus didn't hear about Ulrichs's earlier work until he'd finished medical school, learning of him through a whisper network of older members of Germany's gay community.

In Ulrichs's scheme, homosexuals were people whose psyches did not match their bodies. He called them "Uranians" or "inverts." A gay man (*Urning*), Ulrichs believed, had a woman's psyche in a man's body; analogously, a lesbian (*Urningin*) had a man's psyche in a female body. His terms were of ancient Greek derivation, lifted from Plato's *Symposium*. Hirschfeld would build on Ulrich's thinking, which viewed gay men and lesbians as "countersexuals," to develop his overarching theory of "sexual intermediaries" in which every person is their own unique mix of masculinity and femininity.

Neither Ulrichs's theory that gay men had women's souls nor the medical faculty's conceptualization of homosexuality as a form of insanity linked to pedophilia and trauma jibed with Magnus's experience. Magnus was gay but not particularly feminine; the concept of "inversion" seemed far-fetched, at least in his case. He was attracted to men but not to children, so the idea that homosexuality tracked with pedophilia struck him as pure slander. As for heredity, his extended family were all, as far as he could tell, straight, rather boringly so. He did entertain the notion that his gayness might be nature's way of ensuring that he, the product of his parents' inbreeding, didn't reproduce. But why then were his siblings straight?

If homosexuality was caused by childhood trauma, there's no way Magnus would have ended up gay. His upbringing had been achingly, comically, almost unbearably normal. There was his professional father—a breadwinner who excelled at work but still had time to serve as a pillar of the community. There was his loving mother, with a brood and a maid. And then there were three little boys, all following in their father's footsteps to become doctors, while the sisters were prepared for broods and maids of their own. The only real trauma was his father's death. But he was nearly eighteen by then, and he'd been gay as long as he could remember.

Adulthood augured a queasy mix of pressure and boredom, and Magnus found a way to delay it all. One of his brothers, Emanuel, had moved to America after completing his medical studies, settling in suburban Chicago. Emanuel wangled Magnus an invitation to give a lecture in New York on "The Natural Way of Living," assuring his little brother that his respect for natural remedies was more acceptable in American medical circles than in European ones. Once in New York, Magnus planned to travel the country as a newspaper stringer.

By happenstance, the year Magnus passed his medical examination, 1893, Chicago would be hosting the world's fair. The World's Columbian Exposition had been planned for the four hundredth anniversary of Columbus's voyage to the New World in 1892, but the Americans, not being Germans, had fallen a year behind schedule. The Old World had long been captivated by the New, particularly the metropolis on the shores of Lake Michigan that had burned to the ground in 1871 only to bounce back as the fastest-growing city in the history of the world. The expo offered Magnus a surefire story to sell to German newspapers. With his immigrant brother already there, he had a place to land. On August 27, 1893, Magnus set sail from Hamburg for a destination that billed itself as "the land of the free and the home of the brave." It must have sounded appealing. He knew he wanted to be free. Hopefully, he could be brave as well.

Chapter 2

In Don't-Ask, Don't-Tell America

"The White City" built for the World's Columbian Exposition, Chicago, 1893.

AS MAGNUS SAILED into New York harbor, a bronze-skinned Statue of Liberty welcomed him to melting-pot America. Not far from the docks, in the shadows of the Brooklyn Bridge—a seductive blend of strength and elegance—lay the most densely populated neighborhoods in the world. In Chinatown, Magnus could lose himself in the fantasy that his boat had somehow gone the other way around the world, while a few blocks north, in Kleindeutschland ("Little Germany"), he could reminisce with a taste of his homeland. Down by the river, on the teeming streets of the Jewish Lower East Side, he could hear echoes of the cloistered Yiddish-speaking Eastern European world that his assimilationist grandparents had left behind.

Established New Yorkers uptown dismissed these neighborhoods as "ghettos," but that was something of a misnomer. They weren't walled, and after a few years in the New World, Magnus came to see, immigrants became locals who would be unrecognizable in their native lands on account of their Americanized "appearance, language, dress, attitude, and education." As he later poetically mused on this phenomenon, "Life kneads the dough." Certainly once the urges of adolescence bubbled up, the American-born teenagers raised in these tenements paid little heed to the ethnic borderlines that meant so much to the older generation. Gender lines blurred, too.

This city of strangers from all over the world was sexy, and everyone, it seemed, was getting with everyone else. Right in the center of Manhattan sat the fabled cruising grounds of Central Park—a perfect rectangle on the map but a tangle of shady wooded pathways within. Below the belt of 14th Street, gay bars beckoned, operating as open secrets. The Slide, a basement dive in Greenwich Village, drew crowds nightly till dawn who brushed off the mainstream press's homophobic slander. A short jaunt east, on the seedier Bowery, the famed Excise Exchange drag bar scandalized with its clientele of "MALES WHO BLEACH THEIR HAIR," as a headline in the New York *World* screeched shortly before Magnus arrived in town. The paper gasped over bar patrons who "imitate the dress and manner of women—paint their faces and eyebrows . . . wear bracelets and address each other by female names" before repairing to the establishment's upstairs "assignation annex" for illicit trysts.

Even more scandalous was the Golden Rule Pleasure Club on West 3rd Street, a playful pun on the biblical Golden Rule—"do unto others as you'd have them do unto you." Looking innocent enough from the outside, the four-story brick building contained a long interior hallway lined with small sparsely furnished rentable rooms. As a New York vice detective recorded in his 1894 memoir, each room came with "a youth, whose face was painted, eyebrows blackened and whose airs were those of a young girl." These hustlers, who had all been assigned male at birth, called each other "by women's names" and used "high falsetto voice[s]."

With his insatiable curiosity, both intellectual and sexual, Magnus squeezed in trips to Boston and Philadelphia where he found more *sotto voce* queer scenes. In the Puritan and Quaker strongholds, an informant confided, "a great deal goes on" but typically in private get-togethers. Trans scenes were even more on the downlow. A few years before Magnus's journey, a police crackdown in Washington, DC, obliterated the Black drag ball scene that had been run by William Dorsey Swann, the self-proclaimed "queen of drag," who'd been born enslaved in antebellum Maryland. Invitations to this secretive world generally came in whispers from trusted friends or from contacts at the capital's Black YMCA, which had been founded by free people of color before the Civil War. Ever diligent, Magnus contacted trans individuals in New York and, later in his trip, in Chicago and San Francisco as well. Like the reporter he was, he relied on tips from German expat friends and friends of friends and spent time in the neighborhoods they were known to frequent.

After his natural remedies lecture in New York and his wider American explorations, Hirschfeld met up with his brother Emanuel in Chicago and settled in. On paper, the Midwest was an incredibly repressive, homophobic place. In Chicago, what the local statute books dubbed "the infamous crime against nature" was a felony; "sodomy" convicts in Illinois lost their right to vote and to serve on juries. But out on the streets, the state's great metropolis was a meat market. In broad daylight, gay men spotted each other by walking the streets downtown wearing a red tie, an open-secret uniform. As one local observer explained in an 1890s account, "It is red that has become almost a synonym for sexual inversion [homosexuality], not only in the minds of the inverts themselves, but in the popular mind. To wear a red necktie on the street is to invite remarks from newsboys and others—remarks that have the practices of inverts for their theme. A friend told me once that when a group of street-boys caught sight of the red necktie he was wearing they sucked their fingers in imitation of fellatio."

Sexual freedom via urban anonymity had always been part of Chicago's allure. The City of Big Shoulders began its epic boom when single men poured in during the Civil War to work in wartime industries. Savvy entrepreneurs sprang up to cater to the full gamut of their proclivities. By the end of the war, the infamous Under the Willows bordello, founded in 1861 and nicknamed "the wickedest place in the world," had grown from a single building into a half-block-long complex. The specifics of what occurred in its private cubicles varied from room to room, but all knew hustlers there could be hired for "male degeneracy."

By the 1880s, Chicago boasted more than fifteen bars for every church. The vicinity of Randolph and Dearborn Streets was known for "viperous dives," specializing in live sex shows. The venues segmented the market into different "perversions" and then competed to outdo each other by mounting the most scandalous fare. Some featured lesbian "freak" revues; others put sadomasochistic acts on stage; still others specialized in dwarf sex. One designated block of Clark Street was famed for its drag performers and sex workers. It was here that Magnus met a trans sex worker, "a young Negro woman, within whom a male prostitute was hiding," as he later recounted. One can't help but imagine Magnus swapping out his usual muted-color wardrobe for a red tie to give him access to the widest array of spaces for his hands-on sex research.

While New York hid its sexual underworld in the odd-angled streets of the Village, Chicago flaunted it in its Levee District on the edge of downtown. Chicago "makes a more amazingly open display of evil than any other city known to me," reported one correspondent from London around the time of the World's Fair. "Other places hide their [vice] out of sight; Chicago treasures it in the heart of the business quarter and gives it a veneer."

Shortly before Magnus arrived in Chicago, downtown voters had picked "Bathhouse John" Coughlin to represent them on the city council as the First Ward alderman. The son of an Irish immigrant, Coughlin had risen from the position of lowly "rubber" (steam-room masseur)—first in a low-rent Clark Street operation and then at the posh Palmer House Turkish Baths—to become a chain bathhouse magnate. With his connections in the city's sexual underworld, Coughlin soon hosted an annual sex party as a political fundraiser, the First Ward Ball, that was famed for its drag queens. First elected in 1892, Bathhouse John would hold the seat for forty-six years, until the day he died, but the First Ward Ball wouldn't last. On the eve of the 1908 fête, a newspaper threatened to print the names of attendees, and it broke the Ball. Many guests no showed, and others came with masks and fake beards to obscure their identities. With the media threatening America's don't-ask, don't-tell sexual code, the ball was never held again. Even in Chicago, where kinks were displayed openly, the kinky themselves coveted their anonymity.

The contradictions of America struck Magnus. In the most diverse society that he had ever encountered, he realized that all of the varied communities in America harbored a queer subculture—from San Francisco's Chinatown to Chicago's African American enclave and even, he heard, the Native American settlements of the West. And yet the dominant Anglo culture enforced a Victorian silence about all things sexual and conspired to keep them hidden. He made it his mandate as a budding sex researcher to unearth them.

With America so repressed about homosexuality, the public debate over the impact of over twenty-seven million strangers pouring into Chicago for the world's fair focused on straight single young women. "Never before in civilization have such numbers of young girls been suddenly released from the protection of the home and permitted to walk unattended upon the city streets and to work under alien roofs," fretted Chicago settlement house founder Jane Addams. What young women might get up to once freed from the prying eyes of mothers, aunts, and neighbors terrified America. What young men might do given the same freedom—and access to hair bleach and red ties—was not something that could be discussed in polite company.

On paper, the United States was the most open country in the world, a place where the constitution sacralized the freedom to say and write anything. But in practice, a puritanical culture repressed frank talk about all but the most mundane sexual subjects. This inability to speak honestly about sex, Magnus would come to see, undergirded America's bizarre and backward system of race.

Even as he catalogued America's sexual underworld for himself—material that he wouldn't publish for decades—his newspaper assignment was to cover the fair. At the World's Columbian Exposition, America told the world its official story about itself. The fair presented the United States as the energetic heir to European civilization. What had begun as an upstart nation had now risen to world power. Three decades after its civil war, the racial issues that had sparked the conflagration were finally being resolved, Americans claimed. Under new "Jim

Crow" laws, the country had begun constructing a parallel infrastructure for those deemed "colored" and those deemed "white." It was all soundly scientific, Americans assured the world.

Fair organizers endeavored to showcase the nation's growing sense of itself. On lakefront land, seven miles south of Chicago's downtown, where visitors like Magnus marveled at the world's first skyscrapers, Central Park creator Frederick Law Olmstead was picked to transform over six hundred acres of swampland into a manicured fairgrounds around a manmade lagoon. A talented young architect, Daniel Burnham would manage construction. On Burnham's orders, an endless line of columned, neoclassical buildings rose along the dug-out coastline like some science-fiction ancient Rome undergirded with steel frames. Glowing nightly from a hundred thousand electric lightbulbs, the fairgrounds was nicknamed "the White City." Among the over two hundred buildings, pride of place was reserved for those celebrating American achievements in technology, manufacturing, agriculture, and transportation and those of its constituent states. Foreign countries were given their own pavilions, but they were hidden away on the outskirts. The contributions of half of humanity got corralled away in the Woman's Building.

The newspaper dispatches Magnus sent home from the fair were unbylined, making them impossible to definitively identify today. Undoubtedly, Magnus told readers back home about the Germany Building. The ersatz Teutonic city hall—sturdy, stone built, and topped with a *mitteleuropean* cupola—was divided into orderly sections. One room was done up as a full-scale reproduction of a German church. Another saluted Germany's achievements in education on wooden display panels crowded with text and images four tiers high.

Most fairgoers skipped the Germany Building. The biggest attraction proved to be the Midway Plaisance, a slim mile-long rectangular park jutting inland off the central fairgrounds. Sited a safe distance from the stodgy government-sponsored displays, fairgoers could enjoy a stroll down the Midway as a simulated grand tour with the peoples of the world displayed before them in "ethnological villages." But what billed itself as a showcase of the world's peoples was actually a showcase of late-nineteenth-century racism. Such human zoos were common in the era; Magnus would visit another one back home in Germany in 1896.

The Midway Plaisance was the brainchild of Sol Bloom, a San Franciscan born to Polish-Jewish immigrants. On a trip to Paris at age nineteen, Bloom, a footloose autodidact and entrepreneur, had stumbled upon a staged Algerian village staffed by live Algerians. Sensing that Americans would spare no expense to take in the Arab maidens performing the *danse du ventre*, Bloom purchased the rights to display the village—and its villagers—at future exhibitions.

In Chicago, Bloom was put in charge of the Midway after Harvard ethnology professor Frederick Putnam fell badly behind schedule. Putnam later blurted out that he was relieved to "get this whole Indian circus off my hands." Bloom, for his part, scoffed that putting Professor Putnam in charge had been "about as intelligent a decision as it would be . . . to make Albert Einstein manager of the Ringling Brothers and Barnum & Bailey Circus." Bloom's impresario instincts proved profitable. As he later recalled, "When the public learned that the literal translation [of *danse du ventre*] was 'belly dance' they delightedly concluded that it must be salacious and immoral. The crowds poured in. I had a gold mine."

In Bloom's hands, the Midway Plaisance pandered to the prejudices of the public. In the American mind, their melting pot society was divided by the biological binary of "white" and "colored." "White" was a newfangled pan-European "race"; "colored" was everyone else. Whites could progress into the modern world; everyone else was stuck.

On the Midway, Europeans were presented as charming stereotypes of themselves. At the beer garden in the German Village, tourists tucked into sausages and sauerkraut as lederhosen-clad youths made the rounds garlanding them with edelweiss. The Irish section nearby offered an "industrial village" that highlighted the technological progress that had grown out of medieval craft traditions, presenting Europeans as traditional but not backward.

Non-Western peoples were presented as savages frozen in time. North Africans were, at least, given the dignity of being presented as distinct peoples—Egyptians, Tunisians, and Moroccans all got their own displays alongside Bloom's original Algerians. By contrast, sub-Saharan Africans were collectively depicted in a lone "Dahomey Village" (admission fee: twenty-five cents), where one hundred imported natives forced to play the role of half-naked barbarians stood in for half a continent. Indigenous Alaskans, shipped in to play themselves, were made to dance in their heavy furs in the sweltering Chicago summer. Even the Woman's Building, under the curatorial control of an all-white "Board of Lady Managers," led by "Mrs. Potter Palmer," as she insisted on calling herself, divided women's work into those tasks done in the modern industrialized West and what their exhibit called "Women's Work in Savagery," devoted to the rest of the world.

The racist mindset that a people's characteristics were inherent and fixed forever—one Magnus was painfully familiar with from Germany's new "scientific" antisemites—was the most destructive for America's largest minority group, African Americans. The fair management nixed a proposal for a designated African American pavilion akin to the Woman's Building. Instead, Black citizens were encouraged to submit proposals to the pavilions of the various American states where they faced hostile all-white selection panels. When the fair opened, a Black woman was barred on racial grounds from even taking a seat at a show in the Kentucky Pavilion.

The nation's leading advocate for racial equality, Frederick Douglass, lambasted the fair's sins of omission and commission. During the short-lived Reconstruction era, he noted, African Americans had taken their rightful place in the technicolor American panorama as citizens, voters, diplomats, even senators. But the ideology of fixed racial characteristics displayed on the Midway left no space for development or achievement. "As if to shame the Negro," Douglass railed, "the Dahomians are . . . here to exhibit the Negro as a repulsive savage." *Frank Leslie's Popular Monthly* magazine explicitly connected the Midway villagers to the African American population that had lived in America for nearly three centuries. "In these wild people . . . blacker than buried midnight . . . we easily detect many characteristics of the American negro," it informed its readers.

Frederick Douglass did the best he could to shape the fair. On account of his years as the American Consul General in Port-au-Prince, the Haitian government tapped him to guide their contribution. The Haitian Pavilion, a domed wooden structure with a breezy verandah highlighted Haiti's hybridity—a common phenomenon in the world 400 years after

Columbus but a rarity at the fair. In an 1893 lecture in a Chicago church, Douglass noted that "Haiti is herself French" and that "in the cities and towns of the country the people are largely of mixed blood and range all the way from black to white." Inside, the pavilion presented cultural cross-pollination in its most delectable form: a Franco-Caribbean café, where Frederick Douglass often held court, that served Haitian coffee for ten cents a cup. It's a near certainty that Magnus, a confirmed coffee addict, went in to partake—especially considering that the Haitian Pavilion sat right next door to the German Pavilion.

The Anthropology Building, though hidden away at the edge of the fairgrounds and "liable to be overlooked by the ordinary visitor," as one guidebook put it, undoubtedly drew Magnus as well. It catered to his interests in science and culture and had been designed by Franz Boas, a fellow German Jew. An immigrant professor, Boas was building the new field of anthropology and turning a critical eye to received ideas about racial and cultural hierarchies.

In an ostensible concession to the fair's implicit message that ethnic groups were pure and fixed, the exhibit encouraged visitors to take their own facial measurements with calipers, a metal instrument designed specifically for this purpose. But Boas knew that fairgoers' actual measurements would diverge from those predicted by "craniology," the pseudoscience that maintained each ethnic group had a unique head shape. As attendees moved through his exhibit, they learned that Northern and Southern Italians—many of whom were vehement in their insistence that they were not merely culturally, but biologically, distinct peoples—showed no difference in their heights. In Boas's exhibit, the Old World of Europe was exposed to be ethnically mixed like America, the self-declared melting pot. And his exhibit frankly examined America's unspoken history of sex across the color line. Boas's exhibition noted that biracial people, increasingly classed as Black through the one-drop rule that racialized an American as Black if they had any African ancestry at all, were closer in median height to white Americans than to black Africans. A section devoted to the fingerprints of Native Americans showed that every individual has a unique print with no discernable patterns by ethnic group. Boas's Anthropology Building quietly challenged Americans's assumption that race was a biological reality.

In the end, the counterarguments against racial essentialism from Frederick Douglass and Franz Boas that all peoples were mixed and that modernity was open to all were drowned out by the narratives of white purity and progress that pervaded the rest of the fair. But the dissenting ideas embedded in the Haitian Pavilion and the Anthropology Building planted seeds of skepticism in young Magnus. Like Douglass and Boas, he was predisposed to be skeptical of the racial myths Americans swore by.

To European immigrants like Boas and foreign visitors like Magnus, the racial hybridity of the American population was obvious. When Ottilie Assing, a German-Jewish feminist, sought out Frederick Douglass in hope of translating his autobiography into German, she was as struck by his European features as his African ones. Douglass famously wore his hair in a style that mixed a courtly European part with African volume to create his signature leonine mane. Nonetheless, Jim Crow America viewed Douglass as Black even though he was openly biracial. As he'd written in his 1845 autobiography, "My father was a white man . . . admitted to be such by all I ever heard speak of my parentage." Douglass described himself and the millions of Americans who shared his mixed background as "Anglo-African," though, tellingly, his term never caught on. At the dedication of the Chicago exposition, Douglass specifically called out the fair as "an intentional slight to that part of the American population with which I am identified," employing the passive voice to both condemn American racism and question America's racial categorizations in one breath. Under the American one-drop rule, mixed-race individuals like Douglass and the Dahomean villagers on the Midway were all collapsed into a single racial pariah caste. No one listened—except maybe Magnus. As a designated ethnic outsider in Germany, one could imagine him calling out the analogous injustices of antisemitism as "slights to that part of the German population with which I am identified."

Those who found themselves the most awkwardly jammed into America's ill-fitting racial categorization scheme, whether biracial Americans like Douglass, foreign immigrants like Boas, or European visitors like Hirschfeld, could see clearest through America's racial hypocrisy. All three learned from their travels that racism and racial categorization itself varied with geography. The same individual could be assigned different racial classifications in different places and get treated differently. Douglass had heard countless stories of racist indignities inflicted upon his friends among the Haitian elite when they traveled in America that would never be inflicted in the Caribbean or even in Europe. "In every other country on the globe a citizen of Haiti is sure of civil treatment [except] when he ventures within the border of the United States," Douglass told Chicagoans shortly before the fair opened.

Though Hirschfeld and Douglass could agree on the absurdity of American whiteness, it elevated one and degraded the other. For Hirschfeld, as for Ottilie Assing and Franz Boas, traveling from Europe to America meant shedding their racial otherness as Jews. In the American scheme, Hirschfeld discovered, he was "white."

Becoming "white" in America afforded Magnus broad access to the country—and it also gave him new insights into its psyche. In order for Americans to insist that they had a hard and fast color line, they had to stay silent on sex. Interracial sexual relationships could never be discussed even as the offspring from such relationships walked the streets of every American city. Americans had to ignore Frederick Douglass's disquisitions on the racial hybridity of the Haitians because Americans couldn't honestly face the racial hybridity in themselves.

To Magnus, it presented something of a chicken-and-egg problem: Could Americans not speak honestly about sex because they couldn't speak honestly about race? Or could Americans not speak honestly about race because they couldn't speak honestly about sex? Whatever the flow of causation, he came to see that the American code of silence about sex was deeply entwined with the American system of race. Ultimately, he would come to see that every racial system was undergirded by sex—indeed that race and sex were so inseparable that they could only be understood when examined together.

Chapter 3

The Hirschfeld Scale

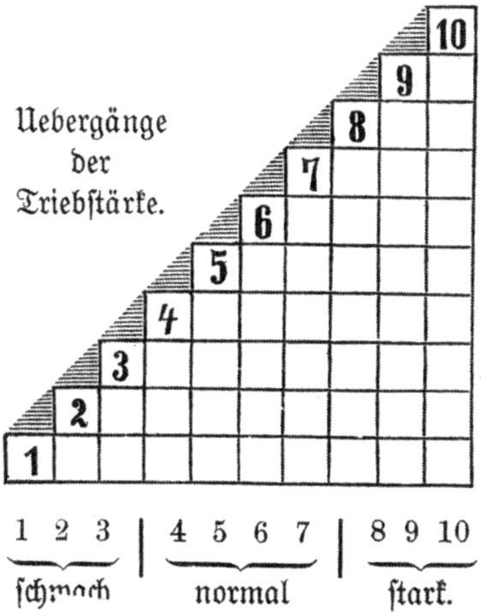

Chart for plotting variations in sex drive and sexual orientation in Magnus Hirschfeld's "Sappho and Socrates," 1896.

AFTER MONTHS IN America following his curiosity wherever it led—to Greenwich Village dive bars and down Levee District alleyways—Magnus returned to Germany to open a medical practice. It couldn't help but feel like a life sentence of boredom. Hirschfeld's medical school thesis advisor, Rudolf Virchow, was scheduled to speak at an international conference of physicians in Rome in the spring and Magnus realized he could delay his return home by attending. Likely buoyed by a mix of savings from his journalism work in America accrued while boarding with his brother and the financial support of his uncles and aunt, when the fair closed down the day before Halloween 1893, Magnus took a circuitous route home. Not due in Rome until late March, Magnus spent a mild winter exploring both sides of the Mediterranean Sea. His ship docked in British-held Gibraltar at Europe's southern tip, and Magnus disembarked. The buttoned-down life of a British colony could hardly compete with the excitement of Morocco, and Magnus promptly crossed the straits to Tangier. Only after exploring North Africa did he return to Europe. It was a captivating trip. Magnus could still vividly evoke the hammams, casbahs, and souks when he finally wrote about queer life in the region two decades after experiencing it.

Even as an accomplished traveler at age twenty-five, Tangier constituted Magnus's first trip outside the West. Europeans with more acquisitive motives had, of course, beaten him to North Africa. By the time of his visit, Tangier was an entrepôt with heavy European influence and Algeria was a French colony. Around tangled historic medinas, Europeans built new neighborhoods of wide straight avenues flanked by cafés, telegraph offices, and train stations, telling themselves that by modeling modernity, locals would eagerly assimilate to their ascendant culture. But Magnus found local traditions resilient.

His European upbringing had surely steeped Magnus in stereotypes about the Muslim world. In his youth, the Continent's libraries were filled with exoticized fairy tales set in faraway lands with genies and snake charmers, its art museums overflowed with paintings of turbaned warriors swinging scimitars in the desert sun. Europeans typically regarded the Middle East as a sexually repressed region where women were kept indoors and only permitted to emerge covered in hijabs, burqas, or abayas. The libertine upper class of salacious sultans and perverted pashas for whom even four wives was never enough provided the exceptions that proved the rule. Behind the palace walls, rumor had it, lay a secret seraglio with voluptuous belly dancers and callipygian slave boys, but out on the streets, it was a straightlaced world overseen by humorless imams.

As his subsequent writings on the region make clear, Magnus quickly found himself disabused of these stereotypes. Upon dropping anchor, it became obvious that Tangier was a fully modern seaport—and a gay cruising ground. In the crowds by the docks, new arrivals were propositioned with varying levels of directness. Rough-hewn hustlers, called "apaches" in local slang, were blatant with unaccompanied male travelers while smooth-faced corner boys, known as "voyous," played it coy. Magnus found similar scenes in the train stations. In major cities like Algiers, he wrote, "prostitutes [can] live entirely on homosexual acts [and] distinguish themselves frequently by assuming a certain elegance, sometimes having definite feminine allure, a tripping and delicate gait, and a languishing look."

In the Middle East, Magnus found, gay-owned barbershops served as queer gathering spaces, with customers dropping by to socialize whether they needed a haircut or a shave that day or not. Certain cafés, serving coffee, tea, and sometimes tobacco smoked from hookah water pipes, played a similar role. And then there were the hammams. The Koran stipulates that observant Muslims bathe regularly, and this religious edict got imbedded in urban space through neighborhood baths. Sex segregation, with specific times designated for men and women, facilitated same-sex assignations; so did the policy at many hammams that permitted patrons to stay overnight for a small additional fee. "Homosexuality blossoms abundantly here," Magnus wrote. "[Gay] brothels are not necessary; they are completely substituted for by Arabian baths—hammams." Reminiscing about these traditional bathhouses, Magnus couldn't help but slip into second person. "Frequently sitting in a row in the reception area, there are agreeable persons of different ages who, besides the actual bath attendants, offer their services as masseurs, or you get your own 'masseur' in the form of the bather beside you," he wrote. Given the fine-grained level of detail, he clearly knows these spaces he'd encountered as a single twenty-five-year-old over a thousand miles from home intimately.

In North Africa, as in Europe, French power meant being forced to be free in exactly the way the French defined freedom. Under the French laws imposed on the region, homosexual acts between consenting adults were perfectly legal (though religious family-law courts were still free to restrict sex acts as they saw fit). But even before the French crossed the Mediterranean, the local culture had been rather tolerant. "With regard to the homosexual question," Magnus wrote, "Islam is more open than Christianity." In North Africa, there was no generalized taboo against men who have sex with men. In most cases, only the receptive sexual partner was seen as being queer, a stigma likely rooted in misogyny.

With his conventionally masculine self-presentation, Magnus presumably faced little stigma in Morocco and Algeria despite his sexual interest in men.

This experience echoed how Magnus changing nothing about himself had gone from a suspect racial other to an exalted white man just by crossing from Germany to America. The same person got slated into different categories—different identities, communities even—depending on geography. The same sex act that rendered one both gay and a criminal in the Levee District of Chicago did neither in an Algiers hammam. As with race, the same person could change their category merely by moving through the world. As Magnus was beginning to see by living his increasingly global life, social categories were arbitrary. They were unintentional commentaries on the observers rather than impartial descriptions of the observed.

Not only were the received stereotypes of the Arab world incorrect, to Magnus the entire concept of an "Arab world" came to seem a gross oversimplification. Arabs had only arrived in North Africa in the Middle Ages, while the Berber mountain tribes were indigenous. Jews were an important minority group in the region, though they themselves reflected a tremendous diversity, typically secular and Westernized in the cities and traditional and religious in the countryside. However one felt about European colonialism, Europeans were now part of the demographic panorama. Many self-described "Europeans" had lived in Africa longer than they had lived in Europe; some had even been born there and had never been to Europe at all. As Magnus wrote, "This mixture of ethnicities [is obvious to] all who know how to travel with their eyes open." Traveling with eyes open was becoming one of Magnus's great talents.

Crossing the Mediterranean back into Europe, Magnus was surprised—pleasantly, we can presume—that Southern Italy hewed to the Middle Eastern conception of homosexuality. Only receptive partners were stigmatized, rather than the universal disdain for men who have sex with men that he knew from Germany and America. The supposed stark cultural border between Europe and Africa, Christendom and the Arab world was proving illusory.

After exploring the alluringly seedy Southern Italian city of Naples,

Magnus headed to Rome for Virchow's speech at the International Medical Congress. The Eternal City, where century was layered upon century, as archeologists unearthed pagan temples beneath Christian churches and imperial palaces beneath modern apartment buildings, held obvious interest for Magnus. Contrary to the notion parroted by his government and schools that history only moved forward, culminating in the Prussian state where he had been fortunate enough to be born, in Italy, queer tolerance increased the further down one dug. In ancient Rome, gay sex was legal, flaunted even. Emperors didn't hide their queerness; they threw themselves fabulous gay weddings to celebrate their relationships with their favorite polygamous partners. Emperor Nero, famously, dressed as a bride—twice. As the ancient historian Tacitus recounted of one of Nero's nuptials, "[the emperor] wore a *flammeum*, the wedding hair net of the female partner." Another historian elaborated, "Dressed as a bride in a wedding gown, [Nero] appeared beside the groom in the assembled senate and settled the amount of the dowry to be brought to the bridegroom. Everyone had to participate in the festivities. He was wed according to the strictest forms of Roman marriage: so did he place himself beneath his husband's absolute power."

It was only the coming of Christianity that restricted gay life on the Italian peninsula. Anti-gay laws and homophobic church teachings didn't stamp out gay life—they only drove it underground. While Roman emperors had paraded their queerness, the Roman popes hid theirs. In 1045, Pope Benedict IX was forced to resign after being implicated in a gay sex scandal. In the Renaissance, an era celebrated as a rebirth of rationality, the proscriptions grew stricter and prosecutions harsher; burnings at the stake for homosexuality actually grew more common in Renaissance Italy than they had been in the Middle Ages.

By the time of Magnus's maiden voyage to Italy in 1894, gay life was less of a target. Though Napoleon's hold on Italian territory was brief, the influence of the French legal code and its decriminalization of consensual sex acts between adults was long-lasting. The modern unified Italy had nothing akin to Germany's Paragraph 175, and it became a popular place of refuge for gay Germans who escaped to the Mediterranean peninsula for vacations or as expatriates. In his explorations of Rome's gay scene, Magnus got tips from members of its queer German expat community. But he never met the most notable gay German in Italy, his queer-rights predecessor, Karl Heinrich Ulrichs. Awareness of the activist and his works had been so thoroughly suppressed in Germany that it seems Magnus had not yet heard of him. Even though Magnus's conference in Rome put him just sixty miles from Ulrich's residence in L'Aquila, where he spent his golden years composing Latin poetry, the man sometimes called "the grandfather of gay liberation," never met Hirschfeld, "the father." Ulrichs died the following year in obscurity.

Returning to his native Germany after the conference, with his voyages to the New World, the Middle East, and Southern Europe behind him, Magnus began discerning a basic fact about humanity. From the American Midwest to the docks of Tangier to Vatican City itself, the reality was obvious to Magnus: everywhere was at least a little bit gay.

Back home and, likely, short on money, Magnus launched his much-delayed medical career. On April 23, 1894, he hung the bespoke porcelain "Dr. Hirschfeld" sign his late father had bequeathed to him and opened his first medical practice in the central German city of Magdeburg. In a place this small it was difficult to specialize, so the sign's text—"general practitioner and obstetrician"—fit the bill. Hirschfeld's father had delivered some babies in his day; for Magnus, obstetrics would quietly signal that his practice was focused on sexuality.

Magnus distinguished himself from other local doctors through his public embrace of naturopathy, an approach to medical practice that relied as much as possible on natural remedies rather than invasive procedures and industrially produced pharmaceuticals. His stance put him at odds with the German medical establishment. For decades, in obstetrics, Germany's invariably male physicians had been using their ability to conduct "scientific" "modern" invasive procedures to sideline the female midwives who used natural remedies and had traditionally served as the primary care providers during pregnancy and labor. A male obstetrician like Magnus openly supporting naturopathy was a traitor not only to his profession—but to his gender.

Strolling the staid streets of Magdeburg, sometimes with a patient in tow for one of his walk-and-talk therapy sessions, Magnus cut a notably restrained figure. Mustachioed and well-dressed, if a little rumpled, he could be easily mistaken for a banker. He was already developing a taste for the good life, enjoying his creature comforts and indulging the love of sweets that would contribute to an early diabetes diagnosis. Looking the part of a well-to-do gentleman, few read him as queer in his sexuality, heterodox in his outlook, or radical in his politics.

Word got around soon enough. Magdeburg was a small place, and Magnus quickly became known as the doctor you could trust with your sexual secrets. Queer patients were soon flocking to his practice. Time and again, new patients told him that there must be something wrong with them, that they must be the only one. As he gently corrected them—their feelings were normal for them; there were similar people all over the world—his office became a place of refuge.

From their confessions, Magnus became aware that provincial Magdeburg was not quite as isolated as it seemed. Though landlocked, it lay on the Elbe River, which flowed up toward Hamburg, Germany's great port city. And even Magdeburg had some churn in its population, with seamen coming and going, and a modicum of diversity from its Jewish community, which had existed on and off, given persecutions and an expulsion, for nearly a thousand years by the time Magnus showed up. Still, the locals took refuge in the past. Most Magdeburgers were inordinately proud of their medieval church—Germany's oldest Gothic cathedral, they would tell you, even if you hadn't asked—while often indifferent to the handsome contemporary edifices springing up all around them. Magnus, notably lacking in medieval nostalgia, settled in the newest section of town.

As queer locals sought out Magnus for therapy, it only redoubled his conviction that gays were everywhere. Sure, queer people flocked to larger cities and even to countries, like Italy, seeking tolerance. But even in little Magdeburg, a notable percentage of the population was queer. And more and more of them made their way to his office.

For his patients, breaking the code of silence governing queer life in Germany, even if only to their doctor, could be liberating. In the new field of psychoanalysis being birthed in Germany and Austria in this era, simply speaking one's feelings aloud was viewed as the first part of the healing process. Telling a trained, impartial third party one's secrets lifted the stress of holding them, lessening depression, anxiety, even suicidal thoughts and deeds. They called it "talk therapy," sometimes even "the talking cure."

In private sessions, Magnus assured his patients that they weren't ill.

Same-sex attraction was a naturally occurring feature in human sexuality and their same-sex attraction was natural to them. When gay men came to Magnus desperately seeking treatment, he suggested the best "cure" would be a boyfriend; for lesbians, a girlfriend. More often than not, this unorthodox advice worked. Patients stopped torturing themselves with feelings of guilt and shame; some accepted his prescription and found lovers and partners.

One patient who seemed to be benefitting from this unburdening was a man Magnus identified in his writings only as "Lieutenant von X"—"lieutenant" because he was an officer in the German army and "von" to signal the man's high-class status. (German surnames preceded by *von* indicate descent from medieval nobles.)

Though the young commander came from a prosperous family and was quickly rising up the military ranks, he was leading a double life. A magician at keeping up appearances, he could project the hypermasculinity expected of a warrior for Bismarck's new Germany of "blood and iron" and dutifully court the wealthy debutantes his parents pushed on him. But after dark he'd slip away, as Magnus recorded, to spend "half the night in the lowest harbor pubs" in the company of the "sailors and men of strength, whom he . . . loved more than everything." Driven by his secret desires, the young officer mastered the rough-and-tumble accents and slang of the regulars so perfectly that no one knew he was an aristocrat slumming it. On the surface, the man was proud of pulling off the ruse but, as Magnus got to know him, he diagnosed him as having "deep mental depression."

Helping queer patients, Magnus himself found only persecution. When a poisoning victim for whom Magnus refused to prescribe the customary pseudoscientific treatment of "invigorating alcohol" later died of sepsis, local medical authorities pounced. Doctors filed suit to have Magnus's medical license revoked. It is likely that they'd gotten wind of the heterodox sexual advice Magnus was dispensing at his clinic. And his public embrace of naturopathy gave Magdeburg's medical establishment an easy excuse for an attack. Though Magnus was ultimately exonerated and permitted to continue his work, the harassment forced him from the city.

In 1896, Magnus left for Berlin. The German capital was only seventy-five miles away from Magdeburg, but life there was lived on a global stage. Magnus settled in Charlottenburg, a posh outlying neighborhood, filled with professionals who craved distance from the city's sootier industrial districts. Magnus's apartment sat a short walk from a palace that was sometimes graced by the kaiser himself.

When he arrived in Berlin, it was no gay mecca. The entire metropolis had just a few queer nightspots. As Magnus later recalled, "When I moved from Magdeburg to Berlin . . . the number of local bars certainly did not exceed half a dozen." The establishments kept a low profile. Too scared to advertise themselves openly as gay bars, Magnus recorded, they were "named only after the landlord or after the street on which they were located."

Gay bars in fin-de-siècle Berlin were invariably modest dives serving beer, schnapps, and the obligatory snacks, often nothing more than salty cuts of cured goose. They didn't host balls or anything that could even be properly called a dance party. At most, there was a piano and a makeshift dance floor created by pushing the tables and chairs up against the wall.

This was an underground community that felt its best days were behind it, still traumatized and reeling from a police raid a decade earlier. As Magnus later reconstructed from community accounts, "in February 1885 in Seger's bar at 10 Jägerstrasse. . . . on a Sunday evening, when all the rooms were packed and cheerful, the Detective Commissioner Wolff . . . suddenly appeared with seven officers." The police blocked the exits and demanded the patrons produce identification—a terrifying prospect in a time and place where it was a scandal to be gay and a crime to act on it. Four customers who refused to produce IDs were booked for disturbing the peace and subsequently sentenced to three months in prison. Worse, the owner and his femme life partner, Paula, were charged with being a john and a prostitute and given longer sentences.

Moving to Berlin, Magnus believed his psychotherapy practice could help heal this cowed community. He soon realized it would take more than talking. Shortly after his move, Magnus, an early riser and a voracious newspaper reader, was leafing through his morning paper and stopped cold by a news brief. A high-born young military officer in Magdeburg had taken his own life in dramatic fashion. On the night of his wedding feast, he'd shot himself through the heart with a pistol leaving his parents, family, and bride-to-be stunned. Magnus flinched with recognition. Later that day, when the postman came, confirmation arrived in Magnus's daily haul. Among the letters was one from Lieutenant von X, a suicide note.

"I could not object to the marriage and confess the truth," it read. "I did not have the strength to tell my parents, who had been urging me, their only child, for years to marry a childhood friend. . . . They would never have understood me anyway." Magnus and his patient had traced this family conflict many times together in therapy, and the late patient hadn't sent Magnus his suicide note to rehash it. He wrote to call him to action. Amidst the self-loathing—the letter referred to his same-sex attraction as "abnormal"—was hope for social change. "It is possible that my voice . . . will die away unheard," the patient wrote, but "the thought that it could contribute to the [possibility of] the German fatherland . . . think[ing] more equitably brightens up my death-hour. . . . This outcry of a wretched person [could be] the salvation of countless people, the same as I, under a . . . curse . . . dragging their life away." The suicide note specifically exhorted Magnus to make the story public as long as he preserved the patient's family's anonymity.

Magnus had long been convinced that his patients weren't sick, their society was. But the logical next step—going public to change Germany's politics and culture—terrified him. Following the trial of gay Irish author Oscar Wilde the previous year, Magnus understood intellectually that only activism could reform society. In his London courtroom, Wilde had bravely martyred himself, openly defending same-sex love rather than denying the truth in a bid to keep his freedom. Now Wilde was serving two years at hard labor while Magnus was doing nothing beyond offering private talk therapy. This reticence now felt like a personal betrayal of his late patient. How many more would follow him to the grave?

But how could Magnus advocate for queer people being queer himself? Sure, audiences would patronize the work of a gay author or playwright if the work was entertaining enough—as Wilde's invariably was. But a gay doctor advocating for gay rights would be dismissed as a judge in his own case, fatally biased. Magnus would have to choose his arguments with utmost care.

Immediately he set to work, feverishly writing what would become his first gay-rights pamphlet. He named the work, which called for the abolition of Paragraph 175, "Sappho and Socrates: How Does One Explain the Love of Men and Women for Persons of Their Own Sex?" On the advice of the only publisher brave enough to put it out, Max Spohr of Leipzig, Magnus decided to publish under a pseudonym: "Dr. med. Th. Ramien," identified only as a Berlin physician.

In the text, published in mid-1896, just months after he'd moved to Berlin, Hirschfeld took on a medical establishment that viewed homosexuality as a disorder caused by childhood trauma. As Magnus surmised from his own idyllic childhood as well as through the life stories of many of his patients who, on paper, were living charmed lives—the late Lieutenant von X, among them—homosexuality was not trauma induced. He ventured that it was inborn. His born-this-way hypothesis had several advantages. Yes, he believed it was scientifically valid. But perhaps more important, it was politically savvy. If being gay was inborn, not a choice, then persecution was both cruel and useless. Why torment someone over an accident of birth? Why police and punish gayness if one could neither be recruited into it nor cured of it?

From talk therapy sessions with a wide array of patients, Magnus had determined that sex drives varied in both direction and intensity. Regarding direction, some were exclusively attracted to the opposite sex; some exclusively to the same sex; and some to both sexes. As for intensity, attraction ranged from nonexistent to uncontrollable, with most people falling somewhere in between.

Playing the educated German man of science to a T, Magnus presented his hypothesis in a series of charts and formulae. In his alpha-numerical scheme, attraction to men was given the heading "A" and attraction to women "B," regardless of the gender of the individual patient. Sex drives were classified in broad categories of weak, moderate, and irrepressible and then into subcategories of increasing strength. Weak sex drives were, in increasing order, "1. imperceptible," "2. almost indifferent," or "3. cold." Moderate drives could be "4. cool," "5. tepid," "6. warm," or

"7. very warm." Irrepressible drives began at "8. hot," ran up through "9. passionate," and peaked at "10. wild lust."

Thus, a straight man with a modest sex drive would be a "B 4." A lesbian woman with a powerful sex drive would be a "B 9." Bisexuals would be assigned two values linked with a plus sign. A bisexual woman, Magnus wrote, who was "equally attracted to both sexes, we would describe as A 5 + B 5," while one with "little . . . love for the opposite sex [and] a wild desire for their own sex, A 3 + B 9." Magnus included a chart where readers could plot their same- and opposite-sex attraction levels for handy self-categorization.

Though this was his first foray into political writing, Magnus proved a natural. He was clear in offering his central thesis—"This classification illuminates the immense variety of sexual inclinations"—and his show of scientific rigor impressed his readers. Indeed, his chart, with its mathematical pyramid of boxes, was a tacit invitation to self-categorize, making accessible his radical claim that human sexuality was astonishingly varied. One can imagine a proper Berlin businessman reading the pamphlet on the train ride home to his wife and taking a second glance at the strapping young conductor walking the aisle. Perhaps our commuter was only *mostly* straight. Maybe an A 3 + B 8? Perhaps bisexuality was less of an exception than the businessman previously believed; maybe it was closer to the rule. In Hirschfeld's conception of sexuality as a continuum, many ostensibly straight people were actually bisexuals who were more powerfully attracted to the opposite sex than to their own sex.

Sexual desire had previously been conceived of as either correct or deviant. In the German language, the binary was stark, literally between the *homosexuell* (gay) and the *normalsexuell* (straight). But, in reality, sexuality wasn't black or white; it was prismatic.

Magnus understood that this insight alone was not enough to guarantee tolerance. As he wrote, "it can be understood that [since] hardly two people have the same feelings . . . one can find it . . . difficult to empathize with the desire[s] of another." Even people who found themselves in the same place on the chart—two conventionally straight B 5 men, say, or a pair of A 7 women—may still find each other's tastes and proclivities hard to identify with. "Let us also consider the endless variety of tastes, according to which one likes blondes, the other dark hair, that one the strong, this one the delicate, that one the smooth, others the hairy, this one a petite foot, another a soulful eye, this one the uniformed, that one a naked person." Faced with the breadth of human sexuality, some might retreat into solipsistic self-regard and claim themselves to be the world's only normal person, dismissing everyone else as a freak.

At the societal level, this type of intolerance could stigmatize—even criminalize—taboo forms of sexuality. This, Magnus explained, was what had happened in Germany with Paragraph 175. Its pseudoscientific defenses were risible, and he systematically debunked them one by one. The first was the most absurd—that straight sex should be legal because it leads to procreation and the continued existence of humanity, while gay sex should be criminalized because it does not. Anyone who has ever met a straight person knows that they do not have sex solely to procreate and often take specific precautions to *avoid* procreation. "Procreation is an effect, but not the cause" of heterosexual intercourse, the physician-pamphleteer wrote. Besides, he noted, if a society wanted to ban sex that did not result in procreation, it would have to outlaw geriatric sex as well. Indeed, if Paragraph 175's goal had been to outlaw non-procreative sex, it would have banned anal sex between a man and a woman, not just between two men, and lesbianism as well.

The source of the gay community's problems, Magnus argued, was not gayness itself but society's persecution of gays. Queer people were first and foremost people, exhibiting the same range of good and bad qualities that straight people did. While Magnus was proud of millennia of gay genius—from the eponymous Sappho and Socrates to Oscar Wilde—the gay community encompassed the full range of humanity. "As with heterosexuals, among homosexuals there are individuals of all sorts, dumb heads and geniuses, good-natured and obstinate, sympathetic and unsympathetic, healthy and sick personalities," Magnus wrote in his pamphlet. Of course, more gays ended up experiencing anxiety and depression—but that was in response to society's hostility, not the result of anything inherently depressing about being gay as he knew from his patients, his community, and his own life. In Germany, coming out or being outed meant risking an entire menu of woe, ranging from arrest and imprisonment to unemployment, blackmail, and disownment. "It is surely obvious," Magnus wrote,

> that to be in constant fear about the secrecy of a congenital [condition], the existence of which one initially perceives as sin and aberration, later as vice, moral crime or mental illness, that the oppressive pangs of pressing conscience, the eternal struggle of the willing spirit against the weak flesh, that constant fear of discovery by extortionists, of arrest, judicial punishment, loss of social status and respect on the part of the family and fellow human beings [must] strongly affect the mind [and] irritate the nerves and can cause neurasthenia, melancholy, hysteria and suicidal thoughts. On the contrary, it is amazing that, on the other hand, not more people lose their minds."

From Magnus's perspective, the relative saneness of queer people living in an insane society was a miracle.

Magnus's born-this-way hypothesis also rendered society's search for the causes of gayness—and possible cures—moot. If queerness was inborn, there would be no child-rearing technique that could alter it or influence it. His theory similarly discredited supposed sociological causes of homosexuality. The large gay communities in major cities led some to claim that city life turned people gay. As Magnus knew from his travels and his recent relocation from provincial Magdeburg to metropolitan Berlin, gay people were drawn to large cities to escape the social straitjacket of small-town life. "The big cities . . . do not produce proportionately more homosexual women and men than the smaller ones," Magnus wrote. "These people often go to the world cities . . . because there they can follow their instincts most comfortably, or because they remain most inconspicuous there."

Similarly, the proliferation of gays within certain professions led some to argue that certain fields turned people gay. Such a disproportionate percentage of hairdressers, actors, and waiters were gay, the thinking went, that surely there was something about those fields—or the elders in them—that converted the apprentices. As with decisions about whether to live in a big city or small town, certain professions beckoned those born queer. Gays, Magnus wrote, "consciously or more often with a deeply unconscious urge are attracted to occupations where they can live out those inclinations more unobtrusively or really well."

In the same vein, left-wing political movements weren't turning people gay. Magnus acknowledged the overrepresentation of lesbians and bisexuals among suffrage leaders but explained that they were naturally drawn to a female-dominated movement that was trying to correct society's underestimation of women. "In our modern women's movement there is unconsciously a good part of . . . homosexuality," he wrote. "These resolute, courageous women, with the beautifully spirited traits . . . these writers, these learned and philosophizing ladies with the serious eye and the simple clothes . . . how diligently they fight for women's rights, how do they love their neglected gender, whose abilities are underestimated . . . today, which betrays astonishing ignorance."

Having made his case, Magnus moved to its clear political implication: the repeal of Paragraph 175. If homosexuality is inborn, then punishment is no deterrent and legalization no enticement. "The legislation . . . hunts down the unfortunates to death with humiliation and disgrace, without being any use at all," he wrote. "Nobody has been bettered or deterred, or even healed, by the punishment." Indeed, as was clear from his experience on the ground, the countries where gay sex was legal, such as Italy, were no gayer than those where it was a crime, like Germany. "France, as well as Italy, Holland, Belgium [and] Luxembourg . . . only punish lewd acts . . . if violence is used or the act is perpetrated on minors or witnessed in public places. In none of these countries has . . . an epidemic-like increase in contrary sexual feeling occurred, as feared by the German legislators," his pamphlet maintained.

"Sappho and Socrates" was passionately argued, cleverly pitched, and slyly funny. Who could argue with an author with a "Dr." in front of his name who produced so many charts and formulas? How could one not laugh at the notion that aspiring hairdressers were straight boys who somehow got turned queer in beauty school? When it hit the streets, the pamphlet created a sensation. Its frank and open discussion of homosexuality shocked readers—and changed many minds. Some were loudly outraged, but many more were quietly relieved.

But what were those convinced by the pamphlet to do? How were they even to contact the pseudonymous Th. Ramien?

Magnus told his publisher that he could connect him to readers who sought him out. But wasn't there some inherent hypocrisy in fighting this fight anonymously?

Chapter 4

The Coming-Out Party

Baron von Teschenberg's carte-de-visite expressing "my true nature."

MAGNUS ALWAYS THOUGHT best while in motion, whether on a talk-therapy walk with one of his patients or navigating the Tangier casbah after a visit to the hammam. On February 15, 1897, as the gray-scale winter landscape glided by on the train from Berlin to Leipzig, he brainstormed a list of reasons why Paragraph 175 had to go. By the time his train pulled into the station a few hours later, he'd drafted a petition.

Magnus was in Leipzig to see his publisher, Max Spohr. Though only in his forties, Spohr was already an old hand in the book business. He'd gotten his start as a teenager working in a bookstore in his native Braunschweig, not far from Magdeburg. Growing in ambition, he'd moved to Leipzig, the country's publishing hub ever since it issued the world's first daily newspaper, in 1650. There, the courtly intellectual, married with three sons, made a name for himself as a daring, politically progressive publisher.

Spohr and Hirschfeld had been collaborating since the previous summer, when Spohr put out "Sappho and Socrates." Nearly a generation older than Magnus, Spohr, with a middle-aged man's accute sense of reputational risk, insisted that Magnus publish under a pseudonym. That fall, as the pamphlet focused public debate on Paragraph 175, the pair debated next steps. Magnus wanted a gay-rights petition—a bold move, from a scrupulously private piece of writing, the anonymous pamphlet, to an overtly public one on which not only its author but supportive readers openly identify themselves. With Oscar Wilde's martyrdom hanging over him, Magnus saw that when it came to achieving progress on gay rights, agitating anonymously was, at best, a hypocritical half measure, maybe even a betrayal of the emancipatory project altogether. The closet was the great ally of persecutors and blackmailers. Frightening as it was to Magnus, the gay-rights movement would have to be a public undertaking and he would have to subject himself and, inevitably, his identity to public speculation.

Considering that Spohr had been so adamant on Magnus preserving anonymity as the author of "Sappho and Socrates," Magnus went to Leipzig to pitch him on the petition in person. Spohr surprised Magnus. He loved the petition idea. The publisher immediately volunteered to cover printing costs and recruit prominent potential signers.

That spring, with Spohr's help, Magnus convened an informal conference in his Charlottenburg apartment. On May 15, a small group of men assembled. Their meeting's resolution stated: "[Based on] research results and personal experience . . . the love of persons of the same sex, so-called homosexuality, is not a vice or a crime but a matter of natural orientation."

Among those present was the neatly coiffed Franz Josef von Bülow, an aristocratic writer and war veteran, and Eduard Oberg, a luxuriantly mustachioed railway official from western Germany. Oberg had been the first reader to finish "Sappho and Socrates" and contact the publishing house in search of the mysterious "Dr. Th. Ramien." As per their agreement, Spohr connected Magnus with every reader who sought the anonymous pamphleteer. The two met in October 1896. Magnus found Oberg "a little gruff and grumpy on the outside, but inwardly very considerate"—perhaps a case of projection since that was precisely the description many applied to Magnus himself. The railroad man told the pamphleteer that he'd read "Sappho and Socrates" and found it convincing. Now both wondered: what is to be done?

At the springtime confab in Magnus's book-filled, lair-like apartment, the clique talked strategy. They knew that their proposal was, for late-nineteenth-century Germany, provocative and concluded that they'd win only if they presented their ideas as a matter of common sense. Rather than call the group the "Committee on the Elimination of Paragraph 175," let alone the "Homosexual Liberation Front," they chose something vaguer: The Scientific Humanitarian Committee. Magnus later explained that the goal was to choose a moniker that was "as innocuous as possible [for] reasons of tact and tactics." The name dovetailed with the argument in "Sappho and Socrates" that queerness was an inborn trait rendering the persecution of gays both wrong *and* pointless. As a motto, the group used the Latin phrase *Per scientiam ad justitiam* ("Through science to justice"), expressing the hope and expectation that a modern society would be a tolerant one. The world's first gay-rights organization packaged itself as nothing radical, just a group championing basic logic.

The founders agreed to seek out as broad a membership as possible, eschewing a gay litmus test for membership. This served two purposes: it allowed members to join without outing themselves and it welcomed straight(er) allies. Hirschfeld's theories in "Sappho and Socrates" had blurred any stark gay/straight distinction.

As the group would soon explain in an annual report, rallying gay men to fight for their rights was only one of its goals. "Our task has been divided into three parts: to win the support of the legislatures for the repeal of Paragraph 175 of the Imperial Penal Code Book, to enlighten public opinion on the nature of sexual intermediaries, and to interest the homosexuals themselves in their struggle for justice." Lesbians, though not directly targeted by Paragraph 175, joined the cause as well. As the report explained, "Although no legal restrictions are imposed on homosexual women in Germany, they also suffer in many ways from ignorance of their nature." Thus, the committee has long interested "intellectually distinguished, especially Uranian [lesbian] ladies . . . and they have [participated in] our events."

In deciding whom to solicit for signatures, Magnus and his Charlottenburg collaborators treated their proposal more like an "open letter" than a political petition—privileging quality over quantity. If major public figures of all sexual orientations were to endorse the repeal of Paragraph 175, the committee believed, it would become a mainstream political opinion. The leadership's respectability politics undoubtedly included a touch of snobbery—they specifically sought out high-status public figures to come out as queer and endorse their movement. But the group was keen to build a mass movement in tandem and made sure not to exclude anyone from membership for lack of funds. Membership dues were paid on an honor system "according to the principle of self-assessment," an annual report explained. "In determining the amount, however, it should be borne in mind that the most important assets of human life, such as honor, rights, prestige and existence are at stake."

At the founding meeting's conclusion, the attendees divvied up responsibilities for their new organization. Magnus would draft the petition, Spohr would manage the finances, and Oberg would work behind the scenes to win supporters in government. All would share the distribution costs for the petition; at the meeting's conclusion, each attendee anteed up gold marks on the table with von Bülow paying extra on account of his independent wealth. "Then we vowed," Magnus recounted, "as long as the legal and social ostracism of homosexuals warrants, to fight against this cultural corruption with all mental powers."

At the May meeting, the activists discussed the content of the petition in broad strokes, but it was left to Magnus to finalize it. He addressed it "To the legislative bodies of the German Reich" and solicited the signatures of those inspired by "the pursuit of truth, justice, and humanity." A political radical in respectable bourgeois clothing, Magnus structured the petition in the conventional stodgy manner, with a long series of "whereas" statements followed by a "therefore" demand for action. The setup closely tracked the arguments Magnus had made in "Sappho and

Socrates" that homosexuality was inborn and thus gays could be neither recruited nor "cured."

In the petition, Magnus Hirschfeld, MD, slyly presented his born-this-way hypothesis as established scientific consensus when, in fact, it was a new and controversial explanation for same-sex attraction. "Scientific research . . . has without exception confirmed . . . that this phenomenon, which is widely distributed in time and location must, by its very nature, be the product of a deep internal constitutional disposition," he wrote. This would become Hirschfeld's go-to argumentative technique. He'd present himself as an impartial man of science with no vested interest in anything beyond the truth. Any disagreement with his conclusions then became evidence of his opponents' inability to reckon with the facts. He'd win his arguments without even acknowledging there was an argument to be had.

The petition ended with the demand that Paragraph 175, being "incompatible with progressive scientific findings" be rewritten so that homosexual and heterosexual acts were treated identically by the law. The only sex that should be criminalized, it argued, was forced sex, sex with minors, and public sex.

After the text was agreed upon, it was sent to Spohr to print. Once produced, the group reconvened in Magnus's apartment to assemble the mailing. Folding the petitions, placing them in their envelopes, stamping and addressing them took hours, but it was one of those Berlin summer nights when the sun sets so late you lose track of time. After midnight, the activists brought their bundles of letters to the front of the post office and, as Magnus later recounted, "entrusted them to the mailboxes like treasures." As the envelopes dropped through the chute, the choice was made. Magnus was leading a public campaign for gay rights. As the letters were opened by notable politicians, jurists, educators, scientists, and medical doctors all over Germany, Magnus was transformed from an anonymous pamphleteer to the country's best-known queer-rights advocate.

When each petition arrived at its destination, the recipient faced the same choice Magnus had weighed: whether to identify openly with the cause of gay rights. Some balked. One came back unsigned with a note reading, "You devote your energies to one of the highest purposes, and

I gladly see how many men of the pertinent sciences and distinguished and influential people want to contribute to the removal of this cruel law, but I cannot give you my signature—because I myself am contrary-sexed [gay]." This response, Magnus wrote, left him "shaken." But others cited personal experiences as the very reason they were signing. One signature came in from an academic who wrote, "Only after the death of a noble young man . . . who pulled the trigger when his contrary sexual orientation was discovered, were my eyes opened and my mind changed. A very humble father thanks the Scientific Humanitarian Committee for its philanthropic work!"

For others, their professional expertise was the impetus for publicly endorsing gay rights. Magnus was encouraged by how many physicians signed. One medical doctor wrote in to second Magnus's hypothesis. People were queer, he wrote, due to "an inborn, natural tendency, not to a faulty upbringing." And he drew the same conclusion that Magnus had that "punishment [must] never be imposed on them, but rather they are at most to be considered people with an orientation that goes against the grain."

As attorneys wrote in with signatures and comments, Magnus was heartened to learn that Paragraph 175 had never been particularly popular in the legal world. Once Magnus made it a matter for public debate, the outcry was widespread. "No educated person could seriously doubt that the petition is justified," one attorney wrote in. "It is hard to believe that this paragraph [175] still exists," wrote another.

Scientists who supported the petition suggested new areas for research which had previously been neglected out of fear it might out the researcher and put reputation, career, and freedom in peril. One biologist noted that he had observed homosexual behavior in animals, bolstering Magnus's inborn theory. The biologist reported, "I totally agree with the petition. The behaviors considered criminal have been observed so frequently not only in Homo sapiens, but also in numerous higher and lower animals, that you really must consider them to be deeply grounded facts in animal nature . . . whose legal prosecution can never change the natural drive. . . . As a biologist, it strikes me as almost comic when, with pen and paper, people think they can uproot such naturally inherited traits or even control them in any way worth mentioning." Spurred by this biologist and others, Magnus directed the Scientific Humanitarian Committee to support and publish scientific research on sex.

A crucial early signer was August Bebel, Magnus's friend and the debonair chair of the Social Democratic Party, the largest political party in Germany. That summer, Bebel took a meeting with Magnus in a Bavarian hill town to plot the petition's presentation in the legislature. A master of parliamentary procedure, the Social Democratic leader requested that he be the petition's primary sponsor in the German parliament, the Reichstag, and he advised Magnus to approach the chair of the petitions committee, a surgeon by training and a political liberal, who would likely be sympathetic to the cause. Bebel also advised Magnus to make sure the first signature on the petition began with the letter *A*. Countless petitions arrived in parliament every year, and they were organized, in a near self-parody of the Germanic fetish for order, alphabetically by the last name of the first signer. Fortuitously enough, Magnus knew just the person—one Dr. Aander-Heyden, an archivist outside Frankfurt, whose surname started not with one *a* but two! The archivist was moved to the top of the list, pushing aside more famous names.

More substantively, Bebel advised linking the repeal of Paragraph 175 to two sex-related bills that were already pending before parliament—a proposal to tighten laws against the publication of obscene materials and another to crackdown on pimping. It was a matter of political strategy. Tightening some sexual restrictions while loosening others might give nervous politicians cover to support the Scientific Humanitarian Committee's petition.

Magnus disagreed. Decriminalizing homosexuality while simultaneously tightening laws on sexually explicit publications, he feared, would invite a regime where gay life got put under a microscope, assiduously policed and patrolled for violations. Bebel overruled him, dismissing the advice from a man not yet thirty, whom he respected morally and intellectually but regarded as politically naïve. With Bebel ready to raise the petition when parliament reconvened, Magnus continued soliciting support from major figures in science, law, and the arts. By the time the petition was formally submitted to parliament in December, it had amassed nine hundred signatures.

At a contentious session on the pimping bill in January 1898, Bebel took the floor to call for repealing Paragraph 175. Addressing his fellow members of parliament in the Reichstag, the grand new legislative hall in the heart of Berlin, he soberly noted all of the prominent signatories that the Scientific Humanitarian Committee had marshalled. "We have a printed petition before us, whose signatories include myself and a number of colleagues belonging to other parties, as well as writers and scholars[,] jurists [and] experts of this area," who all call for "the abolition of the law in question." Perhaps thinking a practical argument would find the broadest support, Bebel focused on how capriciously Paragraph 175 was being applied. "The authorities," he said, "know full well that these laws are systematically broken by a significant number of persons [but] only in the rarest of cases attempt to call on the criminal judge for help." And the capriciousness was inherent, he argued, since systematically enforcing the law was a logistical impossibility. Prosecuting every act of gay sex, even just in the capital, Bebel said, would completely overwhelm the criminal justice system. "I have it from one of the best sources [in] the local Berlin vice squad," Bebel explained, that "the number of [violators] is so large and penetrates so deeply into every level of society, from the lowest to the highest, that, if . . . the police were to do their duty and punish all the people guilty of Paragraph 175, then, in Berlin alone, the Prussian authorities would have to build two new prisons." Bebel's claim that parliament sat in the middle of a queer capital left his colleagues in an uproar with the chair calling in vain for order.

That Berlin drew gay men from all over Germany was an open secret. As traumatizing as the 1885 raid on Seger's bar had been for Berlin's gay community, it did little to push the community underground. Even while the arrested bar patrons were still serving their sentences, new gay bars began popping up in the vicinity of the shuttered Seger's. In quick succession, roughly half a dozen new nightspots opened, and the police seemed largely uninterested in closing them down.

Still, as Bebel found, even the open secret of Berlin's thriving gay community should not be casually mentioned on the floor of parliament. Despite the backing of his Social Democratic Party and the liberal press, the gay-rights petition got firmly rejected. There is no record of the parliamentary vote count, suggesting that the petition was voted down by a show of hands or a voice vote so lopsided that no one made a motion to call the roll for an official tally.

In parliament, much of the opposition came from the religious right, but the Scientific Humanitarian Committee also faced criticism from presumed allies. Some pessimists in the gay community thought that trying to change the law was a fool's errand. Shortly after Magnus began circulating his petition, his high school buddy Richard Kantorowicz (who had now de-Judaized his name to Richard Kandt), wrote him a letter for the first time since leaving for Africa. Kandt urged him as a friend to cease his activism. He quoted a modern poet: "Only he who has crucified his own happiness / Can be a savior for mankind."

Even Magnus's ally, writer Franz Josef von Bülow, a founder of the Scientific Humanitarian Committee, gave up on changing Germany. Von Bülow opted to live free in exile in Italy rather than remain in Germany with Paragraph 175 still on the books. The wealthy aristocrat moved to Venice and lived in the Palazzo Tiepolo, turning the gracious residence into an informal queer community center.

Magnus also faced opposition from a faction within Germany's gay community. A subset rejected his born-this-way hypothesis with a counter theory that homosexuality was a choice—and an elevated one at that. Most were political conservatives who grounded their outlook in the queer culture of ancient Greece, in which bisexuality was widely accepted and married men often had young boyfriends on the side. In antiquity, gay male attraction had been seen as a higher form of love and heterosexuality denigrated as a base instinct necessary only for the survival of humanity. The outlook was rooted in the misogynistic conceit that men were superior to women and, thus, only men could be fully worthy of love. This hierarchical outlook dovetailed with new fascistic intellectual currents in Europe. Those hostile to the liberal creed of human equality could differ on their rankings of humanity. These particular rightists thought gay men superior to straight men. But the general outlook that groups must be ranked into superiors and inferiors, masters and servants, betrayed a fundamental hostility to the revolutionary concept of universal human rights.

In Germany, individuals who placed their queerness in this Greco-Roman tradition formed a right-wing "masculinist" opposition to

Hirschfeld and his Social Democratic allies. Their leader, Adolf Brand, who was married to a woman, set himself up as an intellectual and political rival to Magnus. In 1896, Brand launched an illustrated men's magazine—the world's first gay magazine—and even briefly attended Scientific Humanitarian Committee meetings. But in 1898, Brand broke with the committee over its born-this-way determinism. Brand viewed homosexuality as a cultivated choice. He and his masculinists bristled at the idea first formulated by Ulrichs and only slightly tempered by Hirschfeld that there was something feminine ("inverted") about being a gay man. To them, being gay was the manliest way one could live.

It was not only masculinists on the political right who criticized the Scientific Humanitarian Committee; feminists on the left also took issue with the group. At its founding, the Scientific Humanitarian Committee was entirely male, "an affair of men for men," as one German feminist smarted decades later. Being open to all sexes on paper did not make the committee meaningfully diverse.

The initial decision to seek out petition signatures from the most famous and influential people in a society that rarely permitted women to become scientists, doctors, or attorneys, all but guaranteed a nearly all-male movement. Dr. Agnes Hacker, a pioneering Berlin physician and women's rights advocate, was a rare prominent female signer of the petition—the exception that proved the rule. Even the signer from the University of Strasbourg's Women's Clinic was a man, its director, Dr. Wilhelm Freund. The committee's leadership remained overwhelmingly male despite scores of queer women approaching the group for help. As the committee recorded in an early annual report, "In the course of the year . . . hardly a week went by without homosexuals turning to us for help [including] Uranian women whose marital relations had become untenable." The committee would not diversify its ranks until a proposal to criminalize sex acts between women brought it into an alliance with the radical wing of Germany's women's movement. Even then, the committee's leadership remained overwhelmingly male.

Despite the failure to repeal Paragraph 175, the Scientific Humanitarian Committee's petition made gay rights an issue. Previously unexamined, it was now a question of the day on which scientists, attorneys, journalists, even ordinary citizens were expected to have an opinion.

And once the question was openly posed, it was remarkable how many people came out in favor of equal rights. The Scientific Humanitarian Committee resolved to continue amassing signatures in preparation for some future parliamentary repeal effort.

Presenting the cause as a matter of scientific rationality proved savvy. It allowed public figures to sign the petition without it being read as a public coming-out. The enduring ambiguity of many committee members' sexual orientations allowed Magnus to continue with his self-presentation as a man of science whose own sexual orientation was beside the point. Still, the committee encouraged its members at least to come out to trusted family and friends. Well aware of the hypocrisy that some of the most influential people in German society were secretly gay, the Scientific Humanitarian Committee was tempted to use "outing" as a political strategy. Might not the general public become more tolerant were they to learn that, say, a beloved athlete, a celebrated war hero, or an acclaimed opera star was gay? But since there was no telling how any particular celebrity would react to being outed, the group ultimately rejected this as a "path over corpses."

The heart of the Scientific Humanitarian Committee's strategy would be educating the public. Shortly after their legislative push failed in parliament, Max Spohr published the text of the petition with its eminent signatories alongside Magnus's arguments in its favor in a seventy-one-page pamphlet, "Paragraph 175 of the Imperial Penal Code: The Homosexual Question Judged by Contemporaries."

The short work took the position that anti-gay prejudice was a medieval holdover from the benighted times before the French Revolution. Magnus conjured the horrors of an earlier era, recounting the witch-trial-type hysteria that swept Holland in the early eighteenth century and resulted in "55 [gay men] sentenced to death, choked, singed, burned to ashes and hanged." He then hailed the meeting "in July 1791 [when] the Constitutional Assembly in Paris . . . repeal[ed the antigay] legal provision . . . the first legislative body to take this step."

Despite a few soaring passages, most of the pamphlet argued from simple pragmatism. Whatever one thought of them, gays were everywhere. "There are homosexual men and women among all races, among all nations of the earth," Magnus wrote. "They exist in the highest and lowest classes of the population, in the city and in the country, among the most educated and the most uneducated, among righteous and inferior characters. . . . There are few families among whose nearer or more distant relatives there are not urnish-feeling [gay] ones."

The committee became a hothouse for publications, ranging from monthly reports on its activities to its scientific journal of peer-reviewed research, the *Annual of Sexual Intermediaries with Special Focus on Homosexuality*, edited by Hirschfeld. Its debut issue in 1899 presented several suppressed texts written by Karl Heinrich Ulrichs as well as a detailed questionnaire that Magnus created to plumb the depths of his patients' sexuality. "Does your sex drive extend to both sexes to the same or to different degrees and by how much?" the questionnaire prompted in order to suss out where patients fit on his continuum. Gender identity and nonconformity were addressed in questions such as "Do you have the urge to dress in the clothing of the other sex?" and "Are you or are you not adverse to female occupations, such as cooking, cleaning, hairdressing, design; or male occupations, such as sports, hunting, shooting, fighting. What particular interests do you have (e.g., politics, fashion, theater, horses.)?"

Most of the research published in the journal naturally bolstered Magnus's theories. But it was not dogmatic. The *Annual* published a broad range of articles from different perspectives, even a piece by Sigmund Freud. Magnus's rival was an opponent of the born-this-way hypothesis. The Vienna-based psychiatrist saw homosexuality as a pathology triggered by dysfunctional family dynamics.

Spurred by the biologist who wrote to him about homosexuality in the animal kingdom, Magnus conducted a literature review on the topic. The earliest publication he located was a French entomology text published in 1859. Gay insects were fascinating, but finding homosexuality among our closer relatives in the animal kingdom would provide stronger evidence for his hypothesis, so he commissioned a groundbreaking article on this subject.

The *Annual*'s second issue, published in 1900, included an article by zoologist (and petition signer) Ferdinand Karsch comprehensively cataloguing homosexual behavior observed in animals. As Karsch found, in the fourth century BCE Aristotle himself had recorded lesbian behavior in doves with one female mounting another female, building a nest together, and then attending to the (unfertilized) eggs. More recently, Karsch's contemporaries had observed same-sex intercourse in insects, amphibians, and mammals and confirmed that this behavior occurred even when potential opposite-sex partners were available. In one insect species, the cockchafer, a nineteenth-century scientist discerned that two males were engaged in anal sex that had to be consensual—the smaller, weaker partner was mounting the larger, stronger one and the creature's anal sphincter could be opened and closed at will.

Karsch's article had clear political implications. Opponents could argue—erroneously in Magnus's opinion—that "permissive" cultures like Italy's or Berlin's bred gayness, but there was no equivalent cultural argument for animals.

The assistant director of the Berlin Zoo, Dr. Oskar Heinroth, publicly seconded Karsch's research. Heinroth was an expert on aquatic birds, and he shared his observations of gay ducks acting out the mating rituals of duck reproduction. As he told Magnus:

> In the case of the most disparate of duck species, you can often make the observation that two male or two female animals couple with each other, and to be sure, in doing so it has nothing to do with acts of violent rape. Whether they are two males, called drakes, or females, both partners make the same preparations as for regular copulation. In the case of the so-called *Brautenten*, or "bride" ducks, for example, this consists, first of all, of the male swimming to the female and as a sign of courtship dipping his bill into the water. Whereupon the female sits upon the water dead still, and then, after a longer or shorter period of time of love-playing, pairing occurs. We see a similar game when homosexual acts occur between two males: first of all, both dip their bills into the water; then, one of the partners sits upon the water, and the other does the mounting; also, when two females engage in intercourse with each other, one of the partners plays the passive role, swimming very slowly and calmly, while the other one does the mounting. The love-playing after the act is also the same as after the act between male and female: the active partner swims around the feminine partner, who remains calmly still.

Dr. Heinroth noted that heterosexual assumptions among zookeepers often left queer animal relationships hiding in plain sight. He told Magnus of a pair of inseparable trumpeter swans. Unlike in many bird species, nothing in a trumpeter swan's plumage indicates its sex; male trumpeter swans, called cobs, simply tend to be larger than females, called pens. Zoo staff assumed the couple to be straight and figured the larger one was male and the smaller one female. When the larger of the two died, the smaller was transferred to a zoo in Holland. Soon after intake, the Dutch zookeepers conducted a physical examination of the newly arrived German "female" and discovered male duck genitalia. When the newcomer was put into a zoo environment with a male and a female swan, he showed little interest in the female and mounted the male.

For those who would never read a scientific journal, Magnus included recaps of the *Annuals* in a 1901 pamphlet, alongside the petition and an ever more impressive list of signers. Homosexuality had been observed in animals, the pamphlet explained. It also offered a global outlook noting that numerous non-Western societies have accepted roles for gender nonconforming individuals and "permit their sons to wear women's clothing as soon as they are aware that they are men-women." To target a mass audience, Magnus entitled the pamphlet "What People Should Know About the Third Sex" and offered it nearly for free (it cost the equivalent of two postage stamps). Magnus confessed mixed feelings about the slang term *third sex* for queer people—he would later call it "the common, if not entirely appropriate designation." The term captured the concept that masculinity was not exclusively found in men and femininity not exclusively found in women but failed to convey the deeper concept of human sexuality as a continuum. In place of the binary Magnus was working to debunk, the term *third sex* merely added another category essentially marked "other."

"What People Should Know About the Third Sex" tried to give everyone the argument they needed to accept and decriminalize homosexuality. For the tender hearted, it went maudlin: "The love for one's own sex can be just as pure, tender and noble as that for the other sex, differentiated only in its object, not its nature," Magnus wrote. For laissez-faire liberals, he offered the argument that consensual behavior between two adults should be no concern of the state. For the more practical minded, the pamphlet argued that Paragraph 175 was vague and capricious. Why, for example, was gay male penetrative sex illegal in Germany but not mutual masturbation? He even argued, as Bebel had, that there were just so many gays it was impractical to oppress them. There weren't enough jail cells to hold them all. Magnus even edged into eugenics by asserting that forcing gays into straight marriages was "a danger for their offspring, who are subject to all manner of mental and nervous disturbances." Throwing everything at the wall to see what sticks, Magnus made some arguments that contradicted each other—he usually claimed that the increased incidence of depression in gays was a result of their societal oppression, not their biological makeup. But in the moments when Magnus felt forced to choose whether he was a scientist or an activist first, he chose activism. Eliminating Paragraph 175 was his highest goal.

Those furthest to the right rejected his theories outright. As one newspaper editorialized, "There are only two sexes, the third sex is the invention of polluted brains and perverted hearts." But Magnus was winning over the center. His pamphlet encouraged parents to understand that their children could be gay and to accept them for who they were before it was too late. "How many a mother is unable to comprehend . . . why her daughter rejects one suitor after another," Magnus wrote, or "why her son, despite his outstanding character qualities, despite true goodness of heart, is always so introverted, finds no joy in life until one day he does himself an injury." For queer people themselves, the pamphlet offered help. "Sappho and Socrates" had been published with Max Spohr's private assurance that anyone in need of aid who wrote in would be put in touch with Magnus, but the new tract actively provided resources for those in peril. Anyone being blackmailed on account of their sexual orientation, it explained, should immediately contact the Scientific Humanitarian Committee. It even listed its address—104 Berlinerstrasse in Charlottenburg—down the street from Magnus's home.

In 1902, Max Spohr issued a new edition of "Sappho and Socrates," this time with Magnus's name on it. "The reasons that led me to choose the pseudonym [Th. Ramien] in 1896 no longer exist," Magnus wrote. He no longer had reason to hide.

For all of their stumbles in the political arena, Magnus and the Scientific Humanitarian Committee were winning the battle for public opinion. At its founding, the group had practiced a careful politics of respectability, eagerly touting that Spohr was married with children. By contrast, in 1902, the group published a signed carte-de-visite sent by Baron Hermann von Teschenberg in which the German aristocrat appears in a floor-length white dress and dainty updo. The caption beneath the image reads "Inspired by . . . your efforts . . . I happily give you this image, which reveals my true nature, along with my name for the purposes of publication." A few years later, Teschenberg would become a copresident of the Scientific Humanitarian Committee. The committee had built the cultural space to be openly queer.

Even some of the group's musty peer-reviewed research publications were filtering down to the broader population. After Magnus published scientific evidence on gay animals, it turned out they were everywhere. "People continuously bring dogs to my attention," he wrote, "which, in spite of ample opportunity to have sexual intercourse with female dogs, bypassed the females and, instead, approached male companions in an unmistakably libidinous manner; several of these dogs exhibited 'female characteristics.' "

Magnus took it as a symbol of his success when, a few years later, the suburban Potsdam press gushed over a pair of lesbian doves in the local zoo. Hoping to give them the joys of motherhood, zookeepers placed a fertilized chicken egg in their nest. The two were overjoyed and squabbled over who got to sit on it. The Potsdamers lapped it up.

Most heartening to Magnus was winning over his first gay friend, Richard Kandt. The expatriate contacted Magnus from Africa in a panic. A former lover was threatening to out him and had drained a good part of his inherited wealth in hush-money payoffs. As he had done for patients in the past, Magnus now interceded, ending the extortion racket by convincing Kandt that he had no reason to pay up, since he had nothing to be ashamed of. In the end, Kandt conceded that Magnus had been right all along. As Kandt wrote to him, "If a human right is withheld from us, we must fight until it is restored." Magnus hadn't just won an abstract argument with his old friend. His public gay-rights campaign very well may have saved his friend's life.

Chapter 5

Big Data

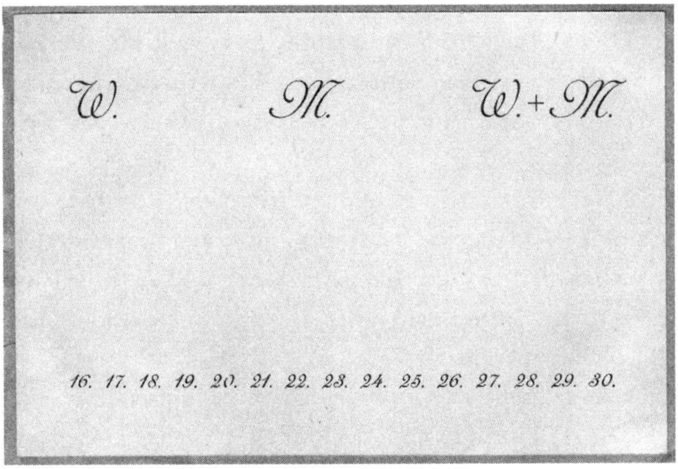

1904 questionnaire card asking respondents to indicate their relative levels of attraction to their own sex and to the opposite sex.

MAGNUS'S TRAVELS IN disparate lands, his therapy patients, and the letters he'd received all suggested that gays were everywhere. But for a scientist, anecdotes aren't evidence. In an 1898 pamphlet, he lamented that "estimating the percentage of homosexuals is impossible at this time." How could one count members of a community whose very existence was criminalized? Undeterred, Magnus made determining the size of the queer population central to the Scientific Humanitarian Committee's research agenda.

Given Paragraph 175 and societal stigma, Magnus presumed most German gays were passing as straight. Magnus termed this phenomenon "external assimilation" and compared it to animals such as chameleons.

"Just as in the realm of nature many organisms blend color and form into their environment in such a way that they can make it uncommonly difficult for predators to find them," Magnus wrote, "so do homosexuals blend into the constructs of their surroundings in such a manner that even educated observers can have difficulty recognizing them."

In high school, Magnus had learned how to pass to protect himself after seeing his more feminine classmate mercilessly harassed. He and his close friend Richard steered clear of sexual topics in fear of the other's response.

Being closeted, even from close family members, was the norm. The gay demimonde was replete with stories of mortifying encounters in the cruising grounds when brothers, cousins—sometimes even fathers and sons—ran into each other.

Psychotherapy was still in its infancy. Many of Magnus's patients had told him that he was the first medical professional to whom they'd confided on sexual matters. And the psychoanalysts' fee-for-service model deterred Germans of limited means. Working-class gays never had money for such extravagances.

Catholic confession, with its pay-what-you-can donation system, was a more widespread form of confidential one-on-one counseling. Catholic priests who secretly sympathized with Magnus's cause anonymously reported that closeted gay parishioners were common. One priest told the committee he first realized how many people were queer when he began asking a follow-up question during confession. Whenever someone admitted to violating the Sixth Commandment—adultery—he would ask whether the affair had been with a member of the same sex or a member of the opposite sex. Occasionally, the individual would admit it had been a same-sex affair. More commonly, though, an awkward silence would ensue, followed by a defensive, unconvincing claim that, of course, the extramarital affair had been with a member of the opposite sex; what a preposterous and unseemly question to ask.

For all the anecdotes, there were no hard numbers. In typical years, only a few dozen men in all of Berlin were indicted on charges of gay sex. That jurists who assumed that the number of prosecutions and convictions under Paragraph 175 was a good guide to the number of gays struck Magnus as ridiculous.

The medical profession thought it had a better grasp on the demographics. Sometimes psychiatrists would ask their queer patients how many other gays there were in their city. But these were guestimates from members of underground, often balkanized, queer communities. One Magdeburg patient pegged his small city's gay community at seventy people, while a patient in the massive port metropolis of Hamburg estimated that city had sixty gays total. Clearly these two reports couldn't both be right. Even for the same city, reports varied widely. One member of Munich's gay community said he knew a hundred other gay people in the Bavarian capital; another said he knew thousands.

Even the gay community's champions found themselves at a loss to define its size. Shortly before dying in self-imposed exile in 1895, Karl Heinrich Ulrichs speculated that rates of homosexuality varied by ethnicity. Ulrichs estimated that among Germans approximately one in every two hundred men were gay while "the relative number of Urnings [gay men] appears to be somewhat higher . . . among the [Hungarians] and Slavs, especially the southern Slavs." Ulrichs based his analysis on his observations throughout Europe, but Magnus figured that Ulrichs was measuring outness not queerness—and that outness naturally increased as one traveled from puritanical Northern Europe toward the more open cultures of the Mediterranean. Magnus was convinced that the percentage of people born queer was constant across time and space but was unsure how to prove it. And a hypothesis remains speculative unless and until there's hard proof.

Earlier scientists had applied quantitative methods to this question, but Magnus found their methodologies embarrassingly lacking. In 1901, an enterprising gay philologist in Berlin had placed a personal ad—"Doctor, twenty-five years of age, in search of [male] friend seventeen to twenty-one years of age."—and collected the results. Even with this prim text, only eleven of the twenty-five publications to which the philologist submitted it would run it. The doctor received 140 replies and brought them all to Magnus, proud of what he regarded as a data trove. Of the 140 responses, 111 were conclusively from gay men seeking a romantic relationship. But from a social-scientific perspective, Magnus asked, what use did it have? The ad ran in just eleven newspapers, and it had run only once. Even loyal newspaper readers don't scan the classifieds every day. Those looking for love in the personals section would surely skew straight precisely because of the taboo against publicly seeking gay companionship. And in a society that persecutes homosexuals, how many gay men might have seen the ad and wanted to reply—but decided not to because it felt unsafe? All this experiment proved was that there were at least 111 gay men in Berlin—not a particularly useful, or even controversial, data point.

A similarly unscientific study was subsequently conducted by Dr. Albert Moll, a pioneering psychiatrist who, though unconvinced by Magnus's born-this-way hypothesis, nonetheless supported the Scientific Humanitarian Committee's campaign against Paragraph 175. Moll's first estimate had been based solely on word of mouth—in 1891, he ventured that Berlin's gay population "at least amounts to 900"—but now, he crafted an ostensibly more scientific study training his doctor's eyes on a men's public toilet. He posted a research assistant to observe a Berlin bathroom from 8 a.m. to midnight, count the total number of users, and discern which of them were gay. He categorized any man who checked out other men, exposed his genitals, or got an erection as homosexual. The research assistant came back with a report that 582 men had used the bathroom and approximately 1 percent of them were gay.

Magnus could hardly contain his mockery. From his personal knowledge of Berlin's gay scene, he knew that all public toilets were not created equal. In every city, some had a reputation for cruising while most did not. In his experience, the best indicator of a cruisy bathroom was phallus graffiti. Studying a single public bathroom at random, as Moll did, would skew the results, probably downwards unless one hit the jackpot. Magnus didn't mince words: "The statistics on observations made in a toilet produced . . . and published by Moll are completely worthless."

Magnus's first attempt to amass better data echoed Moll's initial word-of-mouth impulse but on a larger scale; he asked queer individuals to report back on how many of their colleagues at work or school were gay. This data, he knew, wouldn't be perfect; given how many German gays lived closeted lives, these reports relied more on the observer's gaydar than was ideal. And Magnus believed gay people tended to err on the side of overestimation. But dozens of informants came forward to provide estimates and their reports were illuminating.

A Catholic priest told Magnus that over 3 percent of his fellow Catholic clergymen were queer, which the priest believed must make his field the gayest of them all. But a butcher reported that among master butchers and apprentices, the figure was nearly 4 percent. Actors and theater costume designers self-reported at 5 percent, as did naval officers. The highest figure came from college fraternity brothers and prep school students: just under 6 percent.

Among women, Magnus found it even harder to amass solid data since so many were excluded from the workforce and toiled individually as homemakers. But one lesbian telegraph operator came through. She reported that of her 350 female coworkers in a big-city switchboard office, eight (2.3 percent) were queer.

Magnus made his own estimates for his old high school based on data he had informally collected. "With regard to three of the approximate two hundred students with whom I attended the cathedral high school in my hometown," he wrote, "I know with certainty that they now are homosexual. Because of my work in this field, they disclosed themselves to me." Magnus studiously presented this information in his disinterested man-of-science persona, naming no names—but presumably he and his friend Richard constituted two of the three.

As interesting as these estimates were, they weren't hard data. Magnus's high school experience taught him how difficult it was to guess who was queer and who wasn't. The only way to get solid numbers would be to conduct an anonymous survey.

Magnus was intrigued to learn that Dr. Lucien von Römer of Amsterdam had recently conducted a sexuality survey that touched on some of these issues. His anonymous questionnaire was brief—five questions long—and given to around five hundred adolescent boys. It covered subjects including virginity and masturbation but also sexual orientation. One question read: "Do you have feelings for women, for men, or for both?" Picking up where Römer left off, Magnus resolved to draw up a larger survey focused on sexual orientation. It would be the most comprehensive mass survey on homosexuality yet created. The Dutch doctor, for his part, was flattered; shortly after, Römer joined the executive board of the Scientific Humanitarian Committee.

But sending out sex surveys was risky, as Magnus had already learned from experience. In 1902, he'd sent out the general sex questionnaire he gave his own patients to a wide, anonymous sample of individuals. The questions were never salacious, but they were specific about particular kinks. One question asked, "Have you suffered other sexual anomalies, e.g., sadistic tendencies (torment addiction), masochistic (addiction to being tormented), fetish (love for a body part, such as hands, feet, liver spots, or an article, such as boots, handkerchief), exhibitionism (addicted to showing genitals) or the like?" That this questionnaire went out to women as well as men only raised the stakes in conservative, sex-role–obsessed Germany. Anna von Blankenburg, an imperious Berlin aristocrat, deemed the questionnaire obscene and pressed charges against Hirschfeld. Simply asking her such questions—Did she wield her riding crop solely on the steeplechase course? Had she ever had Lady Godiva fantasies?—was, she argued, an insult to her dignity. Von Blankenburg eventually withdrew the suit, deeming "the inconveniences associated with trial" to be a waste of her time. But Magnus was now on notice.

In the fall of 1903, the Scientific Humanitarian Committee's Statistical Commission members gathered at the Prince Albrecht Hotel in Berlin. Given the trumped-up intimidation lawsuit the previous year, members took pains to inoculate the survey against legal challenge by making it as buttoned-down as possible. They also weighed whom to survey. From his experiences as well as his informants, Magnus knew that some professions skewed gayer than others. It would be crucial not to bias the data by picking an unscientific sample population like costume designers or naval officers. Magnus also wanted to examine—and hopefully debunk—the assumption that rates of homosexuality varied by class. With their fussy etiquette codes, upper-class gents were often seen as more courtly and effeminate—and, presumably, more gay—than working-class men. But the born-this-way hypothesis precluded this possibility.

Magnus and the Statistical Commission decided to survey the college-bound student body at the Technical High School in well-off Charlottenburg and the proletarian membership of a metal workers' union. As Magnus explained, "When polling," they purposefully chose "circles about which we could say in advance that theoretically the number of homosexuals in them would be in no way greater than in the rest of the population: students studying technology and metal workers, both particularly 'manly' occupations." The Scientific Humanitarian Committee justified its decision to only survey men by citing its goal of overturning Paragraph 175, which only applied to men who have sex with men, but there was no doubt some navel gazing in the decision if not a whiff of misogyny. In its research, the committee seemed almost as interested in gay animals as it was in gay women.

In December 1903, the committee sent out three thousand survey cards to students of the Technical High School. To ensure anonymity, the cards required no handwriting to complete, only a series of underlines. Even with its purposefully innocuous name, the Scientific Humanitarian Committee was now well-known and associated in the public mind with the cause of gay rights. The accompanying letter acknowledged its political agenda: "We take it for granted that the results of our survey will be not only of interest in theory but also important in practice, because it will have an eventual impact on legislation, discrimination in society, and, with that, on the fate of a significant portion of our population."

Each student at the high school received a letter in the mail at home from "Magnus Hirschfeld, M.D., for the Scientific Humanitarian Committee" complete with a card and instructions for filling it out. As it explained, "The main question we put before you is the following: Is your love drive (sex drive) directed at women (W), men (M) or women and men (W+M)? We request that . . . you answer the question on the enclosed post card simply by checking and underlining. . . . Please give no names. . . . Strictly adhere to the truth. . . . Everyone is guaranteed discretion."

As the letters arrived, the survey became the talk of the school. There was, of course, some joking in the hallways, but most participants took it seriously. One closeted student initially panicked thinking his secret sexual orientation had been discovered; he calmed down only once he realized that everyone in his class had received the same survey.

As with the committee's petition against Paragraph 175, some respondents sent back unsolicited comments. Several students proclaimed themselves allies of the movement: "May your humanitarian survey find great success," one wrote. "Wishing you total success in your philanthropic efforts!" said another. Some editorialized to proclaim their straightness; one wrote "*Vivant omnes virgines*!" ("Long live young women!") and another, that being attracted to "M simply incomprehensible to me."

When word got out about the anonymous sex surveys showing up in the mailboxes of thousands of teen boys, the right-wing press pounced. The survey, one newspaper argued, was a gay recruitment scheme—the Scientific Humanitarian Committee's effort at the "seduction of" young men. Since gay couples didn't produce offspring, rightists reasoned, the only way the community could replenish itself was by grooming new members. Magnus countered with his born-this-way hypothesis and scoffed that one might as well forbid ophthalmologists from studying color blindness out of fear it would turn their subjects color-blind. More worrisome, an enraged evangelical preacher, Pastor Wilhelm Philipps, organized a student meeting when he learned of the survey. Assailing the questionnaire as an "attack on student honor," he recruited a handful of students and parents to publicly complain.

Even in this contentious atmosphere, most students participated, filling out and returning their cards. Six percent self-identified as queer—a higher percentage than any of the informal workplace estimates Magnus had obtained. And there was an even bigger surprise in the data. Among those who described themselves as not straight, three-fourths identified as bisexual and only one-fourth as exclusively homosexual. In "Sappho and Socrates," Magnus had posited that sexuality was a continuum; now this large cohort of bisexuals was bolstering the case. As his research proceeded, Magnus decided to solicit more information from bisexuals to understand their orientation in more detail.

Before sending out the questionnaire cards to the metal workers, Magnus made a crucial tweak to the instructions. For those who self-identified as being attracted to both men and women, he asked that they make a double underline under either "M" or "W" if their attraction to one sex was more intense.

In February, Magnus wrote to 5,721 lathe operators. His letter opened bluntly: "As you probably already know, the love drive (sex drive) of numerous men is not oriented exclusively toward women, but rather toward male persons from time to time and even exclusively. . . . The undersigned Committee . . . wishes . . . to establish the approximate number of homosexuals." Though the metal workers union was a politically progressive group aligned with the Social Democrats and presumed to be sympathetic to the cause, Magnus assured all respondents anonymity. He also offered "Berlin's freethinking workers" who had not had the opportunity for higher education a thumbnail history lesson that he had not included in his brief letter to the students:

> We know today that homosexuality represents an inborn singularity, which occurs through no fault of one's own and which is harmless. . . . In classical antiquity this love . . . was publicly acknowledged [and] praised impartially by Greek and Roman poets just as much as the love for women, [but] in the Middle Ages superstition seized hold of it and totally suppressed it. . . . Consequently, people were most severely punished for homosexual intercourse . . . by death by burning, which otherwise was the fate only for two other imagined crimes, heresy and witchcraft. . . . The enlightenment of the French Revolution did away with those laws [but] in other countries, Germany included, leftovers of those threats of punishment created by superstition still exist.

The most important difference between the original student survey and this new version was its instructions:

> We ask you now to answer the above question on the enclosed, stamped postcard, simply by underlining the letters printed W, M or W+M, in the following manner:
>
> <u>W</u>   M   W+M
>
> means that your drive always has been directed at women.
>
> W   <u>M</u>   W+M
>
> means that your drive always has been directed at men.

W M W+M

means that your drive always has been directed at women as well as at men.

If the last should apply and if, at the same time, you have made the observation that one of the two orientations of the drive tends to predominate, we request that you underline in the following manner:

W M W+M

namely, that your drive is directed at persons of both sexes; however, the drive toward women decidedly predominated;

W M W+M

on the other hand, means that your drive is directed at persons of both sexes, but that the tendency toward men decidedly predominated.

The metal workers' survey cards went out in February 1904. As Magnus sat back trying his best to be patient until the replies came in, he got dragged back into court. Pastor Philipps had convinced six of the high school students who had received surveys in December to lodge a legal complaint. Chief Public Prosecutor Hugo Isenbiel, a notorious homophobe who had once reportedly said that gays have the "morals of dogs," charged Magnus with having "disseminated obscene writings" through the mail.

On the day of his trial that spring, he bravely entered the courtroom with Siegfried Chodzeisner, his attorney and liberal Jewish Charlottenburg neighbor. The case would hinge on whether the questionnaire "offends the normal popular sense of shame and morality," that is, whether it violated community standards. For the defense, Chodzeisner called an administrator from the Technical High School who told the judges that the student body reaction had been almost universally favorable and sympathetic; out of over three thousand students, only six had objected. Chodzeisner also informed the court that a similar survey had subsequently gone out to members of the metalworkers' union without a single objection. Moreover, the questionnaires were all private and anonymous. How could anyone claim to have been injured by it?

Magnus took the stand in his own defense and scolded the court. While lawyers and judges quibbled over community standards, people were dying. "Just at the beginning of the week," he testified, "a homosexual student I know at the Technical High School committed suicide by taking poison because he was a homosexual. Among the patients I am treating at this time, there is a student at the same institute who attempted suicide by shooting himself because of homosexuality. Only a few weeks ago, in these halls I was present at a hearing for two blackmailers who drove a homosexual gentleman, one of the most honorable men I knew, to take his own life. A second person, threatened by the same blackmailers, could be restrained from doing so only with effort. I could give hundreds of examples."

Given these stakes, Magnus closed, the real crime would be doing nothing: "I believe I would be blameworthy if, in the possession of the knowledge I have gathered for myself in the area of homosexuality, I did not make every effort to stomp out an error whose consequences human language is too inadequate to describe."

Two hours later, the panel of judges filed back into the courtroom to render their verdict: guilty. The law was clear: if a recipient was offended, then the material was obscene. Preserving the respondents' anonymity was no defense; mailing the questionnaire was legally no different from walking the streets asking random strangers if they had syphilis or canvassing the hallways of a girls' school asking passersby whether they were still virgins. The court also entertained the possibility that Magnus's survey could turn some kids gay. "Through such inquiries . . . young, naïve people can easily be confused in their sexual sensibilities and [be] led into the arms of perverse tendencies," the judges' decision warned. There was little solace to be taken in their acknowledgement that Magnus meant well. "The defendant had acted in his eagerness to pursue scientific interests," the panel wrote, "however, the means towards scientific research were wrong."

Upon conviction, Magnus was fined 200 marks (less than $2,000 today) and ordered to pay court costs. He duly anteed up, regarding it all as a modest cost of doing business in his activist struggle. Had he not had the money, he could have spent up to twenty days in jail.

In the end, Magnus believed he'd come out ahead. The trial expanded his fame, with coverage appearing in German language newspapers as far away as São Paolo and Buenos Aires. And though he lost in front of the judges, he largely won in the court of public opinion. Journalists deemed the trial an embarrassing display of backwardness and prudery. One newspaper demanded to know how "such a judgment was possible in 1904"; another expressed a "feeling of shame that such a trial has been possible in Germany."

Editorialists defended Magnus as a martyr to free inquiry. The Social Democratic newspaper the *Forward* likened him to the Renaissance scientist Galileo accused of heresy for insisting that the earth revolved around the sun. A newspaper in Magdeburg, where Magnus had never been universally popular, said he was akin to Giordano Bruno, another early-modern scientist, who'd been burned alive for endorsing the heliocentric model of the universe. A Leipzig paper even compared Magnus to his hero, Socrates, who was sentenced to death for "corrupting the youth." But there were also those who thought the court had not gone far enough in condemning Hirschfeld. One newspaper that opposed gay rights referred to the Scientific Humanitarian Committee as the "League of Perverts" and called for reintroducing medieval punishments: "Not to prison, not to the penitentiary [but] to the stake," its editors fumed.

Even with the courtroom loss, the sex survey proved a victory for science. For a relatively modest expense—printing, mailing, fine, court costs—Magnus had amassed the greatest trove of data on sexual orientation yet collected.

When the cards came back from the metalworkers, 4.3 percent self-identified as queer, with 1.1 percent responding that they were attracted to men alone and 3.2 percent listing being attracted to both men and women. There was some variation between the two surveys—6 percent of the students had self-identified as queer—but nothing that couldn't be accounted for by self-selection among those who chose to pursue a career as a lathe operator. Magnus had picked metalworkers because theirs was a stereotypically masculine job. As Magnus later wrote, "academic profession[s are] pursued more often by urnish [gay] individualities, probably in most cases without their knowledge of their own sexual psyche, than the profession of [say] the locksmith." Such small variations between the academically inclined students and the physical laborers, he thought, largely debunked the stereotype that the working classes were congenitally straighter than the professional classes.

The most illuminating data unearthed by the survey was on bisexuality. By modifying the instructions to request double underlining, the Statistical Commission of the Scientific Humanitarian Committee compiled information that had never before been collected. Among the bisexual metalworkers, roughly one-fifth identified as being equally attracted to both men and women; roughly one-fifth as being attracted more strongly to men; and roughly three-fifths as being more strongly attracted to women.

The central question Magnus had hoped to answer with his surveys was not how many gay students went to Charlottenburg's Technical High School or how many queer lathe operators were in the labor union, but how many queer individuals lived (a) in Germany and (b) on planet Earth. Extrapolating from his survey data to the national level indicated that Germany was a much gayer place than even the most aggressive community estimates had suggested. With sexuality being a continuum, there was no way to definitively sort humans into "gay" and "straight" categories. But for the sake of his computations, Magnus decided to count those who self-identified as being exclusively or predominantly attracted to individuals of their own sex as queer. To err on the conservative side and to safeguard his public persona as an impartial scientist, he left bisexuals who were mostly attracted to the opposite sex as straight for his calculations. According to the data he had collected, 1.5 percent of humans were exclusively gay and another 0.8 percent were bisexual but predominantly attracted to members of their own sex. In sum, this encompassed 2.3 percent of the population. If applied to Germany's population of some fifty million, this conservative estimate would mean that more than a million Germans were queer. If extrapolated globally, the number of queer people would register in the tens of millions. And this was a bare minimum. Undoubtedly some unknown number of respondents had declined to send back their card from fear of outing themselves even in an anonymous survey. Another subset had responded but were, either consciously or subconsciously, unwilling to reckon with their same-sex attraction and had falsely self-identified as straight.

But even with the numbers that the surveys had returned, it was impossible to maintain that heterosexuality was somehow the universal human standard. The German language may call straights *normalsexuelle*, but Magnus no longer would. He began pushing back in his writings, using the term "so-called normal people" (*sogenannten Normalen*). While oppressive laws like Paragraph 175 condemned the "crime against nature," Magnus began referring to his struggle to overturn "a law . . . against nature."

Chapter 6

Unpoliceable City

An elevated train penetrates a Berlin apartment building on an early twentieth-century postcard.

EVEN WITH PARAGRAPH 175 still on the books, when one gay German aristocrat, long expatriated, returned to Berlin, he immediately regretted what he termed his "foolishness." On paper, Berlin could hardly have been more hostile to gay life. Men who had sex with men were officially branded criminals and subject to arrest and prison time. Yet gay life in Berlin was more varied and vibrant than anywhere this man had traveled. As he put in a letter upon his return, I have been "in exile for forty years, only to discover that at the end of my days, in the capital of our country, which I missed so much, urnish life under [Paragraph] 175 is more widespread, more casual, and freer than in any other place."

The simplest explanation for this newfound tolerance was a fortuitous personnel change among Berlin's nightlife overseers. Shortly after the traumatizing 1885 raid on Seger's, the police commissioner who'd ordered it, Leopold von Meerscheidt-Hüllessem, got a new boss. The incoming police president, appointed by the kaiser, was Bernhard von Richthofen, a confirmed bachelor widely believed to be gay. According to rumor, he retained a handler whose chief responsibility was keeping his sex life out of the newspapers.

Under Richthofen, the force came to view their mandate as supervising gay life, not suppressing it. The Berlin police created a new Department of Homosexuals. While ominous sounding, it was modeled on the vice squad that regulated straight life in the city which cracked down only on perceived excesses, like prostitution and exhibitionism. Forming the Department of Homosexuals signaled a significant level of acceptance for gay life in the capital.

As Hüllessem's contacts within the gay community grew, he came to see that the real crime wasn't queer life per se but the blackmail that sprang from its criminalization. Under his leadership, prosecutions for blackmail outnumbered those for violations of Paragraph 175 roughly four to one. Hüllessem even attacked Paragraph 175, lambasting it as hypocritical for outlawing anal sex between two men but not between a man and woman. As he famously quipped, "I do not see why the anus of a woman should have any special privilege." Magnus praised Hüllessem as a "champion of light and justice." The chief personally gave guided tours of the city's queer nightspots to notable visitors. Following the precedent set by Hüllessem, his successors as police chief, Hans von Tresckow and Heinrich Kopp, followed in his tolerant footsteps. As Magnus noted, the enforcement of Paragraph 175 in Berlin had become "extraordinarily lenient [due to the] relationships [that] have developed . . . between representatives of the criminal investigation department . . . and certain homosexual circles."

Attributing the light hand of the law in nighttime Berlin purely to bureaucratic luck was too facile. It grew out of the unpoliceable nature of the new metropolis itself. Unlike the more gracious capitals of Europe—London and Paris with their roots in Roman times—Berlin was a modern industrial boomtown. In the mid-1600s, when the population of Paris was closing in on half a million, Berlin had only six thousand souls. But between 1800 and 1900, Berlin's population increased twenty-fold, to roughly two million. As late as 1870, it was possible to walk across Berlin from end to end in an hour—a messy endeavor in a city whose streets, lined by a rudimentary gutter system, were famously filthy. In 1871, when the decision was made to anoint Berlin the capital of unified Germany it was not on account of the city's size or dynamism but merely because it was the capital of the largest state in the new union, Prussia.

Paris long pulled in great minds from long distances with its Sorbonne, founded in the Middle Ages, while Berlin got a late start, not founding its first university until 1810. Its universities' more practical, secular, and modern outlook attracted open-minded young people—Hermann Hirschfeld among them, and later, his son. The schools also spurred an industrial boom as local innovations in chemistry and pharmaceuticals were commercialized from tiny labs to enormous plants, luring in thousands of workers for factory jobs. Already by 1864, most Berliners were transplants, not natives. By century's end, Germany's come-from-behind capital had become Europe's largest industrial center and the third-largest city on earth. Berlin's greatest creation, it seemed, was Berlin itself.

Observers gawked at the city's breakneck growth. With no natural barriers, development spread across the plains in all directions. New urban districts rose on the former greenbelt of potato farms in an endless cityscape that felt like another industrial product. The growth in the urban fabric was almost numbing. Turn-of-the-century Berlin urbanist August Endell captured the disconcerting feel of the city when he wrote, "the modern city . . . with vanishingly few exceptions . . . is hideous in design. The buildings are garish and yet lifeless, the streets and squares merely satisfy practical requirements without assuming a spatial life of their own; devoid of diversity or variation, they stretch away monotonously. You can walk for hours through the new parts of Berlin and yet still feel like you haven't gone anywhere. . . . It all looks the same." For the city's anarchic manner of growth, urban planners coined a tongue-in-cheek German compound noun: *Planlosigkeit*—planlessness.

With its utilitarian architecture, the German capital felt more like an American city than a European one. In a travelogue recounting his 1891 visit, American author Mark Twain declared Berlin "the European Chicago," adding, "Chicago would seem venerable beside it" as the "mass of the city looks as if it had been built last week." The Midwesterner noted that every street corner in Berlin without exception was well marked with signs. Without them, newcomers would be lost since every part of the city looked the same.

Berlin felt American in a deeper sense. As Twain remarked, the German capital "has no traditions and no history. It is a new city; the newest I have ever seen." Berlin's lack of tradition went deeper than aesthetics: it was socially and culturally open as well, a rarity in Europe.

Becoming the capital in 1871 spurred a white-collar jobs boom to match the blue-collar boom as the number of clerks and officials ballooned to staff the growing government bureaucracy. Sundry professionals—doctors like Magnus and lawyers like Siegfried Chodzeisner—moved in to cater to the growing population's needs. Magnus, for all his uniqueness, was demographically a rather typical transplant. Almost three-quarters of the migrants came from the poorer regions to the east (many from provinces that are today part of Poland). That these eastern migrants were disproportionately Jewish did not go unnoticed, especially by Prussia's aristocrats and the older, more conservative, professional elite who felt pushed aside by the influx of Jewish doctors and lawyers. Jewish students, bigots complained, would come to the capital for college and never leave. The social openness of the city that was a boon to newcomers was a threat to the establishment in what had long been a small insular city.

A growing metropolis of transplants hatched its own distinct culture. So many Berliners had moved in from eastern backwaters that the last thing they wanted was to do everything the way they had growing up. They wanted the best, whether it was local or not—fabrics from France, hats from Vienna, and shoes from America. The cosmopolitan "world city" (*Weltstadt*) was said to operate on its own frenetic pace—the *Berliner Tempo*. The city's faddish impermanence was built into its fabric. Event pillars, eighteen feet tall and the girth of a barrel, were placed at regular intervals on the streets of Berlin. Planted empty, they were soon covered in an ever-changing array of flyers for plays, concerts, lectures, and protests. Every week as the dates passed and the old event notices got pulled down and new notices were pasted up, Berlin was reborn as a different city with different concerns and different obsessions. And yet it was always the same city—the one where the locals were obsessed with the next new thing.

Urban newcomers typically found themselves housed in the structure repeated ad infinitum throughout the newly urbanized districts of Berlin: the tenement apartment building, or "rental barracks" (*Mietskaserne*). Typically five stories tall, each structure contained around a hundred apartments packed with around a thousand residents. Each *Mietskaserne* contained housing for all classes within a single building. The units facing the street were coveted and expensive while those in the back were unfashionable and cheap. Each structure had at least one central courtyard—twenty-eight square meters (three hundred square feet) as mandated by the building code—but some had up to half a dozen courtyards hiding in back if the shape of the lot permitted. Courtyards generally grew darker and dingier the deeper one wandered from the street. Five stories with no elevator created a similar dynamic of desirability vertically. Renting an apartment on the lower floors meant climbing fewer stairs, and they were priced accordingly. Those up top were less coveted and thus cheaper. The poorest residents took in boarders to make rent, turning their bedrooms into dormitories packed with bunkbeds.

The *Mietskaserne* apartment buildings could also contain commercial spaces and sometimes even industrial ones. For those strolling on the street, a line of well-kept boutiques and restaurants formed an orderly streetscape. But the ground-floor units of the interior courtyards could be noisy and dirty with light-industrial workshops, small stores, or dive bars. This array of apartments and social spaces for all, from posh to pauper, conjured the vaunted *Berliner Mischung* ("Berlin mix") which Magnus deemed central to Berlin's sexual free-for-all.

A single *Mietskaserne* housed the entire spectrum of metropolitan society. As Magnus observed, "those in the [well-to-do] front of an apartment building often have no idea who is living in the rear block of the same building, let alone what the inhabitants get up to." A well-off resident might put on a threadbare coat and hat—or a dress and heels—

and spend a night in a dive bar in an interior courtyard in another neighborhood, no one the wiser. Only the richest neighborhoods, such as Charlottenburg, where Magnus lived, and the areas bordering Berlin's central park, the Tiergarten, sprouted buildings made up entirely of spacious, elegant apartments.

Technologically precocious, Berlin was knit together with a circulatory system of trains, subways, and streetcars making it both the ultimate city of strangers and the most accessible city in the world. It began in 1867, when the medieval city walls had been torn down and replaced with a train line, the *Ringbahn*, encircling the city. Initially pulled by horses, the trains were soon steam powered. In quick succession Berlin built the world's first system of electric streetcars; then an elevated electric train system, eight years before Chicago; and finally, in 1902, a subway, two years before New York. All connected central Berlin with the outlying neighborhoods and suburbs making far-flung areas accessible to all in ten minutes on the *U-Bahn*, whether for a business lunch or a tryst.

With its tangle of elevated train lines, the dizzying motion at all levels gave Berlin a futuristic flair. One moment you could imagine yourself in an earlier era, wandering among the venerable old palaces, theaters, and museums on the courtly Unter den Linden thoroughfare, while the next moment an elevated train shot by between the columned facades. Most jaw-dropping of all, some lines rammed through apartment blocks, with trains zipping through a tunnel cut into the building. While locals grew inured to the wonders of their metropolis, visitors stopped to watch elevated trains shoot through the center of a city block.

This first generation of elevated trains ran on brick viaducts that, at street level, formed an endless series of darkened archways. The *Nationalzeitung* newspaper compared them to "aqueducts of Rome." During business hours, many of these brick archways were filled by informal vendors or even formal stores, but there were simply more spaces than could ever be filled. Contemporaneously with each neighborhood getting connected to every other by the elevated trains, the city was becoming a sprawl of furtive spaces, darkened even in broad daylight, where anything could happen.

Berlin's peculiar allure came not in spite of its ugliness but, strangely, because of it. There was something undeniably, compulsively captivating about this city. Magnus had been magnetically drawn to it from stately Magdeburg. Even August Endell, the urbanist who was so blunt about the monotony and hideousness of growth-spurt adolescent Berlin, had to admit, there was in "this woeful ugliness a strange beauty." While the unified German capital's city planners tried to draw eyes toward the heart of the city, with nostalgic neoclassical monuments and museums built in emulation of its venerable European rivals, the strange beauty of this city was in its endless outlying districts. The real heart of this most modern of metropolises was in its margins. The *Mietskaserne* sprawl, Endell wrote, is "the most visible and perhaps most singular incarnation of our present-day lives, the most conspicuous, most complete form of our works and desires."

For Endell and millions of others, the modern metropolis, so unhomey, was home. "City-dwellers are mocked for their lack of *Heimat* [homeland]," Endell wrote, which is conceived "to be the little peasant cottage with the window shimmering in the setting sun." But "our cities . . . are our *Heimat*, because . . . they are as inexhaustible as life itself . . . because every day they speak to us in a thousand voices that we can never forget. [T]hey give us joy, they give us strength, they give us the soil without which we cannot live."

Magnus agreed. Berlin, the metropolis that went unpoliced because it was unpoliceable, was a place where any desire could be fulfilled and maybe even voiced. To Magnus, this city of strangers, of darkened spaces and costume changes, was more a homeland than any provincial town, with its overbearing family members and nosey neighbors, could ever be. Berlin's underworld was no afterthought; it was its essence, built brick by brick into its cityscape.

And Magnus had the rare gift of being able to explain Berlin to Berliners. It was Hans Ostwald, a self-taught scholar of the city, who first identified this talent in Magnus. Born in Berlin in 1873, Ostwald had grown disillusioned with urban life and lived for a stretch as an itinerant craftsman in the countryside. When he returned to his hometown, he saw it afresh. The city was relentlessly novel and improvisational, not only in its architecture and urbanism, he discerned, but also in its people. As a city of transplants, it skewed unnaturally young; men and women in their twenties, footloose and sex obsessed, were the largest single demographic group. In a strange way, these young newcomers could feel more at home in Berlin than natives like Ostwald, since they weren't burdened by memories of the city as it used to be.

Ostwald wanted to capture the dynamism of his hometown in words, but he realized that a single creation could never encompass it. Instead, he launched a series of short books, nonfiction snapshots portraying different subcultures of the city, each written by an in-the-know author. Together, they would form what one contemporary scholar calls a "pointillist" portrait of Berlin.

Drawn to Berlin's margins, in 1904, Ostwald launched his series—Metropolis Documents (*Großstadt-Dokumente*)—with each volume dedicated to a different Berlin demimonde. The books, all around one hundred pages long, blended reportage with sociology. Unlike academic monographs, they leaned into the quirkiness of the city. Individual Berliners were presented in all their flamboyant eccentricity, and the city came alive through vivid depictions of its hidden spaces. Ostwald recruited writers from the omnivorous coffeehouse intellectuals whom he chronicled himself as the "bleary-eyed. . . . elegant. . . . city dwellers [with] something restless . . . in their gaze [who] talk of Nietzsche, of the most recent horse races, of the theater premieres." In the seventh book in the series, his own *Berlin Coffeehouses*, Ostwald explained how in a nonstop metropolis like Berlin, the same urban space could transform by the hour. The Kaiserhof coffeehouse near the Ministry of Justice, he noted, hosted young lawyers during the day while, in the dead of night, it would be filled with "actors, dramatists, painters, and stage designers—waiting amid jokes and laughter for the early-morning editions: have the critics given the premiere a good review?"

With Ostwald's interests and obsessions—and his sense of what would sell—the series focused on the urban underworld. The first volume was Ostwald's *Dark Corners of Berlin*, which led readers on a tour of the most ramshackle taverns and flophouses. His notably sympathetic portrait of sex workers presented them with a degree of agency, making the best decisions they could given the harsh constraints of the raw industrial-capitalist city. For the second volume, Ostwald tapped German-Jewish theater critic Julius Bab to write *Berlin Bohème*, a gossipy guide to the city's underground arts scene. The series, which would grow to include looks at the city's gig musicians and its legendary cabarets, was sometimes salacious but rarely judgmental.

For the third volume, Ostwald asked Magnus to chronicle gay Berlin. Ostwald would name the work *Berlin's Third Sex* despite Magnus's mixed feelings about the term. Most of the material would be Magnus's own personal observations; to a lesser extent, a few trusted sources would help—largely lesbian informants who provided details on women-only spaces that would be hard for any man, even Magnus, to access. Vowing to "depict everything exactly as it is" without either "whitewashing" or overemphasizing the "darkest shades," Hirschfeld's insider's tour of Berlin's queer scene would prove to be the most popular of all fifty-one books in the series, reprinted in edition after edition to keep up with demand. (Another volume that might have rivaled its sales, Wilhelm Hammer's book on Berlin's lesbians, got banned as obscene. This led Ostwald to abandon future titles on even more taboo subjects like child prostitution and sadomasochism.)

Writing for a mass audience was the perfect assignment for Magnus. Long torn between being a man of science and a man of letters, Magnus was struggling to be both. Each morning, he would rise at 5 a.m.—before dawn nearly half the year—and pour hours into his writing before seeing his first patient of the day. In the decade since his brief turn as a foreign correspondent at the Chicago World's Fair, most of his output had been destined for academic and professional audiences—summaries of research findings and the correspondence, memos, and petitions that kept the Scientific Humanitarian Committee running day to day. He worried that his focus on experts was leaving the wider culture little changed—with deadly results.

Given the stakes, taking Ostwald's opportunity to popularize his research and present a sympathetic look at gay life in Berlin to a general readership was, Magnus felt, a moral imperative. In the foreword, he explained, "When Hans Ostwald, publisher of the *Metropolis Documents*, asked me to work on a volume that would address the lives of homosexuals in Berlin, I felt it was a challenge I could not shrug off. While the results of my research into the field of homosexuality have only been published in specialist journals to date, particularly the

[*Annual of*] *Sexual Intermediaries*, it has long been clear to me that knowledge of an area that is intertwined with the interests of so many families, of every class, would not and could not remain forever confined in the closed community of specialists or academic circles."

Magnus's most accessible and popular book opened with the insight that queer life was not marginal to Berlin but central to it. "Any well-informed person," he wrote, "will soon notice that the streets and pleasure spots of Berlin boast not just men and women in the accepted sense, but frequently also those who differ not just in their behavior, but often their appearance as well, such that alongside the masculine and feminine one can almost speak of a third sex." Just as the most observant urbanists in this new city were discerning that the physical margins of the metropolis—its endless outlying neighborhoods and darkened archway underpasses—were actually its heart, Magnus was arguing that the city's social margins constituted the core of Berlin. "If one wished to produce a vast portrait of a world-class city like Berlin, penetrating the depths rather than merely dwelling on the surface," he wrote in the book's first sentence, "one could scarcely ignore the impact of homosexuality, which has fundamentally influenced both the shading of this picture in detail and the character of the whole."

Laying out his born-this-way hypothesis for a wide readership, Magnus explained that the percentage of queer persons was fixed but homophobia drove gays to big cities for a tolerance, born of anonymity, that was impossible elsewhere. "It is [doubtful] that there are more homosexuals born in Berlin than in small towns or the hinterlands, [so] it stands to reason that, whether consciously or unconsciously, those who deviate in undesirable ways from the majority gravitate to places where they might live less conspicuously, and less beleaguered, in the amplitude and mutability of the many," he wrote, notably declining to break the third wall and share his own Magdeburg transplant story.

Anonymity was built into the metropolis. In Berlin, the possibilities for sexual nonconformity, with few, often no, repercussions, were endless. As a city of neighborhoods, a cloak of social invisibility could be purchased for the price of a ride on the elevated train. "Anyone living in the east . . . can meet up with friends in the south for years without those in his circle being any the wiser," Magnus noted. "There are many Berliners in the [prosperous] west who have never seen [the working-class northern neighborhood] Wedding, many in [native-dominated] Kreuzberg who have never stepped foot in the [immigrant-heavy] Scheunenviertel." But more remarkably, anonymity even existed in individual apartment buildings. In this metropolis, one could lead double lives, triple lives, infinite lives and never be found out. Magnus discerned that this city of two and a half million people, as vast as it was, contained more than two and a half million personae.

To capture the breadth of this metropolis with more lives than people in a mere hundred pages, he marshaled the journalistic talents he'd put aside for a decade. As a synecdoche for the entire city, he seized on a single space—Room 361 at the Berlin police headquarters, the missing persons bureau—and drew a captivating portrait of it:

> Have you ever been to Room 361 of the police headquarters on Alexanderplatz? It is one of the most remarkable places in a city scarcely wanting for striking locations. Perched high above the roofs of the metropolis, it is to be found in the middle of a row of rooms in which ten million pieces of paper are arranged in alphabetical order. Each sheet represents a human life. Those among the living are found in the blue cartons, the dead repose in white. Each sheet bears the name, place of birth and date of birth of each person who has inhabited an apartment or room in Berlin since the year 1836. Every registration and deregistration, every change of address is scrupulously recorded. There are sheets that contain thirty or more apartments, others with only one; there are those whose lifespans begin in a cellar in the east and stretch all the way to the Tiergarten district, and others who start off on the first floor of the front of a building and end their days on the fourth floor of a rear block. Anyone seeking to find a missing person in Berlin is directed to Room 361. From eight o'clock in the morning to seven o'clock at night, they climb the steep stone steps in their hundreds, many thousands over the course of a year. Each piece of information costs 25 pfennigs. These are not just people seeking to recover money, those who value others purely by the debt they represent. No, many of those mounting the stairs have returned from distant lands and are now

> trying to determine where (or if) their close relations and childhood friends now live. For the first few years they continued to write to each other, then their correspondence abated, and now the stranger has once more returned to the old homeland. Hearts racing, they write their mother's name and last known abode on the information slip—but she is long dead; they ask after brothers, sisters and friends, all of them, every one of them dead, and with heavy heart the lonely supplicant descends the stairs once more.
>
> How many enquire there, fruitlessly, parents seeking prodigal sons, sisters enquiring after brothers, and girls looking for the fathers of the children whose futures lie in their wombs. "Not registered", "forwarding address unknown", "emigrated", "dead", report the officials always dispassionate, when they return after half an hour and summon the waiting applicant, who then silently, gravely, despondently, all too rarely joyfully, goes back down the stairs to be consumed once more by the tide of the buildings and people in this formidable city, Berlin.
>
> The ease with which one can sink unseen into a city of two and a half million inhabitants greatly facilitates the dual personality so often found in the sexual arena. The professional self and the sexual self, day self and night self are often two utterly distinct personalities in one body.

In Berlin—city of day selves and night selves—one's perceived class, sexuality, even gender, could be switched with a change of clothes. There was the retired gay military officer from one of the most illustrious families in Germany who two or three nights a week "would swap his dress coat for an old jacket, his top hat for a flat cap, his high collar for a colourful kerchief, donning a sweater, boatman's trousers and army boots" and spend the entire night in working-class dive bars. After a 4 a.m. "10-pfennig breakfast with the poorest vagabonds," he would go home, take a nap, and "awaken once more to his existence as an irreproachable gentleman." And there was the gay lawyer Magnus knew who worked in a prestigious office on Potsdamer Platz but, after work, would slink off to dive bars populated by hustlers and petty criminals who went by "Mad Dog" and "Revolver Heini."

Most remarkable were those who switched genders. Judging by the significant numbers who got discovered—most typically when police arrested trans sex workers and didn't realize it until booking at the police station—the number who were passing in Berlin was enormous. "There is more than one woman in Berlin who is known to live entirely as a man at home," Magnus divulged. "I encountered one such [individual] during a function at the Philharmonic. . . . and asked if I might call upon her. The next Sunday afternoon around dusk I rang her doorbell; a young man answered, attended by an excitable dog—the man had a lit cigar in his hand and asked what my business was. 'I wish to speak with Miss X., could you please give her my card.' 'Step a little closer,' answered the young lad with a laugh, 'it is I.' I discovered that this maiden lived her domestic life completely as a man." Magnus had another client who, whenever in Berlin, presented as female, while back home, working as the police chief of a small Central European town, presented as male.

Room 361, stuffed with filing cabinets full of blue and white cartons, overflowed with irony: Berlin's bureaucracy was fanatical about keeping tabs on everyone, and yet the Berliners kept going missing. The German capital was a city where people went to get lost, with newcomers flocking to the city to run away from their pasts and reinvent themselves. Estranged relatives, Magnus noted, could live a few neighborhoods apart and never encounter one another. Boomtown Berlin was, in the words of one contemporary scholar, a "fugitive city."

But the true wonder of the metropolis was how much was hiding in plain sight. For his readers, Magnus decoded everyday phenomena: for starters, the Tiergarten, the thousand-acre park in the heart of the capital, was a notorious year-round cruising ground; one section was nicknamed the "Gay Way." Much of the action focused on the paths around the Victory Column, an enormous ribbed cylindrical monument erected decades earlier by Prussian authorities to salute their manly soldiers. Given the thinness of the foliage in a city with such a short summer, the concomitant exhibitionism was integral to the experience.

Even for those who picnicked a safe distance from the Victory Column, Magnus pointed out, the city's gay scene was getting delivered to them daily in their local newspapers. Mixed in with the straight personal ads were those posted by gay men and lesbians seeking same-sex love through subtle hints—the arch use of scare quotes or a seemingly anomalous reference to classical antiquity. Magnus quoted a few of his favorites:

> Older gentleman, no ladies' man, seeks acquaintance with kindred spirits.
>
> Older bachelor looking for like-minded "connection."
>
> Gentleman, 23, seeks friend. Write to "Sokrates" at forwarding centre Kochstrasse.
>
> Young lady, respectable, 24 years old, seeks pretty young lady as friend.
>
> Lady, 36, seeks friendly exchange. PO 16, "Plato."
>
> Seamstress, 22, seeks "friend", PO 33.
>
> Bosom friend, pleasant, seeks spirited, vivacious lady, 23. Psyche, PO 69.

For kinkier forms of love, Magnus dished about a secret service whereby seekers "verbally, in writing, even by telegraph—place orders for people specifying every imaginable fetishistic hobby, [including] cuirassiers with white trousers and high boots, men in women's clothing, women in men's clothing, brewer's draymen, stone-carriers in work clothes, even chimney sweeps."

Like any city, Berlin had single-sex institutions that while not officially gay, tended to attract a disproportionately queer clientele. Among these, Magnus flagged—to only his most clueless readers' surprise—the YMCA for gay men and for lesbians, the women's suffrage advocacy groups.

Despite his interest in focusing on the more wholesome aspects of gay life in the capital, Magnus duly ran through the underbelly, perhaps at Ostwald's request. "[On] the issue of male prostitution . . . we really cannot avoid this lamentable practice if we wish to produce a more or less comprehensive account of the diverse forms in which uranian life manifests itself in Berlin," he wrote. Each summer, when the beer gardens popped up, they were invariably serviced by sex workers, both straight and gay. It was an open secret that male and female prostitutes had long-established paths in the Tiergarten. As Magnus explained, femme trans prostitutes mixed in along the women's path with little controversy or resentment since, as one veteran sex worker told him, "We know that every john wants what he wants."

What truly distinguished Berlin from other cities—what made it a mecca—was its bar scene and ball scene. New arrivals to Berlin often broke down upon entering their first gay bar. "You can witness homosexuals from the provinces arriving at such drinking spots for the first time, weeping in profound emotional convulsion," Magnus wrote.

By the best available estimates, there were around two dozen gay bars in the capital, though Magnus admitted that this was a very rough guess since even he, the supposed expert, was always hearing of new spots. By gay bar, Magnus made clear, he meant not gay-patronized boîtes but gay-run and gay-staffed places where all of the "publicans, waiters, piano players, cabaret singers are themselves—almost without exception—homosexual."

Even with Berlin's unusual level of tolerance, inside the bars, patrons generally used pseudonyms to safeguard their anonymity. Being known to be gay could cost someone their job, as, say, a schoolteacher or get them pushed out of public life altogether. It was best to err on the side of discretion. As Magnus explained, gay men generally picked female names, often a feminine form of their given name. Ludwig, for example, became Luise. Among lesbians, short, clipped male monikers were popular. Magnus informed his readers that "one-syllable names are preferred, such as Fritz, Heinz, Max, Franz and especially Hans," as well as those of historical figures from politics and military affairs, including Caesar, Nero, and Napoleon.

The most legendary aspect of Berlin's turn-of-the-century queer nightlife was its ball scene, and Magnus was glad to serve as tour guide to what he called this "true specialty of Berlin . . . the youngest of the European metropolises." The first events were held quietly in the 1860s, but by the 1890s, they were no secret. During the heart of the season, running from October to Easter, there was at least one event each week. Costumes were elaborate, with some aristocrats commissioning bespoke dresses from the finest Parisian fashion houses. Local media covered the balls with schizophrenic enthusiasm—looking askance at the outré events but proud of a metropolis open-minded enough to host them. In 1894, the *Berliner Zeitung* newspaper breathlessly reported on a costume ball it called the "Ball for the Enemies of Women." In 1899, the *Berliner Morgenpost* described an all-male ball held at the King of Portugal Hotel where half the guests presented as male and half as female. Over time the parties grew world-famous, attracting touristic gawkers from all over Europe and attendees from as far away as South America.

When Magnus researched drag bars and balls, he reputedly sometimes went in drag himself as "Auntie Magnesia" (*Tante Magnesia*). A dowdy feminine version of his rumpled self, Auntie Magnesia presumably favored frumpy dresses with conservative hemlines and sensible shoes. As a known community advocate in Berlin, Magnus surely could have been admitted to most any queer space in his conventional men's suit. Was he drawn to presenting in drag? Did he think he could only fully understand his patients by (literally) walking in their shoes? Needless to say, he never wrote about going out on the town in drag.

In *Berlin's Third Sex*, when Magnus takes his readers to a recent 800-person New Year's Eve ball, he notes only that he arrived "with a few fellow doctors." At 10 p.m., he reports, the place is empty but the crowd begins to swell around 11 p.m., with the bulk of the guests arriving between midnight and 1 a.m., attendance peaking at the 2 a.m. coffee break. As each visitor enters, an announcer presents them to the assembled guests. "The finest costumes [get] greeted with thunderous fanfare on the signal of the moderator, who leads their bearers through the hall," Magnus explains. "Some . . . arrive well concealed by impenetrable . . . masks [and] come and go without anyone suspecting their identity [while] others remove their masks at midnight." Among the guests were those who presented themselves convincingly as women as well as those who "come as 'women' . . . boasting moustaches or full beards." Magnus editorialized that he found this particular practice "distasteful [and] repellant." It is unclear whether he was trying to ingratiate himself to scandalized straight readers with this aside or whether he thought such half-measures were an insult to the art of drag. (Regardless, we can presume Auntie Magnesia got a close shave.)

Gay male balls were typically open to all; some male attendees took female friends—or even understanding wives. By contrast, lesbian balls tended to be strictly assigned-female-at-birth affairs. To bring his readers into this world, Magnus relied on an anonymous informant—"Miss R."—who provided a vivid description of an event from which even he was barred:

> After eight on a fine winter's evening, coach after coach pulls up in front of one of Berlin's finest hotels, from which emerge women and men in costumes of every land and epoch. Here you see a stylish fraternity member arriving with impressive dueling scars, there a slim Rococo cavalier gallantly helping a lady alight from her coach. The large, brightly lit rooms become ever more crowded; here comes a fat Capuchin monk, accepting the salutations of . . . sailors, clowns, bakers, peasants . . . gentlemen and ladies in riding outfits, Boers, Japanese gentlemen and dainty geishas. A dark-eyed Carmen sets a jockey aflame, a fiery Italian strikes up an intimate friendship with a snowman. The cheerful gaggle of those in the most colourful, dazzling costumes presents an unusually becoming tableau. The partygoers first fortify themselves at the flower-laden tables. The host, in a smart velvet jacket, welcomes the gathering in a brief, pithy address. Then the tables are cleared away. The "Waves of the Danube" waltz starts up, and the couples swing through the night in circles accompanied by cheerful dance tunes. From the adjoining halls comes the sound of bright laughter, the clinking of glasses and blithe song, but nowhere—no matter where you look—are the bounds of an elegant costume party transgressed. Not a single false note brings disharmony to the general merriment, until the last of the guests steps out into the wan dawn light of a cold February morning from a venue where, for just a few hours, they were able to find sympathetic company with which to live the dream of their innermost feelings. Anyone who had the opportunity of attending such a party would spend the rest of his life in honest conviction

> defending uranian women so wrongly condemned, because it would be apparent that good and bad people are to be found everywhere, that the natural homosexual inclination is no less apt to mark a person out as either good or evil than the heterosexual.

As a public champion of gay rights there were few queer spaces Magnus couldn't access. Even at events from which he otherwise might be excluded because of his age, class, gender, or ethnicity, Magnus proudly explained, "in acknowledgment of my work for the liberation of homosexuals I am often asked to attend . . . as a guest of honour."

These included a working-class gay Berliner's birthday party—hardly the kind of fête to which a second-generation medical doctor would typically get an invite. The gathering, held in a tavern on the outskirts of the city, as Magnus detailed, was catered humbly with sausages, Swiss cheese, and potato salad. For entertainment, there was "a female impersonator of the lowest order" followed by a coal trader—"a 'hard lad' with tattooed arms [and] shaved head" who belted out some bawdy songs and danced clumsily though, Magnus winked, "not without effect." Afterward, the tables and chairs were pushed to the side and dancing ensued. The party stopped cold when a police officer walked in. But tension soon lifted when the crowd began twirling the cop around on the dance floor. As Magnus quipped, the officer was "soon vying with the . . . coal carrier for the role of most desired and sought-after dance partner."

Magnus also managed to get inside one of the city's gay weightlifting and wrestling clubs. In this "athletic club which has a homosexual dimension [and] is scented with the curious amalgam of oil, metal and sweat that iron workers often exude," Magnus noted, "strapping athletes" form alliances with more feminine gays like "the madam President or Protectress of the athletic club." These relationships, Magnus explained, sometimes served a practical purpose—protection from violence or blackmail.

Among the queer bohemian scene of intellectuals, activists, and artists, Magnus was fully in his element. He fit right in at the informal debating club of gay academics hosted by "a private scholar . . . in his artistically decorated home," where discussions ranged from close readings of Shakespeare's sonnets for queer content to debates on homosexuality in Catholicism versus Protestantism.

In Berlin's gay arts scene, whether at the literary circle known as the Platen Community or the musical meet-up of the Lohengrin Club, hosted by a wine merchant called "The Queen," that lay the groundwork for Berlin's queer cabaret scene, Magnus wrote, "sexuality as such recedes into the background just as it does in corresponding circles of [heterosexuals]." Magnus told his readers that these regular meetings, like the daily coffeeshop gathering of Jewish lesbian chess players, were less about flirting and coupling than about community building.

The most salient fact of queer life in Berlin was how accepted it was. In a city where only the most outré arrangements caused a stir, same-sex partners found tolerance, at a minimum, and often, familial warmth. Berlin's gay world included a staid middle-aged, middle-class couples' scene. " 'Steady relationships' between homosexual men and women, often of significant duration, are extraordinarily common in Berlin," Magnus informed his readers. "It is something you have to experience—the numerous unmistakable examples of tenderness, the bonds that so often unite one with the other, how they care for one another and long for one another."

Some queer Berlin couples even managed to marry. Though he only wrote about it a decade later, around the time that he was writing *Berlin's Third Sex*, a queer couple Magnus knew tied the knot. As he later recounted, "I myself know of a case in Berlin in which a homosexual woman, who lived as a man, succeeded in getting married to her girlfriend in a registry office and in a church without anyone having an idea of her true sex."

Though public authorities rarely recognized queer relationships, parental acceptance was not uncommon. "In Berlin, it is far from unheard of for parents to come to an accommodation with . . . the homosexual lives of their children," Magnus explained. "In Berlin it is not unusual to find uranian bachelors moving in with their friends' families, where they are treated like any other member of the household. There are mothers, often well aware of the circumstances who exuberantly, happily relate that their son, their daughter has found such a wonderful friend; that these friendships are preferable by far to their sons messing about with girls, or their daughters being courted by men."

But when gays met with parental rejection in this tolerant city, it hurt all the more. Magnus concluded *Berlin's Third Sex* by turning from his sympathetic, entertaining tour to an appeal for his presumably straight readers to accept the gay people in their lives. In a maudlin but affecting section, he showed the sadness of rejection coming most acutely during the holidays.

In the queer community, Christmas was always a weighty time, "[the] gravest of all gatherings," Magnus wrote, "because on this more than any other day, the uranian bachelor feels the burden of his solitary fate." During the holidays, "many think about their shattered hopes, what they could have achieved if old prejudices had not hindered progress, and others in respectable positions ponder the heavy lie they must live. Many think about their parents who are dead—or for whom they are dead—and all in deepest sorrow think of the woman they loved most of all and who loved them most of all—their mother."

Though Jewish, Magnus always loved the wintertime holiday and bragged of how Berlin's gay community came together to save Christmas. "Many would find the evening even sadder were it not for the wealthier homosexuals, one or the other of whom always plays host to waifs and strays," he wrote. He reveled in describing one such party set around "a large silver fir [with] garlands entwined around white candles, icicles, snowflakes, glass globes and angel's hair, draped from branch to branch like spiders' webs, all in the best taste. And high on the treetop a large silver star, on which a trumpeting angel in a light tulle gown proclaims 'peace on Earth.'" The wealthy patron had his servants bring their children and grandchildren, whom the host spoiled with presents as they sang carols in return. As the children caroled, one attendee, a dressmaker known as "Lanky Emma" broke down in tears thinking of Christmases of yore and the celebrations being hosted by estranged siblings with nieces and nephews that night.

In the conclusion of his short book, Magnus worked to personalize the problem of homophobia for those who did not identify as queer. He imagined a hypothetical reader—a proper bourgeois Berlin gentleman, the kind of pillar of the community who thought of himself as modern minded but who might be tempted to defer in certain matters to credentialed conservatives like Pastor Wilhelm Philipps, the evangelical who had engineered the obscenity case against Magnus for his sex survey. Giving this reader the benefit of the doubt—that his prejudice was rooted in cluelessness, not animus—Magnus asked him to look on his world with fresh eyes: "Think of the cook who prepares your meal, the hairdresser who attends to you, the seamstress who makes your wife's clothes and the flower seller who decorates your apartment—are you certain there is not a uranian among them?. . . . Do you know for sure that among those closest to you, whom you love most tenderly, those you adore above all, whether among your best friends, your sisters and brothers—that not one is a uranian?" And given the inborn nature of homosexuality, any parent—or future parent—could end up with a gay child. "There is not a father or a mother who can say that not one of their children will be born [this way]."

"Now consider what I have told you," Magnus concluded, and "weigh it up in your conscience and your heart and decide if there is more truth, more love, more justice among those . . . casting so many stones at homosexuals—or on the side of those who . . . in accordance with the results of scientific research and the personal experience of many thousands of people, wish to finally see an end to the misjudgment and persecution which humanity will one day look back on as they do the witch trials."

Magnus's comparisons in *Berlin's Third Sex* of the persecution of gays in modern Germany to medieval witch trials proved a little too prescient. Even as Magnus's book reached ever more readers and established him as the leading public intellectual on sexual orientation and gender identity, German politics got swept up in a gay witch hunt.

A series of salacious newspaper articles identified Philipp, Prince of Eulenburg, a close friend and trusted aide to the German kaiser Wilhelm II, as the central figure in a clique of gay advisers around the throne. Though Eulenburg was a married man with five children, his gayness was an open secret. Earlier in his career, he'd been forced to leave a diplomatic post in Vienna after being blackmailed by one of his lovers. In royal circles, the newspapers alleged, everyone went by a feminine pseudonym, with the kaiser himself, who was known to enjoy leisure cruises in all-male company, dubbed "Liebchen" ("darling"). Even more scandalous, the kaiser's brother, Prince Friedrich Heinrich, was reputed not merely to prefer men but, compelled by his kinks, to dress up as a groom and turn tricks in the Tiergarten. The articles insinuated that the effeminacy of the kaiser's advisers was weakening German foreign policy, pushing the country to go soft in its decades-long rivalry with France.

When one lower-ranking member of the circle, Berlin military commander Kuno von Moltke, sued the newspaper publisher, Maximilian Harden, for libel, the matter ended up in court. The 1907 trial was held before Judge Hugo Isenbiel, the homophobic former prosecutor who had brought charges against Magnus for his "obscene" sex survey three years earlier. Knowing there would be no physical evidence, Moltke mounted the defense that he'd never engaged in gay sex. The newspaper publisher's legal team cleverly countered that they hadn't accused Moltke of engaging in any particular sex act, merely of having a homosexual orientation. As their expert witness, they called Germany's leading expert on homosexuality: Dr. Magnus Hirschfeld.

To Hirschfeld, as a scientist, Harden's attorneys were correct—an individual can be gay, straight, or bisexual, even if they never act on their desires. But Magnus wanted no part in feeding the homophobic hysteria of the scandal. The moral panic rested on the prejudice that gay men should have no role in affairs of state—a belief that was itself rooted in a misogynistic worldview that conflated masculinity with rationality.

Under oath, Magnus was torn between being an activist and a scientist. Uncharacteristically, he opted for the scientist. "We understand the homosexual," Hirschfeld explained, "to be someone who feels a genuine love attraction for someone of the same sex. Whether that person engages in homosexual behaviors is irrelevant from a scientific perspective. Just as some heterosexuals live celibate lives, so too can homosexuals express their love in an idealized, platonic manner." Magnus's testimony was essentially: Moltke may be gay, not that there's anything wrong with that. He was sincere but naïve—and it proved politically disastrous. Given the well-known prejudices of Isenbiel, Magnus's testimony only fed the homophobic frenzy. In part on account of Hirschfeld's expert opinion, the publisher was acquitted of the libel charge.

Within the German gay-rights movement, some saw Hirschfeld's testimony as a betrayal. In early meetings of the Scientific Humanitarian Committee, Hirschfeld had advised against the "path over corpses," of outing prominent figures in German society as a strategy to gain greater acceptance. Yet now he was in court himself essentially outing a man. Magnus's old rival Adolf Brand pounced, attacking him in his magazine as a hypocrite. "Dr. Hirschfeld, the supposed protector of homosexuals," Brand wrote, "disclosed the homosexuality of [the plaintiff], despite his earlier position."

Meanwhile, open homophobes seized on Hirschfeld's courtroom claim that homosexuality was a part of the normal sexual continuum to rail against him—and harp on his ethnic otherness. An anonymous pamphlet entitled "Dr. Hirschfeld: A Public Danger: The Jews Are Our Undoing" hit the streets. In a tacit threat, copies were left on Hirschfeld's doorstep.

In the aftermath of the trial, anti-gay hysteria appeared to be sweeping the country. Just days before the trial opened, Magnus had been advocating for the abolition of Paragraph 175 in front of a thousand people in a public debate entitled "For and Against Paragraph 175." Now, in its wake, homophobic paranoia ran wild while the gay-rights movement fractured. Even the historically hands-off Berlin police department ordered the city's drag balls shut down.

But ultimately the trial's outing of figures at the highest levels of German society only strengthened Berlin's global reputation as a gay mecca and Hirschfeld's centrality to it. As international media streamed in to cover the Eulenburg scandal, one Russian conservative blamed the blossoming gay scene in Berlin specifically on Hirschfeld and his Scientific Humanitarian Committee. The French press reveled in the airing of their neighbor's dirty laundry, only further entrenching the German capital's public association with homosexuality. In 1904, a French nonfiction writer had published *Vertus et vices allemands* (*German Virtues and Vices*), a salacious account of Berlin's queer subculture, making "*le vice allemand*" ("the German perversion") the standard French slang for homosexuality; now French speakers added the scandal-born term "*Eulenburgue*." In the slang of Great Britain and its global colonies, "the German custom" took on the same meaning. Ever-colorful Italian outdid them all, giving the German capital city pride of place by dubbing every gay man a "*Berlinese*"—an honorary citizen of Berlin.

In German popular culture, Hirschfeld had become a household name. A comedian penned and recorded a bawdy cabaret number, "Der Hirschfeld kommt!," that teased Magnus for making perfectly innocent happenings—male friends who walk hand in hand, married couples who have no kids—suddenly seem suspiciously queer.

Though Hirschfeld and his fellow activists in the Scientific Humanitarian Committee smarted over much of the media coverage, it turned out that there was no such thing as bad press. All over the world, even the most fanatical homophobes were channeling the message that Berlin was the center of the gay universe and Magnus its cultural lynchpin.

Magnus did his part to build up the queer capital. Around the time of the scandal, an anonymous German nobleman from Hamburg, a man Magnus identified in his writings only as Baron X, came to him seeking treatment. The situation was dire. Though attracted to males from earliest childhood, he confided, he was now trapped in a straight marriage and was checking himself in and out of institutions for the mentally ill. In response, Magnus offered his new prescription. Not drugs, not therapy, but advice: move to Berlin.

Magnus would eventually take his own advice. In 1910, he relocated from quasi-suburban Charlottenburg to the heart of the city, putting him in the center of the world he was building.

Chapter 7

Some Bodies

Gerd Katter's Transvestite License (*Transvestitenschein*).

EVER SINCE "LIEUTENANT von X" exhorted him in a suicide note to undertake a public campaign, Magnus had been writing about his patients, sharing their stories under pseudonyms to build sympathy for the cause. But now a patient walked through the doors to his office whom Magnus felt had to tell the world their story in their own words: Martha Baer.

After sustaining a foot injury while carelessly debarking from a Berlin city tram, Baer had gone to the doctor with this rather mundane emergency. But as the doctor soon discerned, the patient's chief problems were not podiatric; they were psychological. Baer was tragically in love with a married woman. Rather than live apart, the couple had made a suicide pact and obtained potassium cyanide. Clearly a case for Doctor Hirschfeld, Baer soon showed up at his office with a referral.

In treatment with Magnus, Baer revealed an even deeper secret. He had been born with ambiguous genitalia, assigned female at birth, and raised as a girl. But despite presenting in women's clothing, Baer had always felt male. After pursuing a stereotypically male career as a journalist and building a life, now, in love with a woman, Baer was in crisis.

To Magnus, this predicament was concerning but hardly confounding. Hirschfeld believed it had a simple solution: transitioning. In the coming months, Magnus would guide Martha's transition to Karl.

With this patient, Magnus put his new theory of gender identity into practice. Magnus had recently expanded his thinking from sexual orientation to gender identity in a paper entitled "Gender Transitions" ("*Geschlechtsübergänge*"). Published in early 1906, Hirschfeld's article began with a photographic gallery of intersex individuals he'd encountered in his medical practice. In Hirschfeld's images, patients were shown masked for anonymity and photographed in stereotypically female clothing and stereotypically male clothing—proving equally convincing in both—and then fully nude. "I chose the most eye-catching examples—mostly from my personal observations," Magnus wrote. In one series, Dr. Hirschfeld himself appears in his three-piece suit and bowtie examining a patient.

He explained that "between the . . . male [and] female 'normal' form[s] exist intermediate forms." Hirschfeld had first examined homosexuality through a lens of gender mixing. Never as dogmatic as Ulrichs with his men with women's souls and women with men's souls, Hirschfeld was always keen to note and document the existence of conventionally feminine lesbians and conventionally masculine gay men, like himself. Now turning to purely physical "intermediate forms," Hirschfeld established through his observations, sketches, and photographs the existence of—and surprising commonality of—intersex individuals. From this, Magnus moved to an overarching argument about gender. To Magnus, pure masculinity and pure femininity were archetypes—platonic forms that do not exist in the real world. Actual human beings were always mixtures of both. "The differentiations between the genders are not so sharp as we previously thought," he wrote.

"There are a great variety of crossovers between the male and female gender and nature isn't, by principle, separated into sexes, which we previously designated as one of the most 'ironclad' laws," he explained. Arguing without being argumentative, Magnus was making a revolutionary claim: not just that intersex individuals exist or even that they are more common than most people assumed but that they're part of the normal human gender panorama. His claim attacked the entire conception of the gender binary. To Magnus, every individual was a unique mixture of masculine and feminine physiological and psychological traits. Individuals with ambiguous genitalia were just the most obvious cases. But it was only a matter of degree.

Encountering patients with ambiguous genitalia, like those documented in Magnus's photographs, his contemporaries, steeped in the rigid gender roles of German society, forced individuals into the binary. On every birth certificate, doctors and midwives were forced to check a box: either male or female. But, as Magnus explained, this strict binary reflected the arbitrary rules of society imposed on the mind of the observer, not the body of the individual being observed.

Magnus's theory of gender dovetailed with Albert Einstein's recently published theory of relativity. In the December 1905 edition of *Annalen der Physik*, Einstein had explained that time was relative and, therefore, perspectival—experienced differently by different observers. To explain what he called "The Relativity of Simultaneity" to a lay audience, Einstein came up with a hypothetical example of how two observers could experience a pair of lightning strikes differently and each be equally correct in their assessments. Einstein asked his readers to imagine an exceptionally fast-moving train passing by an embankment as it is struck by lightning on the engine car and on the caboose. One hypothetical observer, sitting at the midpoint of the embankment overlooking the track, would see the train being struck by lightning bolts at the front and back simultaneously. Meanwhile, a passenger seated on this incredibly fast-moving train would perceive the same phenomenon as the train being struck by a lightning bolt first at the front and then, a split second later, by another bolt at the back. Because the train is in motion, but the speed of light is constant, the flash from the front bolt would reach the moving passenger's eye moments before the flash from the back bolt caught up. Thus, two observers in different positions could disagree about whether this lightning strike was a single event or two separate events and both could be equally right. As Einstein explained, "events which are simultaneous with reference to the embankment are not simultaneous with respect to the train." There was no definitive answer to whether the two events take place simultaneously or in succession.

In Magnus's view, the doctors and midwives so committed to the gender binary were like the individual on Einstein's train, convinced that their experience of two separate phenomena was the definitive reality. But Magnus pointed out that the position of the observer shaped their perception of "reality," which was itself relative. Those who approached every body with the preconceived notion that it must be male or female would inevitably see every body as male or female, no matter what the actual body looked like. Those who came with a different perspective would see some babies as intersex and indeed all humans as their own unique mixture of masculinity and femininity.

Not everyone was willing to give up their privileged position as the arbiter of reality. The same year that Magnus wrote "Gender Transitions" and Einstein published his theory of special relativity, Sigmund Freud published his *Three Essays on the Theory of Sexuality* (*Drei Abhandlungen zur Sexualtheorie*). Freud's essays offered a broad readership an explanation of how humans develop their sexuality, tracing it from birth through puberty to adulthood. Unlike Hirschfeld and Einstein, who thought each observer's perception said more about the observer than the observed, Freud harbored few doubts about his perspective. He was particularly self-assured when it came to diagnosing "sexual aberrations," when human sexual development goes "awry" into same-sex attraction.

To Freud, Magnus's inborn hypothesis was "the crudest explanation" for homosexuality. While he cited Magnus's survey research on queerness and conceded that Hirschfeld had proven that "the number of such persons is considerable," Freud disagreed with the rest of Magnus's conclusions. He attacked Magnus's claim that the percentage of queer people was constant in communities around the world—Freud believed it varied with "climate and race"—and he assailed Magnus's assertion that queerness was naturally occurring. "At its most extreme," the Viennese psychiatrist wrote, individuals become gay at "a very early age." Freud entertained the notion that some people were predisposed to becoming gay but, contra Magnus, no one, he believed, was born this way.

According to Freud, homosexuals were made, not born, turned queer by traumas suffered in childhood. "The early loss of one of their parents, whether by death, divorce, or estrangement," Freud warned, could turn a kid queer. To Freud, the ultimate proof that homosexuality came from nurture, not nature, was that it could be cured through hypnosis. And being a curable condition, it "would be surprising if it were of an innate character," Freud wrote.

Rivals but also colleagues, Hirschfeld and Freud kept it civil. Despite their disagreements, Hirschfeld was, for a time, a member of Freud's Psychoanalytical Society and Freud was, for a time, a contributor to Magnus's sexual science journal. Magnus publicly praised Freud's writings on Leonardo da Vinci, the renowned Renaissance artist, scientist, and queer icon. Like Einstein, Hirschfeld and Freud had both sprung from the same secular-Jewish German-speaking milieu where it was an article of faith that one could disagree, even vehemently so, without being disagreeable. Accustomed to being a minority of one in their classrooms, they moved easily into the role of resident skeptics in European society as they emerged from their hometown backwaters into major cities.

Freud and Hirschfeld argued on the merits as intellectual peers, but sparring in the public square Freud had an advantage: respectability. While Magnus cut a rumpled figure, Freud was debonair. Their personalities were reflected in their choice of adopted hometowns. Freud picked beautiful, buttoned-down, boring Vienna, while Magnus chose raw, seedy, untamed Berlin. For Freud, repressing one's impulses was the essence of civilization itself, and he strove to keep his own—not least his same-sex attraction—in check. Magnus, by contrast, reveled in his kinks, elevating Berlin's cruising grounds, drag balls, and cabaret theaters into objects of study and sites of liberation, perhaps even in his Tante Magnesia getup.

In his attacks on Hirschfeld's theories, Freud mentioned Magnus by name only in footnotes that most readers would never glimpse. In his private correspondence with his protégé Carl Jung, however, Freud savaged Magnus in cruel, homophobic terms as "a flabby, unappetizing fellow, absolutely incapable of learning anything," who exhibits the "[typical] homosexual touchiness."

Firmly ensconced in the haughty position of a doctor treating diseased patients, Freud put little stock in his queer couch-talkers' tales of when and how they discovered that they were gay. "The autobiographical information supplied by inverts themselves on the time at which the tendency . . . occurred [is] unreliable," Freud wrote dismissively. He believed the traumatic experience that flipped a particular patient's sexual orientation "awry" may have been repressed, so even asking about it in therapy was not necessarily useful.

Magnus had long taken the opposite approach in his sessions, and now he began encouraging his patients to go public as well. Beginning with Baer, he not only urged patients to recount for him the development of their sexual interests and gender identities from earliest memories but to share their stories with the world. Rather than take the position of the medical expert who knows individual clients better than they know themselves, Magnus deferred to the patient as long as their autobiography could withstand basic fact-checking for internal consistency and veracity. Magnus defended his autobiographical method of therapy, declaring "there is no reason not to believe the patient's statements."

In the medical community, Magnus raised awareness about intersex individuals through conference presentations, even taking a wax mold of Baer's ambiguous genitalia for use as a lecture prop. More crucially, he pushed his gender dysphoric patients to share their stories. With Magnus's encouragement, in 1907, Baer anonymously published the world's first trans memoir, *Memoirs of a Man's Maiden Years*, which ended with a brief but revelatory epilogue by its prime mover, Dr. Magnus Hirschfeld. Baer wrote under the pen name, N. O. Body. It was a pun and a double entendre: both an author's request for anonymity ("nobody") and a trans declaration of gender independence from one's physical form ("no body"). As the anonymous author explained, "I did not want to write this book, but others convinced me that I owed it to mankind as a contribution to modern psychology and that I should write it in the interest of science and truth."

The memoir "tells a true story [of] probably the strangest youth ever lived," Baer wrote, "the story of the confusion and conflicts that arose for me from my very own nature." When Baer was born, in 1885, the parents promptly got into an argument. Facing their child's ambiguous genitalia, the mother wanted to raise the baby as a boy and the father as a girl. They let the delivering physician break the tie. He decreed, "On a superficial inspection, the shape [of the genitalia] has a feminine appearance; ergo we have a girl before us." Fearing a scandal, Baer's father swore the doctor to silence and bribed the midwife never to speak of it again.

In the memoir, N. O. Body recounts a small-town childhood dominated by alienation and fear, where everything from playing house to going for a swim was terrifying. The girls at school ostracized Baer for being too masculine; when Baer played boisterous games with the boys, adults reprimanded the child, enforcing a strict gender binary.

Things got worse during adolescence as male secondary sex characteristics began to assert themselves. Baer monitored and removed facial hairs as they sprouted, and when Baer's voice changed, teachers responded by revoking their speaking role in the upcoming school play.

Despite the barriers to women's participation in public life, Baer vowed to undertake a career. Moving to Berlin for college, they began writing political coverage for newspapers under a male nom de plume. Sensing correctly that there would be more opportunities as an expert on women's issues, Baer became a leading authority on sex trafficking. After transitioning, Baer would write a book on the subject, *The International Trafficking of Girls*, as part of Hans Ostwald's Metropolis Documents series. On a 1904 work trip to Ukraine to deliver a lecture to a women's association, Baer fell in love with the host, a married woman named Hanna, and the crisis ensued. This love—and the barriers to any legal recognition of a union between two people assigned female at birth—pushed Baer toward suicide. Only Magnus's guidance toward transition saved Baer's life.

Magnus was adamant that the public authorities recognize the transition. Enlisting a sympathetic Berlin attorney, Baer duly assembled physician statements from Magnus and others vouching for the necessity of their transition and filed paperwork to legally be recognized as male. In December 1906, Baer received approval from the German government to officially change genders. Even before permission was granted,

Baer had begun to transition in public life, cutting their hair short and ditching their dresses. "The first time I walked across the road in men's clothing," Baer wrote, "I felt such a great sense of uneasiness [but] this insecure feeling lasted [only] for several days, until at last I grew accustomed to it." The medical breakthroughs of the new century provided options to Baer that had previously been the province of science fiction. Under Magnus's guidance, Baer underwent the modern world's first-ever gender-affirmation surgery, a medically crude, multistage procedure that left them in the hospital recovering for weeks.

Tolerant Berlin accepted Karl. As one contemporary who had been in a book club of young Jewish liberals recalled, one day Martha announced that she was moving to another city. Shortly afterwards, Karl joined the circle. Everyone understood what had happened but being tactful, no one mentioned it.

Baer's portrayal of gender trouble in the memoir was straightforward: "I was born a boy, raised as a girl." In Baer's view, the doctor simply made a mistake, misinterpreting ambiguous genitalia as female that should have been categorized as male. In the epilogue to the book, however, Magnus gave a broader and more revolutionary gloss on Baer's tale, placing this case study in the full panorama of gender identity. Baer saw their tortuous youth as the result of a biological miscategorization by an errant obstetrician but, to Magnus, intersex individuals pointed to a deeper truth: sex and gender weren't synonymous. As Magnus explained, ambiguous genitalia was hardly universal—or even that common—among trans individuals. In many of his gender dysphoric patients, the physical body, with its genitalia and sex hormones, seemed irrelevant. Many humans with ovaries psychologically were male and many humans with testes psychologically were female. Sex found expression not only in physical manifestations—genitalia and secondary sexual characteristics—but in social and psychological ways. As Magnus declared in one of his most prophetic sentences, "The sex of a person lies more in his mind than in his body, or to express myself in more medical terms, it lies more in the brain than in the genitals."

Upon its release, Baer's memoir was widely and sympathetically reviewed, and it proved a hit, going through at least six printings. It would subsequently be produced for the silver screen in two different silent-film versions. Magnus was thrilled at Baer's success. But he'd pushed Baer to publish the memoir in order to share *a* story, not *the* story. Now Magnus worked to bring others into print. Taking on a psychiatric establishment that was skeptical of, even hostile to, queer origin stories, Magnus endeavored to collect and publish as many as he could.

The success of Baer's book brought trans patients flocking to Hirschfeld's practice. And through his nocturnal explorations of Berlin's queer bars, cafes, and cabarets, Magnus met other individuals experiencing gender dysphoria, each one a potential memoirist.

One person who materialized at Magnus's office was already famous. Readers of Berlin's gossip columns all knew about the man whose wife had an affair with their housepainter only to discover that the housepainter, as papers put it, was secretly female. One day, this famous housepainter came to Magnus for a psychological evaluation and a physical. The patient, identified only as "Helene N.," was asked by Magnus to write up a brief autobiography. It was a wild story of world travel and subterfuge—and Helene had photographic evidence to back it up.

On the day of their one and only appointment, Helene arrived at the office in simple women's clothing without makeup or accessories. But even these clothes caused psychological distress. As Magnus recorded, "Whenever she is in men's clothing or at least wearing a man's hat, tie, underwear, and boots, she feels light, happy, and able to work; in women's clothing, constrained and in bondage." (Initially, Hirschfeld referred to patients who had not physically transitioned by their sex assigned at birth. In later years, he would affirm his patients' gender identity even before they had physically transitioned.)

Born in Berlin in 1880, Helene had been a rambunctious youth always drawn to playacting a soldier in the boys' war games. "I had the one burning desire that I really was a boy," Helene wrote.

As an adolescent in a Catholic boarding school, Helene went AWOL, began presenting in men's clothing, and worked a series of male-only jobs, by turns, a coalminer, a locksmith, a peddler, a butler, and a barbershop assistant. Always on the move, Helene landed a dream job working as a deckhand on a Norwegian whaling vessel. Bunked in a tiny cabin built to sleep eight, Helene endured arduous conditions. But that was part of the attraction. Despite "the anxiety that my sex would be discovered," Helene wrote, they loved the seafaring life. Dressed in men's clothing, Helene subsequently took a job on an all-male ship that circumnavigated the globe, with stops in Yokohama, Rio de Janeiro, and San Francisco. Only when homesickness for Germany became overwhelming did Helene return to Hamburg and "commit . . . the gross stupidity of getting married" to a man. After having a baby, Helene donned men's clothing again, abandoned the family, left the child with grandma, and disappeared. Helene eventually settled in Berlin and found work as a housepainter until the scandal ensued.

In Magnus's day, individuals like Helene were often dismissed as being jealous of the privileges of men and their gender dysphoria and decision to present as male explained as their only path to these societal roles and professions. It wasn't so much a desire to be male, psychiatrists would condescendingly explain, as a desire to work as, say, a coalminer, a journalist, or a whaler that underlay the dysphoria.

But Helene's autobiography gave the lie to that. Living for a time in London, Helene heard about an all-female ship where they could easily have landed a position. But the women on the all-female ship presented as women and, for Helene, that killed the allure. "I could not stand being in women's clothing any longer," Helene wrote. This ship "whose personnel consisted only of women and was also managed by women, I could not stand [since] I did not want to be a woman."

As each patient with gender dysphoria arrived at Magnus's clinic, he listened anew. Some individuals, of course, offered archetypal tales. One thirty-year-old trader recounted a childhood of being drawn to dolls and needlepoint despite their mother's and sister's reprimands that "a big boy should be ashamed" of these interests. "I so wanted to be a girl," the patient rhapsodized, "[I] often dreamed about it with my eyes wide open [and] saw myself in my dreams as a girl." Another, identified as "Mr. D., merchant, in his thirties," dreamed of transitioning: "My sexual wish is not to be the woman of the female impersonator, but rather my ideal would be, as a woman, to lead a genuinely physiological love life with a man."

But other narratives diverged from the usual assumptions. One thirty-seven-year-old former US army soldier wrote to Magnus explaining that "the main content of my yearning is to be a woman completely [as I have] no trace of any homosexuality." Indeed, the soldier's greatest sexual fantasy was to penetrate a woman while dressed in women's clothing.

These types of individuals turned out to be much more common than many, including Magnus himself, initially assumed. One thirty-five-year-old married man, who had been drawn to his sisters' skirts and earrings as a child, wrote that he flirted with men while dressed as a woman only to prove to himself that he was truly passing; he had no desire to consummate the flirtation. Most common among these men was a desire to have sex with women but with the woman on top, in the conventionally masculine position, which Magnus confirmed by interviewing the wives of such men. "I personally met six of the wives," he wrote. "It is admirable how they adapt to their special kind of husbands . . . meeting them half-way."

Viewing this vast array of patients, Magnus observed that the conflation of homosexuality with the tendency to dress in gender nonconforming clothing broke down. Indeed, even among drag performers, Magnus found some who were married to women. Among gay men as a whole, Magnus estimated, only half acted effeminately, and a mere 10 percent had the desire to wear women's clothing.

Magnus resolved to record this continuum of experiences and publish it as a series of case studies. Scientists typically used case studies to find individual stories that could be universalized, but Magnus used this approach to prove the opposite: that there was no archetypal individual who wore gender nonconforming clothing. All the varied case studies taken together proved that the common stereotypes—largely drawn from drag performers and sex workers—were mostly false.

The world, it seemed, did not want to hear these truths. Max Spohr, Magnus's longtime publisher and a cofounder of the Scientific Humanitarian Committee, had died in 1905, just shy of his fifty-fifth birthday. Now Magnus wrote up his case studies only to find that no publisher would touch the manuscript, now coming from a man who had been convicted under Germany's obscenity laws.

Magnus's seemingly unpublishable manuscript included seventeen case studies—a mix of narratives he had solicited from his own patients, letters written to him from all over the world, and material he'd unearthed in obscure sources that he hoped to popularize. As his research showed, he was describing a wide-ranging phenomenon yet, he felt, it needed a single moniker. To this end, Magnus coined a new word, "transvestites" (*die Transvestiten*), and made it the title of his manuscript. For all their variety, "what do they have in common, what is typical about the circle of people described here that sets them off from other people?" he wrote. "The strong drive to live in the clothing of that sex that does not belong to the relative build of the body. For the sake of brevity we will label this drive as transvestism (from 'trans' = over or opposite, and 'vestis' = clothing)."

To each narrative, Magnus added only basic information on the age and background of the patient and a short physical description. Using these trans autobiographies, Magnus expanded on the theoretical framework of "Gender Transitions." Just as sexual orientation was a continuum, with gayness and straightness shading into gradations of bisexuality, gender constituted a continuum as well. Some people experienced a clearcut dysphoria: one individual, a German immigrant to America, identified as "John O. of San Francisco," whose narrative Magnus had found in a medical journal, wrote, "I am physically a man, mentally a woman." But others experienced gender beyond the binary. After "a tough battle," wrote one forty-year-old technician, "I accepted that I am a mixture of both sexes." Presenting narratives from patients who saw themselves as one-off misfits, Magnus showed that, collectively, they constituted humanity itself. Though most of his peers in German society "hold fast to the dualism of the sexes," he wrote, "it is a mistake if one imagines that both are two fully separate entities."

In "Sappho and Socrates" in 1896, Magnus had used a mathematical formula to present sexual orientation as a continuum; now he presented a similar scheme for gender identity. Beginning with four broad categories—genitalia, secondary sexual characteristics, sexual behavior, and emotional characteristics—Magnus delineated four subcategories. Even within these, the value assigned could be "m" for manly, "w" for womanly, or "m+w" for mixed as in, for example, ambiguous genitalia. "Every combination imaginable can occur," Magnus wrote, "every possible combination of manly and womanly characteristics."

In total, according to his computations, there were 43,046,721 possible permutations.

External features, like clothing or the facial hair Magnus had noticed on his childhood maid "Madame Moustache," it became clear, were only a small component of each individual's gender. Much of human gender nonconformity manifested only in private, when a woman was drawn to playing the active role during sex as a dominatrix, or in the mind, like when a man finds himself attracted to butch women. Only a tiny portion of gender identity appears on the surface, Magnus wrote, while "the internal is limitless."

In debunking the gender binary, Magnus used humor, presenting a sketch of a fully manly man who embodied every masculine stereotype. Magnus's description of this fellow who would have an "m" for all of the sixteen subcategories in his formula of gender identity reads like a parody of masculinity that few, if any, real men would live up to: "The object of his desire would be the normal (characteristically feminine) woman, and in relation to her he would step forth aggressively . . . he would also depict himself as a powerful and strong manly person in his emotional life [and] in his activities." He would eschew "sewing and crocheting or cooking and such things [in favor of] using his muscles." He would also, of course, "prefer men's clothing over women's clothing."

Even if this he-man were to exist, Magnus explained, he would be just one of 43,046,721 possibilities in the continuum of gender identity. The other 43,046,720 options would be, by varying degrees, less manly. And if only one person in every 43,046,721 fully lived up to the norms considered masculine or feminine, how could one even consider them to be norms?

The point of Magnus's formula was less the precise number of possible combinations than the fact that, as Magnus wrote, "there are hardly two humans who are exactly alike." Gender identity was a continuous spectrum and the gender binary a figment of his society's imagination. As Magnus concluded:

> All of these sexual varieties form a complete closed circle in [which] there are no empty points present but rather unbroken connecting lines. The number of actual and imaginable sexual varieties

> is almost unending; in each person there is a different mixture of manly and womanly substances, and as we cannot find two leaves alike on a tree, then it is highly unlikely that we will find two humans whose manly and womanly characteristics exactly match in kind and number.

If sexual "intermediacy," as Hirschfeld termed it, was all but universal—the sole exception being the he-man parody and his girly-girl mirror image—then the stigmatization and ostracization of people on the basis of gender identity was both absurd and unjust. The most glaring fact of Magnus's seventeen case studies was their variety. No grouping could ever accurately capture sociological reality. The only value a grouping could have—like Magnus's "transvestites"—was in defining a group that was already stigmatized so that it could win equal rights.

In a just society, such group demarcations would be unnecessary. Indeed, in the ancient world, Magnus explained, Roman writers had referred to "transvestism" as a practice but not to "transvestites" as a group since there was no stigma against the behavior. As Magnus had noted in his epilogue to Baer's memoir, the idea that ambiguous genitalia were "deformed" and the pathologization of gender-nonconforming individuals was unique to the modern era. "In antiquity," he wrote, they were simply seen as "special individuals within the human race." More broadly, the Greco-Roman conception of liberty had been more enlightened. "The ancient demand of freedom, equal rights for all, has its roots far more in the differences between people than in their sameness," Magnus wrote. The modern assimilationist policing of who was "normal" and thus entitled to be taken seriously in the public square was a step back from a more pluralistic tolerance in the ancient world.

Outside the West, Magnus noted, a broader conception of gender was still largely intact. Magnus's colleague Ferdinand Karsch, the Berlin scientist who had published on queerness in the animal kingdom, also catalogued gender nonconformity in the non-Western world, documenting instances in Africa, Asia, and among the indigenous peoples of the Americas. Among the Crow people of Montana, Karsch noted, there were individuals known as *Bo-te* ("not man, not woman.") Though born with unambiguously male genitalia, Bo-te dressed as girls and, as adults, were given conventionally female social roles. The French explorers of North America's Gulf Coast found analogous traditions among the indigenous peoples there, as recorded by Dutch geographer Cornelius De Pauw in his 1769 tome, *On the Hermaphrodites of Florida*. The Illini, the Sioux, and the Aleuts had similar practices as did indigenous groups in Mexico and Brazil. In sub-Saharan Africa, a similar phenomenon was identified among the Bantu and Bongo peoples.

Closer to home, in Croatia, local Catholics had their own gender conversion ceremony. As Magnus detailed, "a young woman may go to the priest and declare, 'From now on I want to be considered a man and live as one.' The priest then brings this to the attention of the congregation after Mass and gives the young woman a man's name. Thereupon, the . . . woman puts on men's clothing . . . and from then on is treated as a man by everyone."

Further west, meanwhile, the discovery of trans individuals remained a scandal—though always the same scandal. The story was clichéd: someone in a stereotypically male or female job dies and is discovered by the mortician or coroner to have the genitalia of the opposite sex. There was the sixty-nine-year-old German society lady, a foundation fundraiser, whose penis was discovered at death, in 1883. Then, in 1905, Vasili Popovici, a Romanian monk, died at age ninety. Fellow monks, with whom Vasili had shared the monastery for a quarter century, were washing the body for burial when they discovered Vasili's vagina. The following year, the same posthumous sex-reveal occurred when a mustachioed German professor died in an Italian beach resort.

As Magnus discerned, " 'free' England and America" (scare quotes in the original) "take the strictest action against cross-dressing." Not that this stopped the flow of scandals. In London, an individual legally named Julius Walters but who went by Klara Myer got caught and punished half a dozen times with floggings and imprisonments between 1895 and 1907. In America, President Theodore Roosevelt's longtime cook collapsed in a Westchester County bar in 1904 and was found, as a newspaper report put it, to be "no woman but [rather] a man." Meanwhile a prominent New York lawyer and Tammany Hall politician, Murray Hall, was found at death to have a vagina.

To rebuild the space for tolerance that had existed in other times and places in his modern Germany, Magnus borrowed from revolutionary

France. In "France during the French Revolution," he informed his readers, "the public wearing of the clothing of the other sex" was permissible "with the stipulation that the person in question notify the police." Receiving a *permission de travestissement* pass required a note from a medical professional and a sign-off from the police.

In Germany, efforts to carve out this type of space for trans individuals faced legal barriers. Appearing in public in clothing that did not correspond to one's gender assigned at birth (outside of Carnival time) was not illegal per se but was judged "disorderly conduct" and "creating a public nuisance." German citizens were routinely arrested, tried, convicted, and sentenced for nothing more than wearing what the authorities viewed as the wrong clothes.

To Magnus, reform was a matter of life and death. As he wrote, "persons who are forced into a lifestyle that stands opposed to their nature often thereby fall into depressed mental states that at times even lead to suicide."

In tandem with treating trans individuals in one-on-one psychotherapy sessions and compiling their case studies, Magnus pushed the Berlin police department to issue official photo IDs, what he called *Transvestitenschein* (transvestite licenses). To obtain these permits, in Magnus's scheme, individuals would present a letter from a physician and two ID photographs—one dressed in men's clothing and another in women's clothing. The pass, as Magnus envisioned it, would protect the bearer from arrest for disorderly conduct and creating a public nuisance solely on account of their clothing.

In 1908, a Berlin native whom Magnus profiled under the name "Miss Katharina T." filed an application for Berlin's first trans permit. The twenty-something presented an archetypal case of gender dysphoria. Unlike in Baer's case, Magnus's physical examination revealed no ambiguity in Miss Katherina T.'s genitalia. "The external sexual organs are womanly," Magnus wrote. "Pubic hair, likewise, is of the woman's type." Nonetheless they had felt their entire life, from earliest childhood, that they were male.

As a kid, playing house, they'd always wanted to be cast as the father. Not that they liked playing house; they preferred to play pirate, taking the role of ship's captain, with saber and whip in hand. As an adolescent, all of their crushes had been on women and girls. In those years, they took up smoking in an era when the habit was still strictly gendered as male. By the time Magnus met the patient, they were a regular cigar smoker. A few months before coming to Hirschfeld's office, they'd begun to dress in men's clothing and cut their hair short, risking arrest.

In his medical report for the police, Magnus explained that "her mind stands in glaring contradiction to her body" and therefore "wearing men's clothing is natural for the patient." If gender identity was psychological rather than physical, as Magnus claimed, the clothing that was "natural" would be that which accords with an individual's psychology regardless of their genitalia. Thus, he wrote, "Miss T. has valid grounds for her petition" to be given a male first name and permission to wear men's clothing. In his conclusion, Magnus warned, "Since Miss T. had previously suffered depression in women's clothing, denying her petition would bring her very close to the danger of that ill feeling."

In January 1909, the police department issued an ad hoc permit to Miss Katharina T. that allowed them to wear men's clothing in public, though they still refused to allow Katharina to legally change their first name. (Three years later, under Magnus's guidance, Berlin city officials would begin issuing standardized trans permits, which became colloquially known as "transvestite passports" (*Transvestiten-Reisepässe*). Eventually, other progressive German cities, such as Cologne, issued permits as well.)

With the first permit issued, in the spring of 1909, Magnus decided to celebrate the progress he'd made with a trip to Rome. He was eager to attend a ceremony at the Vatican: the beatification of Joan of Arc. The fifteenth-century Maid of Orleans had famously led French armies against England while passing as a man, guided, she claimed, by the instructions of long-dead saints. Her special mass at St. Peter's Basilica, led by the pope himself, was scheduled for the first Sunday after Easter. Nearly five centuries after Catholic authorities condemned Joan as a heretic and burned her alive, the Vatican was acknowledging its error.

In the posthumous trial the Church had held to vet Joan for sainthood, her defenders highlighted her devotion to the faith, while the opposition counsel, the so-called devil's advocate, smeared Joan as an immodest and hysterical woman. In Magnus's view, Joan was a trans pioneer who, he wrote, "can only be understood in terms of sexual psychology." Needless to say, the ecclesiastical court hadn't vindicated Joan on behalf of trans tolerance, but Magnus still thought the event, half a millennium overdue, was worth celebrating.

According to the meticulous records of the medieval church, Joan was charged with many crimes, but she had been burned at the stake solely for wearing gender nonconforming clothing. Among the twelve accusations in her 1431 trial was Article Five:

> The [accused] woman did say and affirm that, by the command and good pleasure of God, she had taken and borne and continues still to bear a man's dress. Further, she did say that, because she had had God's command to bear this habit, it was necessary that she should have a short tunic, cap, jerkin, breeches, hose with many points, hair cut close above her ears, keeping no garment which might indicate her sex. She did say and affirm that she had, in this dress, several times received the Sacrament of the Eucharist. She had not desired and did still not desire to resume woman's dress, although many times required and charitably admonished so to do. At times she said that she would rather die than leave off the dress which she bears; at times she said that she will leave it off only by the command of God.

In the trial record, Joan's clothing was presented less as an attack on the authority of the Church and more as a betrayal of femininity: "This woman, utterly disregarding what is honourable in the female sex, breaking the bounds of modesty, and forgetting all female decency, has disgracefully put on the clothing of the male sex, a striking and vile monstrosity."

Facing a potential death sentence, Joan confessed to all twelve charges, and her sentence was commuted to life in prison. Three days into her punishment, however, her jailers found her prison uniform on the floor of her cell. In its place, they found Joan in "a short mantle, a hood, a doublet and other garments used by men." When Joan was confronted about her relapse, she countered that prison officials had not let her keep a female companion in her cell as she had been promised, so she was not keeping her promise to wear women's clothes. The next morning, Joan was burned alive in the market square of Rouen.

Now, in 1909, as Magnus watched in the packed basilica, Pope Pius X "blessed a fanatically cheering crowd with pompous splendor." It was the ceremony, not the officiant, that Magnus thought pompous. This pope was quite open about his own all-too-human weaknesses; he was fond of hosting—and watching—young gymnasts exercise in the Vatican gardens.

A satisfied Magnus returned to Berlin. Progress might take centuries, but it was possible. The following year, after being rejected by nineteen publishers, Magnus finally found someone willing to issue his book on his trans patients—a German-Jewish Berlin native and cabaret impresario who ran a publishing house on the side. In 1910, Magnus's *Transvestites* finally came out, detailing seventeen case studies as well as historical examples, Joan of Arc included. Despite its high-minded purpose and sympathetic approach, the book was slapped with a salacious subtitle—*The Erotic Drive to Cross-Dress*—that contradicted the text within. It probably helped move copies. As every club promotor knows, sex sells.

Chapter 8

War on Many Fronts

Kaiser Wilhelm II, wearing a *pickelhaube*, reviews his troops.

MAGNUS HAD LITTLE time to celebrate the hard-won publication of *Transvestites*. His conservative opponents, of course, recoiled at any normalization of queer and trans lives. But more troubling to Magnus was the response of some of his allies on the left who found his championing of the community's most marginalized members to be strategically unwise. Even before *Transvestites* came out, the conservative Munich chapter of the Scientific Humanitarian Committee complained, "We cannot spare Dr. Hirschfeld" our "reproach" for having "overemphasized . . . Berlin's cross-dressing and street prostitution in many of his writings [thus] seriously damag[ing] our cause." They thought it savvier to foreground the most mainstream queer lives—partnered professionals and the like—in the hope of gaining wider acceptance. Instead, Magnus was now devoting an entire book to preaching the most radical forms of self-acceptance and social acceptance. As in the Eulenburg scandal trial, Magnus was swinging back to being a scientist first and a political operative a distant second with, they felt, the predictable results. His curiosity was irrepressible. He would do his research, write it up at dawn, find a publisher, and let the chips fall where they may. His through-science-to-justice creed was, at times, wishful thinking, oversimplifying the relationship between intellectual inquiry and social progress.

Next, Magnus dove into drafting his magnum opus: *The Homosexuality of Men and Women*. In one sense, it would be groundbreaking—the most comprehensive work on the subject ever written. But, page by page, it would be a work of synthesis, offering Magnus's key theories in a single volume alongside a comprehensive global survey of queer life. To complete his tome, Magnus drew on his own research, travels, and clinical work as well as the scientific papers he'd commissioned and published as editor of the *Annual of Sexual Intermediaries with Special Focus on Homosexuality*.

The book ran over a thousand pages and was divided into two five-hundred-page halves—the first on the biology of homosexuality and the second on its sociology. Magnus began the biology section with his born-this-way hypothesis: "Homosexuality is always an inborn condition. [It] is neither a disease nor a degeneration, but rather a part of the natural order." And he concluded with an exhortation to his fellow psychologists to stop trying to "cure" their queer patients and instead encourage them to give their sexual desires "free expression."

To defend his theories against the opponents he took the most seriously—Freud and his followers—Magnus used humor. Freud and those in his circle of Vienna psychoanalysts maintained that homosexuality, being the result of repressed childhood trauma, could be cured through hypnosis. In Magnus's gay Berlin circles, a hilarious anecdote had been making the rounds which he gleefully published as a rebuttal. A German aristocrat with a fetish for soldiers on horseback went to Vienna for treatment. In therapy, the Freudian psychoanalysts whip out their swinging pocket watches and do their best to sway away the gay. Returning to Berlin, the gentleman is pleased to report that the hypnosis had worked. He's been cured! "Cavalrymen don't do much for me anymore," he says, "but artillerymen look better all the time."

The sociology half of Magnus's doorstop drew on his personal explorations of queer communities in Europe, the United States, and North Africa, as well as the global network of gay informants he'd cultivated over the years. Magnus began with the scene he knew best—Berlin's—but then offered chapters on gay life in every part of the world. Even in this scholarly work, Magnus couldn't quite stifle the gossipy tone he deployed in *Berlin's Third Sex*. In Buenos Aires, an agent reported, the shoeshine-boy hustlers proposition customers with the coy inquiry "Are you hot?" Another "long-established expert" from Africa dished on a public toilet near the Johannesburg market square where "the craziest scenes were played out especially on Saturday evenings." Changing his lens from space to time, Magnus sketched the history of queer life in the West, a rise and fall from the tolerant ancient era to the repressions of the Middle Ages. He ended in Berlin, with its enlightened police department issuing trans permits. Unlike Hegel the philosopher, who presented Prussia as the culmination of human history, Magnus saw his homeland as only potentially emancipatory, a work in progress. Berlin offered a new and better society in microcosm but there were still many people to convince and laws to change. Magnus concluded his treatise with an open acknowledgment of his activist aims: "if . . . a change of mind has been produced as a result of . . . this book, then this means it has been a success."

The Homosexuality of Men and Women was published in early 1914, but the window for debating its arguments proved brief. On June 28, 1914, a Serbian teenager assassinated the heir to the Austro-Hungarian throne. International rivalries that had been building for decades burst into a mechanized global war of unprecedented destruction.

Germany, aligned with Austria-Hungary, brimmed with what one contemporary historian calls "patriotic hysteria." Germany had long resented Britain and France's vast empires. Belatedly industrialized, the country now had a war machine to compete with its rivals. Gripped by jingoistic fervor, a million Germans volunteered for the fight. Kaiser Wilhelm II, raised on Hegel's fable that all of human history was a prelude to German preeminence, assured his troops they'd be back home victorious "before the leaves fall from the trees."

German authorities goosed militarism through censorship, banning pacifist writings. A rare anti-war speech given in the Reichstag by Karl Liebknecht, a leading Social Democrat, was stricken from the record. The most radical voices—leftist Rosa Luxemburg's among them—were silenced through imprisonment. In the conservative cultural climate that followed the outbreak of the war, certain articles from Magnus's *Annual of Sexual Intermediaries* were banned as well.

As patriotic hysteria suffused the German-speaking lands, a host of unlikely progressives backed the conflict. Pioneering sociologist Max Weber endorsed the war. So did leading figures in the arts and sciences, including impressionist painter Max Liebermann and theoretical physicist Max Planck, who both signed an open letter drummed up by the German war ministry. In the first week of the fighting, Sigmund Freud expressed his desire to see Austrian troops marching victoriously through Paris. Even mystical-humanist Jewish philosopher Martin Buber saw the war as a "sacred spring" that would bring purification through violence. Seemingly alone in his opposition was Albert Einstein, a lifelong pacifist, who joined a self-styled anti-war patriots group, the New Fatherland League.

Among the more surprising pro-war voices was Julius Bab. The German-Jewish theater critic had once been the king of the Berlin underground. He'd written the book on it: *Berlin Bohème*, the Metropolis Documents guide to the city's arts scene. Now, a decade after its publication, Bab lived far from bohemia, ensconced in a villa in upscale suburban Grunewald with his wife and their poodle. When the war broke out, he turned his literary talents to collecting patriotic poetry which he compiled and published in quarterly installments. His gaudily bound anthologies bore the fanatical (redundant) title, *The German War in German Poetry*.

Perhaps the most surprising pro-war intellectual was Magnus himself. In a militaristic 1915 manifesto, a forty-five-page pamphlet with a blood-red fractur title, "Why Do Other Nations Hate Us?," Magnus presented Germans as a stigmatized group targeted for irrational hatred, much like gays or Jews, from the same toxic brew of jealousy and disdain. To Magnus, his people, the Germans, were the model moderns, builders of the civilization that was the envy of the world.

"This [German] sense of order," Magnus wrote, "determines the punctuality which characterizes our transport system, the cleanliness of our streets and houses as well as the precision and reliability of our modern industry." For Germans, this was a source of pride. Among foreigners, it bred resentment.

England and France, he explained, look down on Germany, as an upstart nation encroaching on their global dominance. Russia, by contrast, resented Germany, having endured two centuries of their tsars and tsarinas importing know-it-all German experts in a fruitless effort to modernize their barbarian subjects. Perhaps Magnus hoped that if straight Christian Germans felt the sting of prejudice, they would embrace tolerance for all? It was an odd gambit.

Many members of Germany's queer community as well as its Jewish community saw the conflict as a way to overcome their neighbors' doubts about their bravery and patriotism. In the wake of the Eulenburg scandal, foreign policy dovishness toward France had been conflated with gay male effeminacy. The Jewish community was similarly plagued by suspicions of disloyalty. As one branch of a global diaspora stretching from New York to Shanghai, German Jews often had family abroad in what were now enemy countries like England, France, Russia, and (once it entered the war in 1917) America. Magnus himself had a brother in the United States. Those facing suspicions of disloyalty were often loudest in their proclamations of faithfulness to the Fatherland. Magnus personally joined the war effort, signing up to work as a prisoner exchange negotiator and a Red Cross doctor tending to the German wounded, who would come to number over a million.

The disproportionate number of Jews among pro-war intellectuals as well as among volunteer soldiers reflected the hope that by cloaking themselves in the flag, they could definitively win acceptance as equals. In the war's early weeks, there was every indication that this aspiration for full acceptance was attainable. In a speech to members of the Reichstag given at the imperial palace on August 4, Kaiser Wilhelm II appealed to "all peoples and tribes of the German Reich . . . irrespective of . . . confession." Taking in the diversity of his subjects, he intoned, "I know only Germans."

It seemed sincere. The kaiser soon used his censorship authority to shut down antisemitic far-right publications in the name of a "civic truce." A leader of the Central Union of German Citizens of the Jewish Faith waxed Orwellian about the Great War as a "divine peace [that has] torn down all dividing walls." Ordinary members of the community agreed. A German-Jewish volunteer on the front lines in France wrote home that "in war we are equal" shortly before he died for his Fatherland.

Queer individuals similarly sought to win societal acceptance by proving their loyalty to the nation. Some gay men who had expatriated in search of greater tolerance abroad rushed home to enlist. While the Jewish community sought acceptance by blending in, the gay community sought freedom by standing out. Queer individuals sought the dignity of serving openly in the military.

In Magnus's worldview, there had always been gays in the military. But for the German military brass, open service was a nonstarter. Early in the conflict, the German minister of war, Karl von Einem, issued an order explicitly drumming gay troops from the ranks. Magnus pushed back, advocating personally and through the Scientific Humanitarian Committee to overturn the ban.

In tandem with public advocacy, Magnus privately counseled gay men on how they could successfully enlist by hiding their gayness. He also worked to help women pass as men in order to serve in combat, since the German military, though open to women, barred them from the front lines. If just one of these soldiers achieved war-hero status and went public, Magnus and his allies believed, the ban would surely fall.

As war swept the Continent, the Scientific Humanitarian Committee began issuing *Quarterly Reports* anonymously highlighting the participation of queer soldiers. In the October 1915 issue, a self-identified gay soldier, writing under a pseudonym, argued that the service of gay troops should earn them the repeal of Paragraph 175. "Many went and risked their lives, many lost their lives and some will yet lose their lives," he wrote. "Should those who come back once again be persecuted by that unfortunate Paragraph 175?"

In the spring of 1916, the *Quarterly* published a narrative from an anonymous author it identified only as "S." on sending his boyfriend off to war. Fighting on the Eastern Front, S.'s beau sustained shrapnel wounds to the legs from a Russian shell that hit his trench. From a fetid field hospital, his heartrending letters arrived on the home front. "I crave a decent mouthful of fresh water, of which there isn't any here," he wrote in what proved to be his final letter. "Above all, write very soon."

In the *Quarterly*, S. contrasted his lover's service abroad with the stigma and criminalization he had faced at home under Paragraph 175. "He laid down his life . . . for the Fatherland, which persecuted him because of a natural orientation that he could not help . . . [P]eople who by nature are orientated towards the same sex perform their duty and their part fully and completely. It is finally time *that the state treat them in the same manner that they treat the state*," he wrote.

Among queer enlistees, those at greatest risk were individuals caught in gender-nonconforming clothing. The military assumed that anyone assigned male at birth who dressed in women's clothing was a spy trying to seduce soldiers, pump them for information, and pass it to the enemy. Espionage was a capital offense.

During the war, Magnus worked urgently to popularize his theories on gender nonconformity as an inborn condition. And he pushed military physicians to include notes in soldiers' files if they expressed a desire to wear gender-nonconforming clothes so that, in the event they were caught and court-martialed for espionage, there would be an exculpatory paper trail.

As the conflagration dragged on, the unified feeling at the war's outbreak collapsed. Each year, as the leaves fell and winter set in, recalling the kaiser's early assurance of a quick victory in the summer of 1914 grew more painful. Facing the stalemate in the trenches and the horrors of chemical warfare, many German liberals and progressives reconsidered their early pro-war stance. In 1916, the Social Democratic Party fractured into pro-war and anti-war wings. Seeing the senseless carnage firsthand, Magnus turned against the conflict.

Ordinary Germans were left grasping at straws to explain why the swift triumph their kaiser had promised never materialized. As German losses mounted on the battlefield, the kaiser further tightened the censorship regime. In the newspapers, victory was perennially just around the corner. But there was no way to explain away all the sons and husbands who never returned home from the front. Nearly 3 percent of

Germany's population died in the war, leaving over half a million widows and a million fatherless children. Somehow Germany was losing more troops than any other country in the war—even though much larger countries, including Russia and the United States, were combatants. And one didn't need to be an economist to see that German industry was collapsing and that the wartime blockade of the country was causing widespread hunger. Rightists hatched a conspiracy theory: enemies at home were undermining the war effort, stabbing Germany in the back. Jewish munitions merchants, they insinuated, made more money the longer the war dragged on, so they'd secretly conspired to prevent a quick German victory. As the war effort continued to falter, some targeted Magnus himself with a new anti-gay, antisemitic myth. Germany was losing, some whispered, because it had marched into battle with an army full of closet cases who shrieked at the sight of blood and cowered at the sound of a howitzer. It had all been engineered by the gay Jewish socialist, Magnus Hirschfeld, who actively counseled his queer patients on how to slip into the army undetected.

While liberals lobbied for a negotiated peace, the military establishment pressed on, and the people began turning on the kaiser. The abdication of the tsar in Russia in March 1917, powered by discontent over the war, should have served as a warning but it went unheeded. Concessions to progressives, including officially honoring Hirschfeld for his contributions to public health in October 1918, placated no one. Throughout that fall, wildcat anti-war actions broke out. German soldiers deserted and workers went on strike. By the time the kaiser and his inner circle understood how precarious their position was, it was too late. Lost in a fog of conspiracy theories himself, Kaiser Wilhelm II vowed not to abdicate under pressure from liberals and radicals, whom he termed "a few hundred Jews and a thousand workers." But his last-minute bid to retain the throne faltered.

On Tuesday, November 5, revolutionaries seized power in several towns near the Danish border. The leader of the Russian Revolution, Vladimir Lenin, had famously joked that German revolutionaries would never occupy a train station without buying tickets first, but the red flag–flying radicals who fought the kaiser did not seem so restrained. By the weekend, almost every major city in the country had slipped from the kaiser's grip. On November 9, a republic was proclaimed from a window at the Reichstag. The kaiser abdicated, fleeing to Holland on November 10.

As the kaiser fled, Magnus took the podium on the square in front of the Reichstag at a demonstration demanding elections for a new parliament. As he began to address the crowd of nearly five thousand peaceful protestors, shots rang out.

Monarchist dead-enders hidden in buildings around the square were firing on pro-democracy demonstrators. Republican militiamen shot back, and a melee ensued. As civilians scattered down nearby streets, Magnus ducked for cover.

The battle proved brief; the monarchists were soon routed. As ambulances moved in to collect the wounded and to recover the bodies of several soldiers who had been slain, calm was restored. Despite the clear risk to his safety, Magnus returned to the podium and continued his speech saluting the birth of the republic.

Trenchant observers, Magnus among them, realized that this was a golden opportunity for reform. As the progressive German architect Walter Gropius wrote on a visit to Berlin at this time, "This is more than just a lost war. A world has come to an end. We must seek a radical solution to our problems."

Now, in his address, Magnus presented Germany's loss of the war as a win for the German people. With the end of militarism, Germans could finally build themselves the just society they deserved. "We want a socialist republic," Magnus intoned. "Socialism means: 'The union of all citizens of Germany, mutual care for one another, the evolution of society into one organism, equality for all.'" He disavowed his earlier jingoism, pledging to "fight against national chauvinism," and offered the crowd a prediction: henceforth, Germany would never be ruled by the dictates of one man. "Never again," he intoned, "should the will of a king be the law of the land. The only law will be: 'Everything will be decided by the people for the people.'"

"Long live the free German Republic!" he concluded, as cheers erupted in the crowd.

Though the new democracy was proclaimed in Berlin, the authors of the new German constitution would gather to write it in the small central German city of Weimar out of fears that Berlin was too unstable for such a gathering. Germany's first experiment with democracy would thus be known as the Weimar Republic.

Every day, it seemed, brought new freedoms. The new democracy meant women had the right to vote. The Scientific Humanitarian Committee had supported women's suffrage for decades, and Magnus had cowritten a pamphlet on the subject with his brilliant sister Franziska Mann. Now the moment had finally arrived. Press censorship was abolished three days after the republic was declared. Magnus promptly took advantage of the newly freed press to voice new ideas. In 1919, he published a fifteen-page, 50-pfennig pamphlet entitled "What Unites and Divides the Human Race," his first attempt to apply his idea of the human panorama, developed for sexual orientation and gender, to race.

In his pamphlet, Magnus developed an argument about human sameness and difference. Upon close examination, "there is nothing identical in the world, only similar things: we are not even able to find two identical leaves on a tree, not even identical grains of sand are present on earth, let alone two identical people. . . . The small raised parts of the fingertips make it easy to recognize and identify a person."

While a botanist could separate the leaves of a tree into two groups by an infinite variety of metrics—lighter or darker than a certain shade, say, or smaller or larger than a certain size—the groupings would be determined not by the underlying physical reality but by the metric the botanist chose. The groupings would say more about the scientist doing the grouping—which qualities they deemed most important—than about the actual specimens being grouped.

The same insight, Magnus explained, should be applied to people and their categorizations by social scientists. "In order to summarize individuals with a large number of similar characteristics, i.e., similar, not identical, certain collective terms are used in natural and human sciences," Magnus wrote. "One speaks of species, of tribes, of peoples, of races, of classes, in order to connect beings that are similar in many respects to each other. But all these classifications are uncertain and fluctuate, and the deeper one explores nature and life, the more the borderlines augment [and] the opposites become completely blurred." The criteria a social scientist uses to sort human beings into tribes or races are no less impartial than the criteria a botanist uses to sort the leaves of the tree. Again, the groupings say more about the social scientist than about the people being categorized.

Under the manipulation of the power hungry, these arbitrary groupings can be weaponized. Understanding this, Magnus hoped, could inoculate people against such manipulation. "People are 99% equal to each other, at most 1% different from each other," he wrote, nearly a century before DNA evidence from the human genome backed him up. "For this one percent it is really not worthwhile to insult and destroy each other."

For Hirschfeld, human subgroups found unity through shared experience, not racial biology. He'd discerned this during his journey to America when, he recounted, he stuck out as foreign even though his physical features matched those of many Americans. In a nation of immigrants, Magnus was marked as a foreigner not by his skin color or hair texture but by his culture. It was his formal European clothing and his libertine Continental views that marked him as different. And it struck him as a cruel absurdity that many Americans were more eager to embrace him as one of their own on the racial grounds of "whiteness" than their English-speaking, baseball-playing, hotdog-eating "colored" neighbors whose families had been in America for centuries.

Magnus dreamed of a universal equality that would embrace the world's diversity. Breaking with earlier democratic theories that often made conformity the price of freedom and offered democracy only to those deemed racially worthy, Magnus announced, "Today we base the demand for the greatest possible freedom for the greatest possible number of people on diversity."

Though laudable, Magnus's rhetoric was growing disconnected from German realities. Extremist political parties in Germany did not share a commitment to democracy at all. Under the guise of providing security at rallies, some parties formed paramilitaries that brawled with rivals in the street and assassinated opponents. When Germans now spoke of "peacetime," they meant the era before the Great War, not the time they were living in. Exacerbating the postwar instability, in 1919, Rosa Luxemburg and Karl Liebknecht, who had left the Social Democrats to become Communists, launched a left-wing coup attempt modeled on Lenin's Russian Revolution. Fearing dictatorship, mainstream Social Democrats, who had patched up their internal breach over the war and were preparing to lead the new government, made common cause with the right-wing paramilitaries who put down the revolt and executed the two radicals. This bad blood between the center-left socialists and far-left communists would make it difficult for them to unite against later threats from the right.

Even among avowed liberals, Magnus's pluralist conception of democracy put him on the outs with the ascendant vision of the allied war victors. According to US President Woodrow Wilson's Fourteen Points, in the postwar world as empires collapsed, Central European peoples like the Poles and Hungarians who had long been dominated by more powerful neighbors would be granted independence. This ostensibly liberal call for national self-determination across Europe was tantamount to a scheme for a continent of ethno-states. In place of Magnus's grand pluralist democracy with diverse individuals participating as equals in a shared project, Wilson called for each ethnic group to have its own separate democracy.

Magnus's theories shined a light on the shortcomings of the Wilsonian view. In Hirschfeld's scheme, the borders between peoples were far too blurry to draw clean national lines around them. Not only were peoples spread beyond the borders of any potential ethnic-majority state—Russians in Latvia, Bosnians in Serbia, Jews in Poland—but after centuries of coexistence and comingling, all boundaries between peoples were arbitrary. Centuries of sex—overt and covert, consensual and forced—had made the peoples of the world impossible to sort back out into pure races even if one imagined that pure races had once existed.

Ironically, Woodrow Wilson's family embodied the shortcomings of his own approach. He hailed from Virginia, a state which maintained a strict system of segregation between its "white" and "colored" populations. Yet, ironically, the state's leading families prided themselves on their mixed-race backgrounds, claiming (often on flimsy evidence) to be descended from the colony's English founder, John Rolfe, and his indigenous bride, Pocahontas, daughter of the local king. As aristocrats in an ostensibly democratic society, elite Virginians believed their membership in the indigenous royal family bolstered their right to lead the commonwealth. Wilson's wife, Edith Bolling Galt Wilson, herself claimed descent from Pocahontas on her father's side. Hoping to justify a white supremacist system run by openly mixed-race elites, the state's leaders crafted a byzantine racial classification system that permitted a Virginian to be biologically biracial and still remain legally "white" as long as none of their non-European forbears had been born in sub-Saharan Africa.

Magnus had seen the white/colored system close-up on his 1890s trip to America, and he balked at Americans foisting something similar on Europe. Magnus argued against it not merely in writing but with facts on the ground. The polyglot libertine Berlin he had long been building, which could finally flourish under the new Weimar Republic, would be his best argument. Even as it struggled to recover following the disastrous war, he hoped his metropolis could be a microcosm of a new society—one based not on false hierarchies of gender and phantasms of racial purity but on freedom and diversity, indeed, on a true freedom that can only exist amid diversity.

Chapter 9

Moving Pictures

Conrad Veidt and Magnus Hirschfeld in a still from the film *Different from the Others.*

"FROM OUR STANDPOINT, the great revolution of the last week can only be greeted with joy," Magnus wrote at the dawn of the Weimar Republic. "The new era brings us freedom of speech and publication, and with the liberation of all who were formerly oppressed, we may with certainty assume that those upon whose behalf we have worked for many years will also receive an equitable assessment."

Surely, he figured, the new republic, founded on principles of universal human rights, would finally repeal the notorious Paragraph 175. He swiftly drafted an amnesty proposal for all men sentenced to prison for their sexual orientation under the old regime and presented it to the new president of the Prussian cabinet.

Magnus and his allies won an early victory on trans rights when, in 1919, the new government loosened the process for legally changing one's name. What looked to those outside queer-rights circles like a small technical modification lifted a huge burden for trans Germans. For one trans man, the change meant he could finally marry his girlfriend. Previously, he'd been barred on account of the female first name on his official documents. Another individual, now free of the legal name Hedwig that had been assigned at birth, could get a job in conventionally male lines of work unimpeded by their dead name.

In his activist efforts, Magnus had always played the inside game of lobbying the powerful and the outside game of rallying the public. But in this new world of democracy, the public became more important. And the end of censorship coincided with the development of technologies that afforded powerful new means of mass persuasion.

Magnus grew captivated by the new medium of film and felt compelled to use it. Invented in France in 1895, when the Lumière brothers captivated the world with their minute-long documentary of a crowd leaving a building, by the time of the Great War, the first feature-length silent blockbusters were arriving in theaters. These major releases shaped public opinion—for better or for worse. D. W. Griffith's 1915 *The Birth of a Nation*, a favorite of President Woodrow Wilson who screened it in the White House, infamously spurred a revival of the Ku Klux Klan. But Magnus also saw film's potential for good. In 1919, he endorsed the medium saying, "those who work to educate people about sexual matters not only have the right, but the duty to use film, in addition to the spoken and written word."

Berlin quickly became a leading global center of film production and consumption. A leapfrog city, getting a late start and then overtaking its venerable rivals, Berlin was able to adopt cutting-edge technology ready-made without going through the cumbersome trial-and-error stages. As more-established European capitals struggled to convert their ornate historic theaters into screening rooms, Berlin built vast modern cinemas from the ground up with poured concrete facades topped with bold all-caps signs.

At the birth of the republic in 1919, Germany already boasted over two hundred film companies releasing some five hundred movies annually. And the revolution eliminated the country's main disadvantage in comparison with France and the US: the kaiser's onerous censorship regime. Since films were silent in this era, the relative obscurity of the German language was irrelevant. With a few new text panels subbed in, a compelling made-in-Berlin film could be exported anywhere, just as easily as one made in Paris or Los Angeles. At home, this cornucopia was screened in Weimar Germany's three thousand cinemas to an audience of one million moviegoers a day. Overseas, global audiences gobbled up the German film industry's prodigious output. German film stars, most famously the dour enchantress Marlene Dietrich, became icons worldwide.

Weimar Germany's love of film could not entirely be chalked up to the good looks of its matinée idols or the country's frequent spells of drizzle and sleet. Film offered escapism on a budget—an irresistible proposition for postwar Germans. The country had lost so many young men in the war that few families were left untouched. The economy was in shambles. And the nation's spirit was broken. For ordinary workers, often survivors of combat trauma, the plentiful jobs and stunning economic growth they had taken for granted growing up had vanished. Educated Germans raised on Hegel's theory that the modern Prussian state was the pinnacle of human civilization had to face the reality that the unified Germany had been humiliated by an alliance of Britain, France, and America—stodgy European powers in league with a philistine New World upstart. German filmgoers proved an eager and impressionable audience.

The world's first films had captured the magic of motion—galloping horses, chugging trains, and the like. Then slapstick comedies and tear-jerking melodramas pulled in the crowds. But in the aftermath of the Great War, social thinkers and activists like Hirschfeld came to believe this new medium could shift public opinion in progressive directions. In the months after the end of Germany's censorship regime, socially engaged directors flooded theaters with a new type of cinema called "enlightenment films" (*Aufklärungsfilme*). The trick was to entice audiences with a risqué subject and then, once you had their attention, win them over to the cause of reform. Some films, with names like *The Chamber of Seven Sins*, *Hyenas of Pleasure*, and *Paradise of Prosti-*

tutes, leaned more titillating than didactic. But others, made with input from expert scientists and political operatives, were sincere attempts to instruct and then spur reform. In 1919 alone, over one hundred such enlightenment films were released or went into production. These German projects tackled taboo subjects that were rarely, if ever, the focus of films made in other countries at the time.

The most prominent director and producer of enlightenment films was Richard Oswald. A Berlin transplant born Richard Ornstein to a secular Jewish family in Vienna, the bespectacled Oswald called his specific subgenre the "social hygiene film." An audacious auteur, he'd been creating these films long before they were fashionable—or even legal. Oswald's first effort, an anti-war pic entitled *The Iron Cross*, was set to launch at the height of war fever in 1914 but got banned by the authorities. In 1916, Oswald released *Let There Be Light!* to raise awareness about sexually transmitted diseases. In this melodramatic work, the protagonist contracts syphilis from a sex worker and then passes it to his pregnant wife and, ultimately, their newborn baby. The film was a hit, so Oswald turned it into a series. For the fourth installment, on the dangers of back-alley abortions, Oswald enlisted Hirschfeld as a scientific advisor. Magnus shaped the film's arguments for legalizing abortion, which was then, under German law, a felony for both doctor and patient. The movie poster for the premier gave Magnus nearly equal billing with Oswald, a testament to Dr. Hirschfeld's prominence.

Now Oswald proposed a collaboration with Magnus to expose the social cost of Paragraph 175 and build support for its repeal. "It should be," Oswald suggested, "a work of art, presented as a personal documentary in the framework of scientific knowledge."

Magnus was enthralled. In film, he could bring his views to individuals who would never read his pamphlets let alone hunker down with issues of his scientific journal. He began plotting how he could make all of his key points—the born-this-way hypothesis, the long history of queerness, the panorama of human sexuality—for a mass audience on the silver screen. In his most popular writings, Magnus had appealed to emotion. Film offered endless possibilities for melodrama. But it also contained didactic possibilities in those written panels flashing on screen. By its nature, silent film was a hybrid medium—part live-action drama and part literature. Torn between dramatizing a gay man's terror under Paragraph 175 or simply filming his own lecture with a series of long text panels, Magnus chose what he called "a unification of both approaches. At the centre [would stand] the lecture of the sexologist. Entwined around it [would be] a simple life story . . . that is only all too familiar to the knowledgeable."

A month after the revolution, Magnus and Oswald were already collaborating on the world's first feature film with an explicitly gay theme. Under the working title *Paragraph 175*, shooting began in February 1919. As public relations materials for the film explained, "Dr. Magnus Hirschfeld, the famous physician and psychiatrist, has taken upon himself the task of writing the story for a drama, and . . . the brilliant director Richard Oswald has transformed this story into a dramatic film of gripping power."

In advance of the premiere that spring, the film's legalistic-sounding *Paragraph 175* was swapped out for something more poetic: *Different from the Others* (*Anders als die Andern*). The new title signaled a turn away from a narrow focus on repealing Paragraph 175 to Hirschfeld's broader goal of projecting the full breadth of the human sexual panorama. In Hirschfeld's view, every human being is unique in their sexuality, every member of society a sexual minority of one, every individual different from the others.

Shot and edited in a matter of weeks, the film was first screened at a May 24 press preview held in Berlin's cavernous Apollo Theater. "The film you are about to see for the first time today," Magnus told the assembled media, will win "science . . . a victory over error, justice a victory over injustice and human love a victory over human hatred."

The lights went down, and the audience watched the most traumatic experience of Hirschfeld's career—learning of the suicide of his patient "Lieutenant von X"—transformed into on-screen drama.*

As the film opens, concert violinist Paul Körner, played by the bisex-

* The narrative arc of *Different from the Others* is discernable even though only a portion of the film—approximately fifty minutes of the original ninety—exists today. Upon taking power, the Nazis attempted to destroy all copies of the film. The fifty-minute remnant, screenable online through the Internet Archive, is largely drawn from materials found in a Soviet film library.

ual matinée idol Conrad Veidt, leafs through the newspaper. Veidt musters his deep reserves of silent-film-actor melodrama, his gaunt, striking face framed by a rakish collar and wave of dark hair. He betrays increasing levels of panic as he reads article after article detailing a mysterious string of suicides. The first case is unmistakably a roman-a-clef version of Lieutenant von X: "Suicide of the factory owner H. on the day before his wedding. Motive unknown." Then another: "For unknown reasons, the respected circuit court judge H.W. took his own life by shooting himself." And another: "The student W. E. poisoned himself with cyanide. His parents are distraught about the incomprehensible deed of the young man." In a depressive daze, Veidt drops the paper. "He senses a common thread" that connects all of these seemingly unrelated suicides: "the sword of Damocles that is Paragraph 175."

In Hirschfeld's hands, this contemporary suicide epidemic gets situated within the 2,000-year history of gay oppression in the West. As Veidt stares off into a daydream, "in his mind's eye he sees an endless procession . . . from all times and countries, passing in review." In the elegant waistcoats, robes, and ascots of times past, a procession of gay men marches forth, their heads held high, beneath a banner inscribed "§ 175" hanging from a sword. Among the marchers are gay notables including Leonardo da Vinci, Peter Tchaikovsky, King Frederick the Great of Prussia, and Oscar Wilde.

From there, the plot unfolds. Veidt and his student, a violin prodigy, are star-crossed gay lovers. The student's sister, played by a nineteen-year-old Anita Berber, Weimar Berlin's infamous wild child, falls hard for her brother's unattainable teacher. Meanwhile, a blackmailer extorts Veidt after spotting him and his lover strolling in the Tiergarten even as his parents try to pressure him into marriage. Veidt is arrested for violating Paragraph 175, but in a plot twist, a sympathetic judge sentences him to only a week in jail. But a lone judge cannot overcome the full weight of a bigoted society. The protagonist returns home to find a letter from his talent agency reading, "We greatly regret to inform you that because of this scandal, we cannot continue your concert tour. Moreover, we wish to cancel our contract with you." Distraught, Veidt grabs a bottle of prescription pills, popping them one by one for dramatic effect before finally slumping down dead in a sequence that takes well over a minute. On the off chance that anyone has still missed the point, at Veidt's funeral, Berber lashes out at his father: "You and the rest of society have his death on your conscience!"

True to Magnus's method of winning an argument by not even conceding there is anything to argue over, *Different from the Others* makes its strongest points through its nonchalant portrayal of urban gay life. The film brings viewers into gay spaces that are unthreatening in their ordinariness. The gay lovers' walk through the Tiergarten feels no different from a heterosexual couple's stroll. A scene set in a queer-friendly Berlin café shows couples twirling on the dance floor, including two elegant gentlemen and a pair of lesbians in vests and hats who briefly put down their cigarettes for a waltz. Everyone seems to be enjoying themselves except the blackmailer, consumed by greed and bigotry, who looks miserable.

A formal drag ball is presented as almost comically wholesome. Pairs of attendees are cast in couples' costumes—two gay men come as a cowboy and a bullfighter, two lesbians appear as a jockey and a newsboy—and dance in an orderly circle as a sedate band plays. A waiter makes the rounds with champagne flutes that almost no one takes. By contrast, in a flashback to the protagonist's boarding school days, his straight classmates drag him from his studies to a brothel where prostitutes ply him with booze and paw at him despite his mortified lack of interest.

Magnus makes several cameos as an unnamed "physician and sexologist" who is obviously himself. By his own account, "I would ask that my participation in the film not be construed [as assuming] the role of an actor. It is an actor's high calling to embody figures other than himself. In this instance clearly that is not the case." The famously dowdy scientist was a difficult candidate for a movie-star makeover; for the shoot, the makeup crew successfully waxed his walrus mustache to fine points and the costume designer put him in fashionable minimalist specs. He appears, rather woodenly, in several dramatic sequences. In one, Veidt seeks out Magnus after the hypnosis treatment he underwent fails to cure him of his same-sex attraction. Magnus tells him, "Love for one's own sex can be just as pure and noble as that for the opposite sex. . . . Don't despair! As a homosexual, you can still make valuable contributions to humanity."

Much of Magnus's scientific and social theory was embedded in the dramatic elements of the film. The scene that debunks hypnosis as a way to cure same-sex attraction, for example, hints at Magnus's larger scientific outlook. But he clearly couldn't resist making a more overt case for his ideas. For those more complicated lessons, Oswald and Hirschfeld have the characters attend a lecture given by the unnamed physician and sexologist himself in a candle-lit academic lecture hall.

Magnus presents his principal theories through a series of on-screen text panels. "Nature is boundless in its creations," he opens and goes on to present an accessible summary of his groundbreaking 1906 paper "Gender Transitions" complete with its photos. After showing that gender is a continuum, Magnus explains how same-sex attraction sometimes maps onto that spectrum and sometimes doesn't. "Femininity and homosexuality often occur together [in men], but by no means always," he says. The same applies to masculinity and lesbianism in women.

Then the history lesson ensues, from tolerance in ancient Greece and Rome, to persecution in the Dark Ages, to liberation under Napoleon, to backsliding in the unified Germany. Now, the Weimar Republic offers hope for reform. "May justice soon prevail over this grave injustice, science conquer superstition, love achieve victory over hatred!" Magnus concludes to unanimous applause. A crowd of well-wishers mobs him at the podium.

In a kind of cinematic wish-fulfillment, the final text panel of the film announces vindication: "Over an open law book of the German Republic, a large hand appears, holding a brush. Drawing a large X, it strikes out once and for all §175, that horrible law to which clings so much blood and tears."

Outside the fantasy world of the cinema, in this unstable era, science sparred with conspiracy theories. Those seeking to discredit the film began spreading salacious rumors about Magnus. A whisper campaign alleged that he was sexually involved with Anita Berber, the teen actress who portrayed the protagonist's sister. The famously androgynous Berber, a renowned cabaret performer in Berlin, was the embodiment of all that was alluring and scandalous about the bohemian underground. Lithe and slim, no one knew until showtime whether Berber would take the stage nipples out in a corset dress for her famous "Cocaine" dance or appear in her "Eton boy" drag-king persona, complete with bowler hat, bowtie, monocle, and cane. The famed "priestess of depravity" was a porno pioneer, among the first individuals to dance nude on film. Berber and her collaborators in Berlin's burgeoning cabaret world reveled in making campy mockery of their sexually repressed opponents, from bourgeois conservatives to rigid authoritarians.

Over Berber's short life—she would die of tuberculosis at age twenty-nine—she was romantically linked to both men and women, many of them bisexual themselves. While there is no doubt Hirschfeld and Berber were close friends—Magnus was one of a small handful of nonfamily members who came to her funeral—given Magnus's lifelong residence on the far end of the continuum of queerness, a romance between them seems highly unlikely. As with all of the best rumors, it is "confirmed" only by the least reliable sources.

In the weeks Magnus was allegedly seducing Berber, he was indisputably beginning an affair on set with Karl Giese, the strapping actor who played Conrad Veidt's character in the flashbacks to his youth. Giese had turned twenty shortly before shooting began. Hirschfeld, famously fond of younger men, was fifty. Soon after meeting, the pair established what Magnus called their "physical, psychological bond." From filming onwards, Karl and Magnus were inseparable. They moved in together later that year.

Giese's star turn in *Different from the Others* is brief. He first appears clad in a sailor's V-necked tunic that shows off his hairless chest. The costume choice was an in-the-know wink to sailor garb as a signal of same-sex interest on the streets of Berlin. In his next sequence—the closest thing to a gay love scene in cinema up to that point—a pajama-clad Giese moves in to kiss a fellow student in their shared dormitory. Just before their lips meet, a faculty member barges in, grimaces in melodramatic horror, and vows to have the young seducer expelled. The film cuts to a faculty panel rendering harsh homophobic judgment. The scene, with the moon-faced, flowing-locked Giese unbowed before his bigoted judges evokes the trial of Oscar Wilde, where the accused writer had famously dubbed the "great affection of an elder for a younger man" as the "Love that dare not speak its name."

It was more than just years that separated Karl from Magnus. They were a case of opposites attract. Karl was born in Berlin in 1898 to a large working-class Christian family. His strong, hardy physique contrasted with Magnus's rumpled, portly self, and his feminine affect played counterpoint to Magnus's conventionally masculine self-presentation. The British writer Christopher Isherwood, who boarded for several weeks with the couple in the 1920s and later birthed *Goodbye to Berlin* (the source material for the musical, *Cabaret*) called Karl a "sturdy peasant youth" and reported that the young lover affectionately referred to Magnus as "Papa." Magnus, for his part, sometimes called his partner by the diminutive "Karlchen" ("Little Karl").

As life partners, Karl ruled the domestic sphere, handling interior decor, overseeing a much-needed upgrade to Magnus's wardrobe, and checking his aging, diabetic lover's addiction to sweets. The physical attraction between the two men was strong, but they were not entirely compatible in bed. Karl was a masochist and Magnus was no sadist. Ever the modern man of science, Magnus came up with a logical solution: he permitted Karl to get the whippings he craved from their mutual friend Erwin Hansen, a burly, blond, military-trained leftist. Magnus was similarly nonmonogamous. He reputedly had a weakness for sanitation workers and a very particular foot fetish for men with large feet. As the encouraged each other's outside explorations, Karl and Magnus remained committed to each other, in keeping with Magnus's sage adage: "sex tends to polygamy, while love tends to monogamy."

Karl and Magnus's first professional collaboration, *Different from the Others*, made a splash. Even with the timidity of the near-miss gay love scene, audiences had never seen these themes portrayed on screen. In some showings, viewers couldn't sit silent as cries of "*Huch nein*!" ("gasp, no!") and a scandalized "*aber Schwester*!" ("but sister!") rang out in the theaters. Reviews were mixed but the controversy made it a must-see. In advance of its May release, Oswald prepared around three dozen prints of the film and dispatched them from Berlin to distribution points in Frankfurt, Cologne, Hanover, and Vienna. By summer, the film was screening all over Germany, often to sold-out crowds. Reaching a new vast popular audience that had eluded him in his scientific writings, Magnus was soon deluged with letters from viewers. Most were fan mail, often unsigned. But the film also aroused opposition.

By the time *Different from the Others* dropped, the religious right was already enraged over enlightenment films. An earlier movie, *The Vow of Chastity*, about philandering priests, had sparked a riot in Düsseldorf where audience members stormed the stage and destroyed the screen. At showings of *Different from the Others*, hecklers were soon the least of theatergoers' worries. Several screenings were halted by stink bombs. In one incident, someone released live mice as the projector rolled. In Oswald's native Vienna, an incensed ticketholder let loose shots from a revolver injuring several audience members and terrifying the crowd. But controversy and headlines only made people more eager to see the film. *Different from the Others* was still running in Berlin nearly a year after its original release.

Coupled with these wildcat cinema outbursts, an organized censorship campaign against the film took shape. Social conservatives held influence during the Weimar era through the Catholic Center Party which was a partner in all of its coalition governments. Those who'd never supported the new republic's free speech free-for-all now used the controversy to push for reinstating a system of censorship. One conservative pastor wrote in an official "Call for Censorship" that "with *Different from the Others* the realm of the perverse has been entered." A Prussian legislator sponsored a measure to ban the film in Germany's largest state for "glorifying" homosexuality. By contrast, a film version of Karl Baer's trans narrative, *Memoirs of a Man's Maiden Years*, released the same year, drew less ire. The Baer biopic was banned only in the ultraconservative southern state of Bavaria.

Opponents of *Different from the Others* insisted that it wasn't necessary to actually watch it to support its being banned; ordinary citizens could trust them to view the perverted film on their behalf. To defend themselves, Hirschfeld and Oswald scrambled to arrange screenings for opinion makers and politicians to prove that their film had educational merit.

Among the film's most powerful opponents were the Berlin League to Fight Public Immorality and the Greater Berlin Committee to Combat Smut. "Shamelessness [and] perversity [are] the order of the day in Berlin," League members wrote to the Prussian state government in 1920. Indeed, Berlin was shameless about its perversity, proudly broadcasting it nationwide. From the capital, the group alleged, "the filth flows over the whole of Germany [through] movies, theatre, dance performances, erotic and perverse literature and periodicals."

The leader of the self-styled smut brigade was Karl Brunner, a one-time high school history teacher who, in his words, worked to protect the "moral development" of his young charges from the "threatening print materials [that are] chiefly guilty for today's 'sexual emergency' [among] our youth." Before the revolution, Brunner had worked as a professional censor, serving nearly a decade as the head of the Theater and Film Censorship Office of the Berlin police. The 1919 revolution put him out of a job.

Seeking to confront his enemies in person, Brunner crashed one of Hirschfeld's and Oswald's special screenings. In the midst of the showing at Berlin's Central Institute for Education and Instruction, an enraged Brunner leapt out of his seat denouncing the film as "swinish filth."

Oswald stood up. "If anyone calls this film swinish filth, he himself is a swine," the director yelled before calling out "Herr Professor Brunner" by name.

The audience, peeved at the disruption and eager to watch the film to the end, gave Oswald an impromptu standing ovation and didn't let up until Brunner exited the theater several minutes later. The projectors rolled on, but Brunner sought his revenge by pushing for a nationwide ban.

The censorship campaign doubled down on the antisemitic-inflected homophobia that had been wielded against Hirschfeld in wartime. *Different from the Others*, a creation of Hirschfeld, Oswald, and a disproportionately Jewish cast and crew, was animated by the tolerant outlook that was common among Berlin's liberal secular Jews but was hardly limited to them. For Brunner and his allies, it was easier to invoke shadowy racial conspiracies than to openly make the case against a free society.

The antisemitic campaign, waged in both private whispers and public newspaper screeds, highlighted the filmmakers' ethnic backgrounds and wielded well-worn stereotypes against them. Oswald, a risk-taking auteur and committed reformer, was slandered as a smut baron destroying Germany's social fabric for personal profit. Hirschfeld, a native-born Prussian and decades-long Berlin resident (as well as an avid celebrant of Christmas), was painted as a racial outsider. As one Christian rightist put it, "Hirschfeld is Jewish, that explains something. . . . Although he appears to be an assimilated Jew, [he] is still in no condition to empathize with our German people. . . . With his scientific movie-trash, he did an extremely bad service to our German people."

Reeling from the outcry over *Different from the Others*, the German federal government worked to reestablish a censorship regime. While the national authorities moved slowly, efforts at the state level to ban the film succeeded in conservative regions, even while liberal locales continued to screen it for packed houses. Since regional bans required the local police to certify the film as obscene, there was no chance of banning it in Berlin where Magnus had won over the police leadership years before. Heinrich Kopp, Berlin's police chief, not only attended one of Magnus's screenings for government officials, he even served on the postscreening question-and-answer panel.

Only in May 1920, a full year after the release of *Different from the Others*, did the Reichstag finally pass a national film censorship law. Despite its exemption for films of a "social or philosophical slant," the legislation was quite strict. It applied similar standards to print media. In Hirschfeld's remarks at the prerelease press screening in 1919, he had all but predicted the backlash. "I am conscious of the fact that whoever wants to use intellectual weapons to fight for human progress must overcome attacks and opposition," he'd said. "The first scholars who, after they had discovered the printing press, put their ideas into letters were also violently attacked."

Weeks after the new film censorship law was enacted, a tribunal of scientists was empaneled to decide the film's fate. Ominously, two of these three "experts" maintained that homosexuality could be cured through hypnosis. And certain adolescents, they believed, could be turned gay through "recruitment," a process they worried could be aided by films like *Different from the Others*.

On October 16, 1920, the board ordered a nationwide ban, albeit on a technicality: the film was not explicit *enough* in its depiction of gay male love. *Different from the Others* never depicts gay sex, instead using clothed caresses and knowing fades-to-black to intimate sexual intercourse. But under Paragraph 175, the panel noted, only penetrative gay male sex was illegal—and that is never shown. "Whereas the criminal code penalized specific homosexual practices, this film suggested that a homosexual orientation itself was punishable," the panelists wrote in their decision. "'Impartial and especially uneducated viewers' might easily arrive at the conclusion that the protagonist was sentenced to prison simply for stroking his pupil's head or placing his arm on the blackmailer's shoulder. Such erroneous understanding of § 175 would necessarily confuse the audience, arousing fears that simple gestures of friendship were punishable and thereby damaging the image of the judiciary and the state." The panel clearly wanted an excuse—any excuse—to ban the film.

With the new censorship law, what was legal and what was banned came to depend on the experts called to judge individual cases. Magnus himself sometimes served in this capacity, and when he did, he tried to mitigate the worst impacts of the legislation. Ironically, Brunner's own ultranationalist publication *German Deeds* (*Deutschen Taten*), which ran hagiographies of fearless German soldiers from the Great War, got censored under the law he'd championed, when a Frankfurt panel ruled that it glorified violence.

The republic's two-steps-forward, one-step-back broadening of free speech also opened new avenues of attack on Hirschfeld and his allies. Adolf Brand's masculinist wing of the German gay movement was now reaching more readers than ever. Brand's minions published an anti-Hirschfeld magazine, *The Aunt* (*Die Tante*), which mocked Germany's leading gay-rights activist as an effete, intellectual, cross-dressing, sissy Jew. Against Hirschfeld's vision of tolerance for all, it offered Brand's fascistic race-and-gender hierarchy.

With the censorship law applied on a case-by-case basis by different judges informed by different experts, Weimar culture became a never-ending game of whack-a-mole. Social conservatives—rarely the most in-the-know scenesters—would happen upon some performance or publication they found objectionable and make their case. Sometimes they'd win, but even their victories proved pyrrhic. Whenever they prevailed, some other work would invariably spring up to take the place of whatever had just been banned.

As one conservative Berlin prosecutor lamented, "Nothing has been as demoralizing for the *Volk* [German people] as the inundation of the market since the [revolution] with obscene and lewd print media of different sorts. One filthy magazine is barely driven out of the public realm when more of the same character appear." The censorship regime was littered with loopholes, and Magnus and his allies brazenly exploited them. When Magnus's gay weekly *Friendship* (*Die Freundschaft*) was successfully, albeit briefly, banned, he simply put out an alternate publication called *Friend* (*Der Freund*).

Under the republic's censorship regime, the same publication could be off-limits in some parts of Germany while permitted in others. With censors in provincial cities more successful at closing down local publications, the Berlin-based press became ever more important. The capital's cultural reach was vast, and its taste spread far and wide. Weimar Berlin's newsstands were packed with nearly two dozen gay and lesbian magazines, and Magnus himself marveled at what he called the "absolute flood" of queer publications on offer. Unlike Magnus's own pioneering *Annual of Sexual Intermediaries with Special Focus on Homosexuality*, newer queer publications presented themselves as purely popular—good clean (or dirty) fun—with no pretense of scientific rigor. One publication aimed at trans readers was mostly fashion tips and makeup advice.

With such a cornucopia of queer literature available at Berlin's newsstands, closeted readers could safeguard their anonymity by buying the publications in far-flung neighborhoods. One reader of *Die Freundin* (*Girlfriend*), a lesbian magazine that sometimes ran a trans insert, recalled that carrying the publication home "was like you had a bomb in your bag." Meanwhile, out and proud Berliners would further the cause by reading the publications in public and then leaving their finished copies on park benches or subway seats for others to discover.

Even far from Berlin, readers could get a taste of the city's open culture by subscribing to queer publications written, edited, and printed in the capital. Spurred by calls to action from publications like Magnus's *Friendship*, gay-rights organizations formed even in small locales.

These popular publications arguably did as much for the gay-rights cause as the agitation of actual political organizations. Soon, the mainstream was shifting in response to queer culture. The short, boyish haircuts that had begun in the lesbian underground became the *de rigueur* pageboy cut, the *Bubikopf*. The old-school girly-girl blonde braids (*Zöpfe*), popular before the revolution, were now seen as hopelessly passé. Similarly, women smoking tobacco, once seen as a lesbian quirk, was now embraced as a hallmark of the Weimar-era "new woman" and of flapper culture worldwide.

With a sympathetic police force and enlightened local authorities, Berlin remained a remarkable zone of free expression. Even after it was banned, *Different from the Others* was a cultural touchstone. And screenings of the film never actually stopped. Shortly after the revolution, Magnus began building his Institute for Sexual Science. By the time his film was banned, Magnus had a private screening room where he could continue to show it to visiting scientists and physicians from all over the world. If anything, the frisson of tasting forbidden fruit added to the film's allure. What could be sexier than a private screening of a banned queer film in the heart of Weimar Berlin?

Chapter 10

Here It's Right!

Berlin's Eldorado drag club with the motto "Here It's Right!" on the marquee.

SUMMER IN BERLIN was like a magic trick. It stayed light out past 10 p.m. as long days melted into raucous nights. The first summer of the republic felt particularly auspicious, no moment more so than the evening that Magnus opened his Institute for Sexual Science on the edge of the Tiergarten.

The July 1, 1919, inauguration ceremony at the mansion-turned-institute, formerly the residence of the nobleman and diplomat Count Hatzfeldt, began with a musical number. It was sung by Leo Gollanin, a gifted baritone and committed ally of Magnus's gay-rights campaign. In his day job, Gollanin served as the cantor to Berlin's largest progressive congregation, the imposing Moorish-domed New Synagogue on Oranienburger Strasse that, viewed from certain vistas in the city, appeared equal to the city's main cathedral, the Berliner Dom. As Cantor Gollanin's participation underscored, Judaism and liberalism had become nearly inseparable in the capital.

After Gollanin sounded his final note, Magnus rose to speak. The goal of his institute, he explained, was "two-fold: scientific research on all of human sexuality [and] to make use of this research for all." Then he ushered his guests and the assembled press in for a tour of the building, highlighting its museum and clinics.

Magnus had long dreamt of opening the world's first institution dedicated to the scientific study of sex. Decades before, while penning "Sappho and Socrates," he came to see that only a public education campaign could save his patients. Now, with the regime change, it could become a reality. As he told his audience, "Our Institute can be called a child of the revolution."

Magnus had moved to this park-side neighborhood from semi-suburban Charlottenburg in 1910, and the Scientific Humanitarian Committee had been headquartered up the street since 1912. In early 1919, he'd bought the mansion and then an adjoining property using a grant from the Ministry of Internal Affairs, his own savings, and donations from anonymous funders. Rumors abounded that his donors were wealthy closeted individuals who supported Magnus's gay-rights crusade in secret. A short walk from the center of political power, the Reichstag, and the capital's main train station, the Lehrter Bahnhof, this was the perfect location for what Magnus termed his "facility for research, teaching, healing and refuge"—part thinktank, part community center, and part tourist attraction. The park-side site was also ideal for Magnus's walk-and-talk therapy sessions.

Inside, the sprawling mansion channeled the previous century. As the gay British writer Christopher Isherwood, who boarded at the institute as a young expat, later recalled, the "furniture was classic, pillared, garlanded, [the] marble massive, [the] curtains solemnly sculpted, [the] engravings [impressive]."

This nostalgic feel put visitors at ease as they encountered a glaringly modern institution. On the ground floor, Magnus lived with his partner, Karl, who ran the archive and often served as tour guide. The good looks and arresting stage presence that had served him in his brief acting career were assets in this new role as he led visitors through the exhibit halls, his hair punctiliously parted, a debonair pocket square peeking out of his sport coat. When the hosts entertained, they'd open their living quarters to strangers who spilled out of the mansion's ballroom. This too was a form of public education, wordlessly inculcating the lesson that a gay couple's living space was fundamentally no different than a straight couple's, just more tastefully decorated.

In the heart of the institute, visitors took in the permanent exhibition, the "Wall of Sexual Transitions." Presented in German, English, and French, it visually instilled Magnus's core theory that human sexuality was a continuum. Museum goers were confronted with photographs of ambiguous genitalia. Instinctually, of course, they'd try to slot them into categories of male or female. When they threw up their hands in exasperation, Magnus offered them an elegantly simple way out: dispense with the binary.

Through explicit images, the Wall of Sexual Transitions illustrated Magnus's theory that masculinity and femininity were archetypes. In the real world, everyone was a mixture of both. As the exhibit showed, transitions between male and female occur in every area in which sexuality is expressed. In the genitals, a mixture of maleness and femaleness can manifest in the ambiguous genitalia of intersex individuals. In the secondary sexual characteristics, it showed up in boys who develop breasts at puberty (gynecomastia) and in women who sprout facial hair, like Magnus's childhood maid. In the sex drive, transitions can manifest both in same-sex attraction or in people who play against type during heterosexual sex. In the psyche, the exhibit explained, some individuals experience "the urge to present and conduct oneself in the outer raiment of the sex to which a person does not belong—as regards the visible sexual organs" and must change their clothing or even transition physically. As always, Magnus chose extreme cases to illustrate his points while insisting that these cases differed only by degree from all humans—including, of course, you, walking through his exhibit. If everybody is in some respect queer, what's left of "normal"? If everyone is a hodgepodge of masculinity and femininity, what's left of gender?

Beyond the central exhibition halls, visitors found facilities as sprawling as the institute's mission. A psychotherapy room, fitted with heavy drapes and cozy furniture, was available for counselors who, unlike Magnus, preferred to work indoors. In the psychotherapy studio, Dr. Felix Abraham, a progressive psychiatrist who specialized in gender dysphoria, offered gender-affirming counseling.

Pioneering medical professionals gravitated to the institute to practice their craft. In a spotless, spartan medical clinic, patients received hormone treatments and, under Dr. Ludwig Levy-Lenz, the head of the institute's gynecology department, underwent the world's first comprehensive gender-affirmation surgeries. Advances in medicine and endocrinology now allowed institute doctors to perform sophisticated surgeries that made Karl Baer's 1906 procedures look rudimentary by comparison. All institute facilities treated patients on a sliding scale based on ability to pay.

In the library, whose collection would swell to twenty thousand volumes, casual visitors and committed researchers discovered the world's greatest trove of books about sex. The core of the holdings came from Magnus's personal collection, amassed over decades. It included works from all over the world, such as the Kama Sutra, the Indian subcontinent's fabled sex guide, and rare copies of recovered texts by "the grandfather of gay liberation," Karl Heinrich Ulrichs. The institute's visual collection would ultimately include some thirty-five thousand photographs, slides, and movie reels, which anyone could view in the institute's screening room, safely insulated from Germany's censorship law. As a thinktank of sorts, activists and legislators gathered in the institute's offices and meeting rooms to formulate policy reforms and scheme to get them through parliament. In addition to repealing Paragraph 175, the institute, in coalition with German feminist leader Helene Stöcker, pushed for legalizing abortion and no-fault divorce.

Local couples poured into the institute's auditorium for question-and-answer nights geared toward young people entering into heterosexual marriages. In this first marriage counseling center in Germany, Magnus and his staff presented sex education and family-planning basics in talks such as "What is the best way to have sex without making a baby?" Public programs also disseminated information on venereal diseases and warnings about inherited disorders that could be passed from parents to the children they would conceive. Attendees who were too shy to voice their questions were invited to anonymously submit them in writing. In the fourteen-year life of the institute, over fourteen thousand question cards would be turned in, many answered by Magnus personally. For those unable to attend, the institute brought its sex education to couples far from Berlin by publishing a popular magazine entitled *Marriage*.

At times, the institute's family-planning teachings veered into eugenics, though it is crucial to distinguish the institute's health-based goals from the racist aims of the institute's opponents. Magnus kept a long list of traits he considered to be "degenerative signs"—some as mundane as varicose veins and big ears—that made matches between two carriers undesirable. And he was concerned that inbreeding led to unhealthy children. Indeed, he thought his own health problems might be a result of his parents' decision to inbreed within two not-too-distant branches of the same German-Jewish family tree. As a believer in the concept of hybrid vigor, Magnus taught that intermarriage could help couples avoid hereditary diseases that were common in certain parts of the world and in certain ethnic groups. To him, interracial marriages were the healthiest marriages. This put him diametrically at odds with racist eugenicists who believed racial purity could be achieved—and a master race bred—through a government-enforced policy of racial inbreeding and a concomitant ban on "miscegenation."

For all its sprawling mission, the main draw for the general public was the exhibit space, which was so closely associated with its founder that it was sometimes referred to as the "Hirschfeld Museum." When it first opened, the institute mostly drew physicians and medical students, but as word spread, it became a must-see for any curious tourist, the most quintessentially Berlin of all Berlin attractions. As one visiting American doctor, a birth control activist from New York, observed, "It is an institution absolutely unique in the whole world . . . which I [wish I could] establish in the United States but which I [know] would not thrive on account of our prudish, hypocritical attitude to all questions of sex."

The museum's mission was clear—to convert visitors to Hirschfeld's tolerance-inducing concept of the sexual panorama—but it wasn't above using salacious displays to get them in the door. As a therapist, sexologist, and urban explorer, Magnus had spent his life acquiring an encyclopedic knowledge of kinks. His psychotherapy patients keyed him into their fetishes, and he encountered others as an observer of—and participant in—Berlin's libertine nightlife. The "Darwin of the Berlin sexual underworld," as one contemporary scholar calls him, put every kink known to him on display in his museum.

After taking in a complicated mathematical chart—the $e = mc^2$ of sexual relativity—that explained the forty-three million gender possibilities and walking past posters detailing the Soviet Union's legalization of abortion, visitors could wander through the world's greatest collection of dildos. The institute held carved phalluses from as far away as Central Africa, Polynesia, and Japan. Some, the plaques explained, served indigenous religious purposes. Others were purely for pleasure, such as the foot-pedal-operated penetrative device on display that was proudly made in Germany.

Past the dildos, a vast array of condoms appeared under glass. The ancient invention had been revolutionized by the vulcanization process in the nineteenth century to become a mass-produced commodity. Now condoms were distributed widely despite strenuous objections from contraception opponents in many Western countries. Most scandalous, they could be purchased anonymously at vending machines which, by the early 1930s, numbered more than 1,600 throughout Germany. At the institute, alongside the clear tube that was Germany's best seller and the newfangled reservoir tip version, there was a stunning array of kinkier options. The tiny "capot" only covered the head of the penis leaving the shaft nude for maximum stimulation; the ribbed condom, according to the text panel, could combat a woman's "frigidity." And then there were the whimsical shapes available on the black market: one in the shape of a stocking with a foot on the end, another in the shape of a hand, complete with four fingers and a thumb, presumably for those turned on by complex decision-making in the heat of passion. Historical contraceptive devices made appearances as well, including an authentic medieval chastity belt.

In the midst of this menagerie, only the most salacious items stood out. In one room, the back wall was loaded up to the ceiling with paintings, drawings, and etchings by gender-nonconforming artists. But who could focus on those when the center of the room featured a collection of leather military boots donated by a fetishist who had mounted roughly a dozen of them on a wooden disk? As the anonymous creator explained in an accompanying note, "This collection . . . was completed after immense effort on 18 September 1919. I took delight in [it] because I passionately enthuse about knee-boots and behold in this footwear a piece of art, an aesthetic work, especially when a young man wears knee-boots. What I find most beautiful are hussar boots, which, unfortunately, have become something of the past. Let whoever discovers this note laugh at this curiosity—it gives me much pleasure."

Beyond the boot fetish, the institute displayed images and paraphernalia illustrating the foot fetish, the fingernail fetish, the hair fetish, the fat fetish, and the asphyxiation fetish. The lesser-known fetish for children's clothing was depicted through photographs of one of Magnus's patients, a balding middle-aged man clad in a sailor's suit with knee-pants who appeared bravely unmasked. The man was married to a woman but could only consummate the relationship when dressed as a fifteen-year-old boy. "The exposed knee is very important to him," Magnus noted. The institute's exhibitionism display included a trench coat worn by a real-life flasher, and the voyeurism fetish was illustrated with a stick-mounted mirror confiscated from an actual peeping tom who'd used it to look up women's skirts in a movie-theater lobby.

Arguably, the centerpiece of the Hirschfeld Museum was its sadomasochism collection. Magnus had unusually open access to the S&M underworld through Karl, his masochist partner. Over a glass-topped cabinet full of whips, photographs and illustrations explained their various uses. Another displayed a cuff with rubber teeth, meant to be worn just beneath the head of the penis. The images of S&M fantasies went on and on. One set of drawings featured navy men flogging each other in various configurations. In a photographic series, four naked men playact a medieval execution, part of an initiation rite for a right-wing gay masculinist group. The leader, with a cross painted on his bare chest, wields the sword while his assistants—one in a hat and cape, the other in nothing but a hat—restrain the kneeling initiate, pinning his head to the ground.

The museum also detailed a type of gender play Magnus called "metatropism"—when heterosexual couples play against stereotypes with the woman dominating the man. In one photograph, a man, on all fours, wears a bridle and blinders, while a dominatrix holds the reins in one hand and a riding crop in the other. In another, a dominatrix in a low-necked, high-hemmed nightie and leather ankle boots stands, reins in hand, atop a prone man, who wears nothing but a rough loincloth that suggests horsehide. The text below explains to museumgoers that, in the sober Latin taxonomy of sexual science, this horse-and-jockey position is termed *Equus eroticus*.

"What was collected here," institute doctor Levy-Lenz later reminisced, was "a labyrinth of human passions and aberrations! We had countless objects that had served to satisfy sexual fetishisms: a collection of a hundred pairs of women's kid leather shoes in all colors; boots, including some that were laced-up well past the thigh. In the same museum room, there was an exhibition case filled with braids and locks of hair that one single braid-cutter had cut off and collected. From a panty fetishist we inherited a selection of the most beautiful, varied, exquisite, and intimate pieces of lingerie that have ever been worn." One of the harder-to-categorize fetishes was illustrated by the pair of lacey women's underwear one Prussian World War I soldier felt compelled to wear under his battle uniform.

The variety was endless—and that was the point. "The number of fetishes is unlimited," Magnus wrote in 1920. "From head to toe there is not a single spot on the body, and from hats to shoes there is no fold in a garment that cannot trigger a fetishistic pleasure."

As the Hirschfeld Museum drew crowds to the heart of Berlin and blew up their ideas of what was normal, even possible, sexually, the borders between the day tourism of the institute and the night tourism of the city's cabarets began to blur. For some museumgoers, information on the wall panels about massage parlors where tables came equipped with restraints for those who craved them, served as advertisements.

Even the museum's most sophisticated scientific displays could take on a tawdry second life in the alleyways of the capital. The Wall of Sexual Transitions exhibit included a picture of a thickly bearded individual labeled "Anna H., a waitress." At the Berlin bar where they worked,

Anna became the tourist attraction. Other nightlife venues put nude intersex individuals on stage and called it the evening's entertainment. The acts didn't so much perform as simply smoke, smile, and wave from a chair as audience members looked on.

As each new kink was discovered, documented, and displayed at the institute, it was only a matter of time before it would appear on stage. Many sex clubs featured "themes" inspired by the institute. The artist Francis Bacon, who spent two months in 1927 as a young queer expat in Berlin, recalled tableaux vivants on stage that looked like the sketches, drawings, and lithographs on the walls of the Hirschfeld Museum come to life. This feedback loop could also run in reverse. A phenomenon would surface on stage in Berlin, draw a crowd, and then get documented at the institute.

On the seedier streets of the capital, touts bundled against Berlin's chilly nighttime air offered hints of what lay inside. "I remember these streets of clubs where people stood in front of the entrance miming the perversions that were going on inside," Bacon reminisced. Tourists with little or no knowledge of German relied on this miming to decide which show to watch. As for so many others, Bacon's brief time in Berlin was transformational. "There was something so extraordinarily open about the whole place," he recalled. "You had this feeling that sexually you could get absolutely anything you wanted. I'd never seen anything like it, of course, having been brought up in Ireland, and it excited me enormously. I felt, well, now I can just drift and follow my instincts."

If you were, like Francis Bacon, a citizen of one of the victorious allied powers, the German mark's ever-worsening exchange rate against your currency was a boon. This favorable exchange rate helped draw some two hundred thousand foreign tourists a year to Berlin. Many stuck around for the excitement and the low rents as expats. Soon envious locals were referring to flush visitors from "Dollarika" (the United States), "Guilderland" (Holland), and "Yeniwara" (Japan). As desperate Germans moved to the capital to find work, Berlin became a booming city in a sinking country. All too often the only jobs available required demeaning oneself for the amusement of foreigners, scraping for tips in a hospitality job, performing dirndled and lederhosened clichés of Germanness on stage, or turning to sex work as a last resort. As one contemporary scholar explains, in these years "prostitution, male and female, became more noticeable and more widespread, the product of Weimar's sexual tolerance as much as of its economic failure."

As the newest European capital, Berlin had no equivalent to Rome's Coliseum or Paris's Louvre to wow tourists. All it had was novelty. Arriving late to the party of modernity, Berlin found the typical roles already taken and had to improvise. Christopher Isherwood joshed that this was the real reason Berlin was so kinky and so queer. "Paris had long since cornered the straight girl–market" with its skirt-lifting cancan revues, he noted, "so what was left for Berlin to offer its visitors but a masquerade of perversions?" This was, of course, what drew Isherwood to the city. In his heavily autobiographical novel *Down There on a Visit*, he paraphrased his mother's warning about Berlin: "You couldn't find anything more nauseating than what goes on, quite openly, every day." And his reaction: "Then and there I made a decision . . . that, no matter how, I would get to Berlin."

The city's hustler dive bars, like the Cozy Corner near the Halle Gate, were Isherwood's weakness. As he put it in a memoir, my "chief motive for going to Berlin [was that] Berlin meant Boys." Pushing aside a heavy leather curtain by the entrance, Isherwood entered the simplest watering hole imaginable, decorated with just a few images of burly boxers and strapping cyclists tacked up over the bar. In this stifling dive, Isherwood reveled in a rough-trade world of young, perpetually underemployed working-class teens. As he recalled, "because they knew it excited their clients (*die Stubben*), the boys stripped off their sweaters or leather jackets and sat around with their shirts unbuttoned to the navel and their sleeve rolled up to the armpits." With his posh background and internalized British-bred homophobia, Isherwood could initially consummate relations only with guys below his class, the less English spoken the better. For Isherwood, bars like the Cozy Corner offered liberation from the constricting class structure of England. He seemed less keen to face the German economic realities that led young locals, disproportionately war orphans, to places like this.

For other scenes and fetishes, Berlin offered other bars and clubs. After the fall of the kaiser and the opening of the institute, the number of queer establishments roughly tripled as did the size of the capital's queer population. Weimar Berlin boasted some 135 gay bars and 85 lesbian establishments.

Gay men into facial hair gathered at the Moustache-Lounge. The elite gathered at the Boheme-Bar, which declared itself "The Gentlemen's Bar." Its ads conjured a roaring twenties world of all Gatsbys and no Daisys, where men in black tie, with slicked-back hair, elegantly puffed cigarettes at tables topped with champagne on ice.

Weimar Berlin's tolerance was etched into its urban fabric. The institute sat in the heart of the capital and the city's red-light district was literally around the corner from the police headquarters on Alexanderplatz. The city's brothels, both female and male staffed, duly registered with the department and were generally left alone. In the tangle of streets bordering the vast plaza, everything was on offer—as long as you could read the codes. A streetwalker in red shoes was a dominatrix for hire; more blatant ones simply held a whip. Only the most clueless of newbies were at a loss. One American visitor complained, "At night along the Unter den Linden it was never possible to know whether it was a woman or a man in woman's clothes who accosted one."

Between the city's diverse nightlife and the comprehensive scientific research at Hirschfeld's institute, Berlin was bringing the then-new concept of market segmentation to sex. From his perch in prim Vienna, novelist Stefan Zweig quipped that "the Germans introduced all their vehemence and methodical organization into perversion," while Berlin drama critic Klaus Mann, the gay son of famed novelist Thomas Mann, called his city "our department store of assorted vices." One could mock the German fetish for order or one could simply enjoy it. Catering to every class and subculture, Berlin's underground was so methodically organized that whatever your itch, you could scratch it.

Whether partaking or merely peeking, visitors found that no Berlin trip was complete without exploring the city's queer nightlife. Even conventional guidebooks listed the best gay, lesbian, and trans bars. Most were written from the perspective of the straight voyeur. One guide sneered at the Adonis Lounge, a gay hustler bar—but still deemed it a must-see! There, as it detailed, the more "disreputable element" assembles and the "evil alliances are more numerous than the good ones. From the white poison (cocaine) to love of all kinds, everything is traded here that can be exchanged with money."

Of the scene at the legendary Eldorado drag queen bar, another Weimar-era tour book dished primly, "This place, one of Berlin's most popular, recruits its patrons mainly from circles where the arithmetic of love is not without its mistakes. Here men do not only dance with women but with men. And women dance with women. And the nice gentleman from Saxony, who dances with the blond singer, doesn't have the slightest idea that his blond lady is a man." One can imagine some nice gentleman readers from Saxony dropping by the Eldorado purely to take in the scene—and others going there to make just this kind of plausibly deniable "mistake."

The Eldorado, called by one popular music composer "a supermarket of eroticism," actively sought out press coverage and ran ads showing tables with same-sex couples that promised "what you don't see elsewhere." The club, expressly founded by a veteran lesbian nightlife impresario to be the least underground space in her empire, sat squarely in the heart of the queer nightlife hub around Nollendorfplatz, a magnet within the city and beyond. After decamping from the institute, Christopher Isherwood moved a few blocks away and vividly chronicled the neighborhood, bestowing on its short-lived cabaret world a cultural immortality. Unlike more down-low nightspots, the Eldorado welcomed straight tourists with money to burn. As one in-the-know journalist explained, the drag queens in the venue put on a show "for the people from the provinces, and they live off the tips." Magnus was an Eldorado goer, rumor had it in drag as Tante Magnesia. However he presented, he was no doubt drawn to the wide-ranging scene that unfolded beneath the marquee reassuring all comers that "*Hier Ist's Richtig!*" ("Here It's Right!").

A notable exception to the holier-than-thou straight-gaze guidebooks arrived in 1928 when Ruth Roellig, in collaboration with Magnus, penned *Berlin's Lesbian Women*, the world's first lesbian travel guide. In his foreword, Hirschfeld hailed the work as the landmark that it was. Such a volume, he noted, could never have appeared under the old censorship regime—or even in ostensibly freer countries, like Great Britain. Ever since the fall of the kaiser, the book reassured visitors, "people have become more tolerant."

Roellig's catalogue of the various bars, clubs, and cafés where lesbians congregated as well as trans spaces for those the author called "women who prefer to appear in men's clothing" constituted an integral part of Hirschfeld's from-science-to-justice crusade. All too often, Magnus noted in his foreword, lesbian women got pressured into straight marriages; they'd be psychologically healthier, he wrote, if "they keep their [true] sexual nature." For lesbian readers, Magnus explained, the guidebook itself could be a form of therapy, helping them in their journey to self-acceptance. The work would also be important to nonlesbian readers, he wrote, since it would demystify lesbianism and lessen "the ingrained bias" against queer women.

Much like Magnus, Roellig didn't deny her queerness, but she wrote about lesbians in the third person. Still, she could wax poetic about queer "love that is sacred, pure, and beautiful in itself." Roellig could also write grippingly about sex: "caresses of soft and pliant hands, nail and tooth, soft bites and pulling of hair, and finally, after great tension, an utter free-fall . . . into a moment of measureless bliss."

The heart of her book detailed the Berlin built by lesbians for lesbians. "They build a world of their own—in their homes, in their lounges, in their literature, and especially in their love practices," Roellig wrote in a close third person. Following the highbrow foreword by the eminent medical doctor and her own heartfelt introduction, she led readers on a tour of her Berlin cataloguing roughly a dozen lesbian bars in the capital without the puritanical gaze typical of the guidebook genre. Indeed, Roellig openly mocked the upper-middle-class straight couples who visited Berlin's queer clubs as if on human safari.

The world Roellig documented was vast. With Germany's male population winnowed by the Great War, many formerly male-only jobs, such as tram conductor, had been opened to all. In the wake of the war, women made up 36 percent of the German workforce. Women flocked to Berlin for these new opportunities, giving the city a lopsided gender ratio that skewed even more heavily lesbian, in keeping with Magnus's theory that queer individuals are disproportionately likely to migrate to a metropolis. Under Hirschfeld's big-tent definition, he estimated that the city's queer female population during the late-Weimar era stood at four hundred thousand, meaning roughly one in five Berlin women were at least queer-curious. Even under a more conservative definition, based on subscribers to lesbian publications and membership in the city's various lesbian social organizations and sports leagues, it was nearly one hundred thousand.

The city's lesbian scene, as portrayed by Roellig, was, if anything, even more meticulously segmented than its gay male scene. Like a carefully curated exhibit at the institute, the lesbian world was siloed by gender expression into ultrafemme *Mädis*, pert *Gamines*, and butch *Bubis*. Powerful business-class lesbians, who wore tuxes at night, were called *Dodos*.

Well-to-do lesbians gathered at The Monokel, which, its founder declared a "glamorous, elegant dance bar for fastidious women." An ad for the self-declared "bar for ladies" showed a statuesque lesbian couple ballroom dancing, one leading in black tie while her partner follows in an evening gown. The Meyer-Stube catered exclusively to *Dodos*—and the women who loved them. Nights there were said to end in a business deal as often as a make-out session. For every upscale bar like The Monokel, there were numerous dives like the Taverne, which smelled of stale beer, played host to the occasional bar fight, and was renowned for its house band leader, a genderqueer individual with one eye.

Despite its size, Berlin's lesbian nightlife could be opaque to outsiders. In an era when journalism was a male-dominated profession, those most likely to catalogue the scene were barred from it; many lesbians considered allowing men into their spaces to be "treason." The Monokel famously posted a bouncer out front toting a riding crop to ensure that no man entered. Even Magnus, who had written about the city's lesbian scene for decades and collaborated with Roellig on her guidebook, had to rely on female informers for many of his depictions of the city's lesbian demimonde.

Given these restrictions, the best-known queer spaces of the era were simply the most accessible ones. Among lesbian venues, the Toppkeller was legendary largely because it embraced mass tourism. By the late 1920s, visitors could book packaged bus tours of the city's queer underworld. The London-based Cook Travel Agency offered late-night guided bar crawls, picking up tourists at their hotels at midnight. The requisite lesbian stop was the Toppkeller, a dive whose "sad-looking walls [were] covered in cheap tinsel," according to the 1931 *Guide to "Depraved" Berlin.*

Affording a frisson of clandestine fun, the tourists stumbling out of the coach bus found this nightspot hidden away from the street in the back courtyard of a classic Berlin *Mietskaserne* apartment building. After crossing the interior courtyard and being scanned by two intimidating, cigar-smoking *Bubi* bouncers, guests entered beneath a sign reading, "We are the New Spirit. / We do it with Brazenness." Once inside, a mistress of ceremonies—nom-de-guerre: Napoleon—presided over the festivities for a mash-up of the city's various lesbian scenes and an eclectic mix of local bohemians, slumming notables, reporters on assignment, and gawking tourists. Midnight at the Toppkeller meant Black Mass, when the militaristic emcee issued orders to the crowd: Stand! Kneel! Fondle! Later, spin-the-bottle-type games ensued dictating liaisons between guests from different scenes, classes, and gender expressions who would never have coupled otherwise.

Headliners on stage at the Toppkeller varied from the omnisexual Anita Berber to the iconic butch cabaret singer Claire Waldoff. Neither performer cared a whit for the Weimar Republic's increasingly restrictive obscenity laws. Waldoff was renowned for belting out the era's leading gay-rights cabaret anthem, the "Lavender Song" (*Das Lila-Lied*), which was dedicated to Hirschfeld and name-checked his 1919 silent film in the sing-along refrain, "We are different from the others [but] we have the same rights!"

Berlin as a city was now different from the others. It had become the Western world's first trans mecca, as was evident to all in the sequined and feathered world of the city's drag queen bars. The Mikado, the grande dame with its Japanese-lantern interior, had graced the city since 1907. But in the Weimar era, Berlin's trans community built a wide-ranging scene of its own. Its varied subculture stretched the panorama from older, heavy-set *Aunties* in their dowdy dresses to *Androgynes*, who plucked their eyebrows and cultivated a vampish look. Genderqueer *Garçonnes*, a cute, intentionally ungrammatical feminization of the French word *garçon* (boy), sported close-cropped hair and wore the latest men's fashions from Paris guided by the lesbian magazine of the same name. *Garçonnes* congregated at the Mali and Igel nightclub where the windows were blacked out and a sign permanently hung on the door read "CLOSED FOR PRIVATE PARTY." As the scene grew with wider acceptance and new medical advances in the late 1920s, the Violetta Dance Club, which had previously catered exclusively to lesbians, launched a weekly *Transvestitenball* every Wednesday night.

Trans folks of all stripes came together at the Club d'Eon. Their association was named after the chevalier d'Eon, a French noble, assigned male at birth, who had remained a fixture in the highest levels of European society dressed in elegant women's clothing. A lady-in-waiting to Marie Antoinette, the chevalier had been famously presented as a woman to the Russian court in St. Petersburg. The group's namesake was well known in Berlin from a portrait on the wall of the Hirschfeld Museum.

To institute doctors, these social clubs and nightspots were themselves a form of therapy. When gender-nonconforming individuals arrived at the institute, they got referred to these organizations and social spaces. For one patient, Gerd Katter, staff psychiatrist Dr. Felix Abraham wrote out a prescription with three items. The first was the name and address of Paul Wriggers, a founder of the Club d'Eon. The second and third were the names and addresses of two trans-friendly bars—the Mali and Igel and the Ariane. Abraham wrote it on his official prescription stationery as if prescribing medicine. In a sense, he was: hit two bars and call me in the morning.

For Katter, the nightlife really was therapy. Born in Berlin in 1910, they had been assigned female at birth and named Eva. When Katter's mother discovered queer publications hidden in their room during adolescence, she had the presence of mind to take her sixteen-year-old to Dr. Hirschfeld's clinic. Institute staffers immediately affirmed Gerd's masculine gender identity even as the authorities continued to address Gerd in official correspondence as "Frauline Katter," but they balked at the teen's request for chest masculinization surgery. Their deliberations were likely the world's first discussion on the medical ethics of trans healthcare for minors. Institute medical staff reversed course when Katter returned to the clinic days later having attempted to perform the surgery on themselves, sans anesthetic, with a razor blade. At age eighteen, Gerd Katter received a transvestite license (*Transvestitenschein*) from the Berlin police.

The German capital was now a magnet for queer youth from all over

Europe and beyond, and the institute became their community center in the city. Newcomers to Berlin who hoped to transition were taken on their first shopping trips for gender-affirming clothing by institute staff members. Within the walls of the institute, everyone could be themselves. As one government functionary recorded after a routine visit to the building, "Like the director himself, the small number employed by the Institute (including domestic and office workers) appear to be homosexual. And there was a young man, a supposed student, evidently feeling quite at home, who left a small impression of being homosexual."

Each afternoon, Karl Giese would hold court over coffee. Shedding the buttoned-down bearing he presented to the public as a tour guide, he would indulge in lighthearted gossip. Karl relished teasing social-climbing working-class gays from his arch takes-one-to-know-one perspective. Christopher Isherwood, who was going in the other direction—slumming in Berlin to distance himself from his upscale upbringing—ate it up.

"The atmosphere of Karl's sitting room had none of the Institute's noble seriousness," Isherwood recorded. "In repose, Karl's long handsome face was melancholy. But soon he would be giggling and rolling his eyes. Touching the back of his head with his fingertips, as if patting bobbed curls, he would strike an It-Girl pose."

With Karl free to expose what Isherwood dubbed his "peasant . . . girl's heart," everyone felt liberated. Erwin Hansen, the one-time army man and Karl's designated dom, projected a butchness that contrasted with Karl's femme demeanor. As Isherwood recalled, Erwin was "a big muscular man with blond hair close-cropped, ... rough and ready manners and pale roving blue eyes." Other attendees, Isherwood recounted, "were in drag, which was never mentioned." Before his Berlin sojourn, Isherwood confessed, he'd considered transwomen to be "loud, screaming, willfully unnatural creatures," but those at the institute were "quietly natural [and] accepted by everyone else as a matter of course."

In the evenings, things loosened further as nighttime social events offered space to present new gender personae. The best institute parties rivaled anything the city's clubs could offer. At one such event, Magnus wore a conventionally male suit while fresh-faced Karl came in drag, wearing a billowy black dress. Other attendees included an older queer couple decked out like Louis XVI and Marie Antoinette, in a ruffly waistcoat and a bustle-y evening gown, while the younger generation came in simpler getups and vamped for a camera that recorded it all. Karl's mother, who lived a short distance but a world away in her Berlin neighborhood, also attended. The camera captured her looking admirably serene in a high-necked, structured, rather funereal number.

Particularly after hours when the facility was closed to the public, the institute became a supportive cocoon for those transitioning. Trans folks who needed jobs often found them there. One employee, who went by "Herr Alfred," was a middle-aged parent from Bavaria, assigned female at birth, who presented as a man. Most of the institute's domestic staff were transwomen. Even in open-minded Weimar Berlin, Dr. Levy-Lenz explained,

> few places of work were willing to employ transvestites [so] we did everything we could to give such people a job at our Institute. For instance, we had five maids—all of them male transvestites, and I shall never forget the sight one day when I happened to go into the Institute's kitchen after work: there they sat close together, the five "girls" peacefully knitting and sewing and singing old folk-songs. These were, in any case, the best, most hardworking and conscientious domestic workers we ever had. Never ever did a stranger visiting us notice anything.

Some institute staffers were also institute patients. Dora Richter, who served as a maid in her standard-issue black dress and white apron, had been assigned male at birth and named Rudolph. From earliest youth, Dora, called "*Dorchen*" ("Little Dora") by Magnus, told doctors she'd felt female. As the institute developed new gender-affirmation treatments, time and again Dora would sign up to be the first experimental patient. Beginning with rudimentary hormone treatments in the institute's earliest days, in 1922, Dora volunteered for an orchiectomy, the surgical removal of the testicles. Later, under the guidance of institute doctors Levy-Lenz and Abraham, she would undergo further gender-affirmation surgeries. Others who worked part-time at the institute, including dancer Charlotte Charlaque and artist Toni Ebel, also underwent surgery. All three transwomen would appear together in *Mystery of Gender* (*Mysterium des Geschlechtes*), a 1933 Austrian film made in consultation with Dr. Abraham that interspersed shots of the trio—both clothed and naked—with graphic operating room footage of the procedures, blood, gauze, and all.

As the renown of the institute grew in Berlin and beyond, its enemies grew ever more furious. Shortly after inauguration night in 1919, a right-wing newspaper called for the institution to be shut down lest it recruit young people through "homosexual seduction." Rightists fumed that the German population, already decimated by the Great War, would dwindle even further if Hirschfeld and his allies were permitted to turn the rising generation queer. Not only had Germany lost so many of its young men in the war, its shocking weakness on the battlefield suggested a wider crisis of masculinity. Some thought that the only solution was a return to one-man rule.

Far-right demands to investigate the institute were rebuffed. As one sympathetic Berlin police official wrote, scientific research into "sexual life [should] be welcomed." After all, the institute was merely promoting the "not uncommon opinion that homosexuality is not a vice, but rather an inborn predisposition." In the capital, at least, Magnus's born-this-way hypothesis was becoming conventional wisdom. But in the more conservative Germany beyond Berlin, Magnus was held up as Exhibit A for the claim that the republic's freedoms had gone too far.

Germany's first democracy, so late in arriving, was fragile from the start. And its enemies were not above using violence to fight it. In March 1920, monarchists led by reactionary government functionary Dr. Wolfgang Kapp launched an ill-fated coup attempt, and Magnus found himself mentioned by name in their antisemitic flyers. That summer's elections were held as planned, but voters flocked to the illiberal fringes of politics with many drawn to the fascist right. Parties committed to democracy won less than 50 percent of the vote and would never recover their majority.

Dire economic conditions in Germany were undermining stability. The Treaty of Versailles, which ended the Great War, required the losing countries to pay onerous reparations to the victors. Already during the war, the German government was spending more than it was taking in, assuring itself it would come out ahead by annexing prosperous industrial regions after its victory. Now, the scramble to pay off this war debt plus the new reparations sparked runaway inflation. At the beginning of 1921, the exchange rate stood at forty-five German marks to one US dollar. By summer, the mark had fallen to sixty to one; by fall, one hundred to one, and by year's end to one hundred and sixty to one. It kept getting worse, soon running into the thousands, then the millions, then the billions, and finally the trillions. Parents began giving their children stacks of worthless notes to use as toy building blocks. Working-class Germans now asked to be paid at lunchtime, since their wages would be less valuable by dinner. And even that trick didn't always work. Stories abounded of people ordering a coffee off a menu and finding that the price had risen by the time they asked for their check. The *Daily Mail* correspondent reported to readers back home in Britain that a copy of the paper had cost 35,000 marks the previous day and now cost 60,000.

Ordinary Germans with money in savings banks were ruined, while those wealthy enough to have investments abroad—or fortunate enough to have family in other countries—better weathered the storm. Having family abroad in more stable countries, like the US and UK, was rare for German Christians but relatively common for German Jews, some of whom had emigrated after earlier antisemitic flareups. The appearance of unequal levels of suffering during the economic crisis only ratcheted up antisemitic resentment further.

Magnus himself was well-enough positioned to avoid an uncomfortable financial appeal to his big brother in America. Real estate holdings insulated the upper middle class from the worst of the inflation—currency could become worthless, but land would always have value. Indeed, those who had taken out mortgages to buy real estate in better times had seen their debts inflated away to a pittance. Now they owned their properties at a deep discount or, if the timing was right, almost for free. Magnus's decision to buy the Tiergarten properties just after the war now looked prophetic. He was also commercializing impotence treatments globally. His Viagra-like products—which combined traditional aphrodisiacs, like African yohimbe bark and Atlantic Ocean clamshells, with more recently discovered sex hormones—were sold in both a prescription version (Testofortan) and over the counter (Pearls of

Titus). Marketing and selling the products beyond the borders of Germany helped protect Magnus from his homeland's economic troubles.

The unequal pain of inflation was a boon to the far right which, in place of a sophisticated macroeconomic analysis, pointed to scapegoats. The increased visibility of Hirschfeld and other Germans of Jewish descent in positions of fame and authority in the republic led fascist elements to present the republic itself as the result of a Jewish coup. Antisemites began to speak of "the Jewish November revolution" that brought down the kaiser and of the "'Jewish' republic" that Germans now lived under.

Despite the political instability, Magnus brazenly lectured all over the country. At a September 1920 presentation in Hamburg, far-right hooligans set off firecrackers during his talk but then got jeered out of the hall. Later that fall, on the eve of a lecture in Munich, Magnus received death threats, but he refused to call off the event. The southern city was a hotbed of far-right parties and their affiliated paramilitary groups, among them the National Socialist German Workers' Party (NSDAP, or Nazis), which had been founded in the Bavarian capital earlier that year.

In his lecture, Magnus retraced recent research on sex hormones and the implications for patients who hoped to transition. As in previous talks, a small clique of hecklers made their presence known but were quickly shouted down and ejected. But after the program let out, as Magnus walked the streets, fascist goons assailed him from behind with a fusillade of stones. He fell down unconscious on the pavement in a pool of his own blood and woke up in a hospital bed.

The attack on the famed Berlin sexologist made headlines around the world. Hearing of the severity of the assault, some newspapers prematurely published Magnus's obituary. In America, *New York Times* readers learned that "Dr. Magnus Hirschfeld, the well-known expert on sexual science, died in Munich today of injuries inflicted upon him by an anti-Jewish mob." Recovering in the hospital, a bemused Magnus chuckled over the greatly exaggerated reports of his death. For the rest of his life, he would revel in telling the tale of reading his own obit.

But when news of his survival broke, the threats resumed. An anonymous assailant sent him a letter in the hospital expressing misgivings over the incident only because he had pulled through. A far-right Dresden newspaper similarly lamented, "We regret that this shameless and horrible poisoner of our people has not found his well-deserved end." A fascist southern paper warned "The Apostle of Sodomy" never to leave his "swine . . . stall in Berlin [since] his skull might be crushed . . . the next time."

One particular Munich-based rightist saw in Hirschfeld's activism a vast anti-German conspiracy. In the aftermath of the attack, Adolf Hitler accused Hirschfeld of the "spiritual murder of thousands of German racial comrades" and fumed that he was "deliberately poisoning our people's souls in order to destroy us from within."

Despite threats of further violence, Magnus continued to lecture nationwide, but the situation was increasingly precarious. Beyond the fractious politics in parliament there was politics in the streets, where paramilitaries brawled. On June 24, 1922, young far-right militants assassinated the highest-ranking Jewish official in the German government, Walther Rathenau, the foreign minister. In the fall of 1923, Hitler riled up a goon squad in a Munich beer hall in a shambolic attempt to take over the country. The Beer Hall Putsch, as it became known, of November 8, was a spectacular failure, collapsing in the early morning hours of November 9. But in prison, Hitler had time to write his rambling memoir, *Mein Kampf* (*My Struggle*). In it, a naïve young Great War veteran moves to Vienna in an ill-fated bid to become an artist and leaves with new insights into race.

Hitler wrote of his arrival in Vienna, "Confused by the mass of architectural impressions and crushed by the hardness of my own lot, I was at first unaware of the stratifications of the people within that immense city." He went on, "Although Vienna then counted something like two hundred thousand Jews among its population of two million, I failed to see them." For over a century since Napoleon's invasion, Jews had lived integrated lives in Viennese society. They had long ago swapped out their caftans for three-piece suits and their yarmulkes for top hats, bowlers, and fedoras as the fashion trends dictated. They no longer spoke their Hebrew-inflected dialect, Yiddish, but rather the High German of Goethe. And, as Hitler came to see, they had even intermarried and reproduced with their Germanic neighbors, making themselves difficult to distinguish physically.

After discovering "race," Hitler explained, he could finally make sense of the city. He had long puzzled over why Viennese newspapers were so liberal, so critical of their own society, so unpatriotic. Now he felt he understood: "The writers were — Jews."

The more he examined Vienna through the lens of race, the more secular Jews he unearthed. "Was there any shady undertaking, any form of foulness, especially in cultural life, in which at least one Jew did not participate?" Hitler wrote. "On putting the probing knife carefully to that kind of abscess one immediately discovered, like a maggot in a putrescent body, a little Jew who was often blinded by the sudden light."

To Hitler, Germanic civilization had become infested; it had been secretly conquered from within by cleverly disguised aliens. And the gay, socialist, filmmaking, Christmas-caroling Dr. Hirschfeld would be Hitler's perfect foil as he grandiosely cast himself as his civilization's exterminator-savior. But in 1923, few took his ravings seriously.

After all, who wanted to curl up with Hitler's disjointed, 700-page screed when you could go to the cinema and ogle Conrad Veidt and/or Marlene Dietrich? Or wander a museum chock-full of dominatrix whips and Japanese dildos? Or find a nightclub where you could meet a perfect stranger who, miraculously enough, shared your niche kink?

Even as clouds gathered in Germany with tightening censorship laws, no progress on Paragraph 175, and brazen fascists in the streets, Magnus took solace in the global scene, in which Germany was one small part. In 1921, he'd organized his first worldwide confab, the International Convention for Sexual Reform on a Scientific Basis, with attendees arriving in Berlin from as far away as Tokyo, Beijing, Moscow, and San Francisco. In the institute's exhibition halls, he highlighted countries that had enacted progressive reforms in areas like contraception and abortion rights. In the summer of 1926, he went abroad to examine the society that had embraced the most wide-ranging sexual reforms thus far, the Soviet Union.

At the behest of the Soviet government, Magnus was hosted in Moscow and Leningrad where he marveled at the government's radical policies decreed after the October Revolution: gay-rights protections, abortion on demand, freely available contraception, acceptance of unmarried cohabitating couples, and no-fault divorce. Always a social democrat but never a communist, Hirschfeld was sympathetic to aspects of the new regime while open to seeing its faults. The Soviet health minister told him that the revolutionary nation was trying to "pursue the fight against prostitution, but not against prostitutes" and gave him a tour of a reeducation facility where former sex workers were taught to sew as an alternative career path. Magnus thought it a laudable goal—he had always believed economically coerced sex work should be countered with social welfare benefits rather than prohibition—but he could see how far it was from becoming a reality. On his evening walks near his hotel in Leningrad, he was repeatedly propositioned by streetwalkers, who pegged him as a wealthy—and straight—foreigner.

On his journey eastward, Magnus also visited Latvia, one of the new ethnostates launched on President Woodrow Wilson's model after the Great War. In Riga, the capital, he attended a medical conference where he found himself bemused that attendees in this mixed-up stretch of the Continent were so deeply invested in their mythic racial divisions. The supposedly distinct Russians (Slavs), Latvians (Balts), and Jews (Semites) all looked pretty much the same. No one could tell, Magnus later wrote, "who . . . belonged to one race or the other."

Returning to Berlin, Magnus redoubled his efforts to build a global movement for sexual tolerance. He planned a second international convention to be held in Copenhagen in 1928 even as Germany's instability made it an open question how long his progressive movement could continue in Berlin. It was encouraging that parliament moved, in 1927, to make abortion a misdemeanor rather than a felony, but the far right was ever more emboldened—and Magnus was the man they loved to hate. In the fall of 1928, the Nazi Party's flagship daily, the *Racial Observer*, lashed out at him after a lecture he'd given to a socialist student group. The headline called him a "homosexual," as if it were a slur and as if Magnus was closeted enough that he could still be outed. In February 1929, Hirschfeld was featured on the cover of the antisemitic tabloid *Der Stürmer*. Beneath a caricature of a wrinkled, bespectacled sexologist, the article alleged that he endorsed pedophilia, pure libel. More worrisome to Magnus, were attacks on his reformist agenda. A subsequent issue of *Der Stürmer* alleged that the right to abortion wasn't a legitimate feminist policy proposal but a money-making Judeo-Bolshevik plot. Jewish physicians like Dr. Hirschfeld, it claimed, were getting Germans sexually excited by selling them pornography and salacious sex museum exhibits and then making money on the back end by terminating the resulting pregnancies. It was outlandish and unhinged, but more and more of his countrymen bought it.

Still, Magnus could look around proudly at the world of tolerance he had built at least in one city. In Berlin, a transwoman could ride the tram unafraid, a *Transvestitenschein* safely tucked into her purse, as an out lesbian conductor piloted the vehicle into Alexanderplatz. In his institute and his city, at least, sexual misfits from all over the world could find freedom.

In this Berlin of ultra-niche subcultures, one space stood out: *Alles Eine Familie* (All One Family). Abbreviated to *Aleifa* by those in the know, this nightspot catered to all, whether they defined themselves as gay, straight, or bi, cis or trans. A nighttime analogue to Hirschfeld's Institute, *Aleifa* viewed human sexuality as infinitely varied and thus, ultimately, unified in its diversity.

Against this cosmopolitan all-one-family conception of humanity, the Nazis offered a narrower concept, the organic Germans-only racial community. As one eighteen-year-old who attended a Nazi rally in this era recounted, he was impressed by the speaker's "sincere commitment to the German people as a whole, whose greatest misfortune was being divided into so many parties and classes. Finally, a practical proposal for the renewal of the people! Destroy the parties! Do away with classes! True national community!" But of course, this call for "community" relied on a stark division between those who could belong to it and those who never could. For those deemed internal outsiders, Magnus among them, the Nazis saw only one solution: removal by force.

Chapter 11

On-the-Run Tour

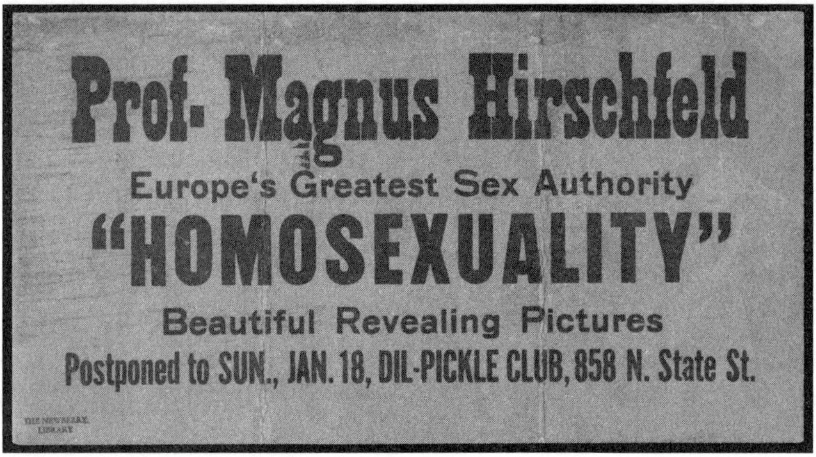

Advertisement for a 1931 Magnus Hirschfeld lecture at Chicago's Dil-Pickle Club.

IN THE LATE 1920s, inflation in Germany briefly eased, opening a window for progressive reform. In the 1928 elections, the Social Democrats took nearly a third of the Reichstag. As the largest party by far, they formed what they called the Grand Coalition with smaller parties that shared their commitment to democracy. Though short-lived, it would prove to be the most stable and effective government of the Weimar era.

The progressive coalition swiftly took up reform of the German penal code. After decades of agitation from Hirschfeld and his allies, in mid-October 1929, a parliamentary committee voted to abolish Paragraph 175. The measure squeaked through by a vote of fifteen to thirteen and was duly sent to the full body for consideration.

At the Institute for Sexual Science, baskets of flowers pinned with notes saluting the hard-won victory poured in for Magnus. Even his enemies were conceding defeat—at least for the moment. The Nazi Party's *Racial Observer* editorialized, "We congratulate you, Mr. Hirschfeld, on the victory in committee. But don't think that we Germans will allow these laws to stand for a single day after we have come to power." (According to Nazi ideology, Germans no longer ran Germany since the Weimar Republic was a Jewish state.)

Yet for Magnus, this victory was not clear cut. In the legislative give-and-take, Paragraph 175 was slated for repeal, but gay sex would be regulated anew under a proposed Paragraph 297. In these new rules, male prostitution would be formally outlawed (under earlier laws, prostitution was a crime only women could commit) and the age of consent would be raised—from fourteen for all to sixteen for women and twenty-one for men. Under the compromise proposal, consensual gay male sex would finally be legal, but paying another man for sex, using a position of influence to pressure another man into sex, or simply being on different sides of the twenty-first-birthday line would all be grounds for prosecution.

As the bouquets arrived, Magnus's celebration was tinged with anxiety. He had paired off with Karl Giese on the set of *Different from the Others* several months before Karl's twenty-first birthday. In the eyes of the new Paragraph 297, as under the old Paragraph 175, their partnership had begun with a crime. Magnus and his allies also worried that criminalizing something as vague as using a position of influence to pressure another man into sex could provide fodder for homophobic prosecutors and jurists. Could this provision also apply to his partnership with Karl? After all, when it began, Magnus was a screenwriter and scientific advisor, while Karl was just a young man from the wrong side of Berlin getting a shot at stardom.

Already wracked by these personal conflicts, Magnus was buffeted from all sides in Germany's balkanized politics. Some on the left thought the compromise ceded too much. The three Communist Party members on the parliamentary committee had all voted to repeal Paragraph 175 as part of the broader coalition but broke with their more moderate allies to vote against the adoption of the new strictures. Even less dogmatic leftists were uncomfortable with the new rules proposed to govern queer relationships. Albert Einstein, a social democrat, condemned Paragraph 297 as "prudery."

Meanwhile the rightists fumed over the attacks on Paragraph 175. The anti-gay law, they believed, needed to be strengthened, not scrapped. Shortly before the repeal vote, the Nazis lavished praise on the decades-old homophobic statute and urged its extension to what theorists of totalitarianism would later dub "thoughtcrime." To the Nazis, it wasn't just queer sex acts that threatened their proposed ethnostate of loyal, fecund, Aryan race-breeders—it was queer desire itself. As their ideologists wrote in an official party statement:

> It is not necessary that you and I live, but it is necessary that the German people live. And it can only live if it. . . . exercises discipline, especially in matters of love. . . . Anyone who even thinks of homosexual love is our enemy. We reject anything which emasculates our people and [w]e therefore reject . . . homosexuality, because it robs us of our last chance to free our people from the bondage which now enslaves it. . . . Might makes right. And the stronger will always win over the weak. Let's see to it that we once again become strong!

Even within the Scientific Humanitarian Committee, debate raged over whether to welcome the reform compromise or condemn it for giving up too much. Younger activists who had been mentored by Magnus now challenged him from the left. They were led by Kurt Hiller, an attorney nearly two decades Magnus's junior.

At first, Hiller had seemed like a model protégé. Born in Berlin to a prosperous Jewish neckwear manufacturer, Hiller had joined the Scientific Humanitarian Committee in 1908 soon after completing his law degree. His thesis, "The Right Over One's Self," was a philosophical defense of gay life grounded in a libertarian argument for bodily autonomy. The state, he argued, had no business in people's bedrooms. In 1922, Hiller published *Paragraph 175: Outrage of the Century*, a work largely in line with Magnus's thinking and activism. But in time Hiller grew increasingly radical. By the late 1920s, Hiller was endorsing gay separatism and suggesting that queer people secede from mainstream politics. Rather than work to win over sympathetic straight liberals, Hiller argued, gays should form their own political party to advocate for themselves in the Reichstag.

The protégé was always more public about his private life than the mentor. As a well-to-do teen, Hiller had begun frequenting the Tiergarten's Gay Way to pay for sex. His first time was with an older man he met on a park bench, a muscular fellow who, as Hiller was surprised to learn once he'd gotten him naked, was covered in tattoos. Paying for sex became a lifelong kink, one he'd come to publicly champion. As he would write in his memoir, "the general criminalization of male prostitution is a scandal."

To Hiller and his allies, the proposed parliamentary compromise seemed a deal not worth taking. "The decriminalization of sex between men is a pressing necessity for a free society," he wrote, "but a law like this is useless. It seems to bring decriminalization, but by criminalizing male prostitution (and by setting the age of consent at twenty-one years—what ridiculousness!) it makes decriminalization an illusion."

Magnus, of course, had mixed feelings about the legislative sausage-making. He'd never believed that sex work by adults—be they male, female, or nonbinary—should be against the law. And changing the age of consent to twenty-one no doubt felt like a personal attack on his lifelong partnership with Karl. Still, he was inclined to take the win. After fulminating against Paragraph 175 for over three decades, its repeal was finally within reach. He was stunned by the internal opposition within his own Scientific Humanitarian Committee.

The two sides clashed at a meeting held five weeks after the committee vote. Hiller and his band of young radicals showed their strength, and Magnus and his allies were helpless to outvote them. The organization Magnus had founded in 1897 to overturn Paragraph 175 spurned the proposed repeal. Shocked and hurt, Magnus resigned his position as chair of the Scientific Humanitarian Committee on the spot.

To Magnus, the defeat felt as much personal as political. He'd always thought of himself as a kindly mentor to the new cohort of activists. Now it was clear that they found him domineering and obtuse. He was disillusioned having been shown up by the radical clique led by Hiller, whose preternaturally youthful moon face only underscored the critique that Magnus had become an old man out of step with the new era. In Magnus's official resignation letter, he hid his bitterness from public view, stating simply that he was resigning to spend more time on his scientific research and on his institute. Once Magnus left, Hiller took his place as chair of the Scientific Humanitarian Committee.

Following the fractious meeting, the group, now under new management, informed its members that it was rejecting the compromise on account of the new age-of-consent rules and the male prostitution ban. "Paragraph 175 has not fallen!" the official statement read. "The conclusions of the penal code reform committee with respect to homosexuality constitute one step forward and two steps backward. The demand that we have made for decades—that the law be applied in the same way to the homosexual minority of the population as it is to the majority—is in no way met. Our Committee must keep fighting."

With its rejection by Germany's first and most important gay-rights organization, the reform effort lost momentum. Squabbles between the Social Democrats and Communists stalled the penal reform platform from ever going before the full Reichstag.

Less than two weeks after the committee's repeal vote, America's stock market crashed. By wintertime, the effects were rippling through the global economy and hitting an already weakened Germany particularly hard. Half of the financial institutions in Central Europe went under; in January of 1930 alone, the number of unemployed workers in Germany more than doubled. Unhoused men, possibly numbering half a million, became fixtures on city streetcorners and in neighborhood parks. Many Germans grew too poor to even drown their sorrows. Per-capita beer consumption dropped 43 percent over the next four years.

The Nazis packaged the economic instability as the inevitable result of modern chaos—political, cultural, sexual, racial—and in March 1930 their MPs offered a bill to turn interracial sex into a capital offense. It was an unhinged response to a macroeconomic crisis, but desperate voters now gravitated to the extremes. In the national elections that fall, the uncompromising Communist Party made large gains, and the biggest winner was the Nazis. The NSDAP won enough votes to increase their representation in the Reichstag nearly tenfold to become the second-largest party. In the wake of the election, any hope of repealing Paragraph 175 was gone. Not only could Hitler and his fascists block any repeal of Paragraph 175, they fantasized about ending the republic, criminalizing queer desire, and turning gay-rights activism into a capital crime. Fulminating against Hirschfeld, Hiller, and other secular Jews who were disproportionately the public face of the German gay-rights movement, the *Racial Observer* fumed that "Among the many evil instincts that characterize the Jewish race, one that is especially pernicious has to do with sexual relationships. The Jews are forever trying to propagandize sexual relations between siblings, men and animals, and men and men. We National Socialists will soon unmask and condemn them by law. These efforts are nothing but vulgar, perverted crimes and we will punish them by banishment or hanging."

Having resigned from leadership in the Scientific Humanitarian Committee, Magnus had more free hours than he knew what to do with for the first time he could remember. As he confided in a diary he'd begun keeping, it seemed his life's work had been for naught and he worried about his health, his safety, and his finances. He'd now struggled with diabetes for years, made worse by his inability to resist sweets, and now, in his sixties, he no longer had youth on his side. The official newspaper of what was now Germany's second largest political party was publicly threatening him. Reeling from twin traumas—the public shock of his countrymen voting in droves for his noxious enemies and the personal pain of having his protégés turn on him—Magnus decided to get away. It had been nearly four decades since his turn as a foreign correspondent in America and now seemed like an opportune time to return. He could hide out for a few weeks or months in New York and Chicago—long enough, he hoped, for the fascist tide to safely recede in his homeland.

Reaching out to an American physician who'd attended his Copenhagen sex reform conference, Magnus drummed up a speaking invitation in New York from a German American doctors' group. Just two months and a day after the catastrophic election, Magnus sailed out from Bremerhaven for the New World aboard the *Columbus*, a German ship. Karl Giese remained behind in Berlin as his eyes and ears at the institute, instructed to tell him when it was safe to return.

The lecture tour was largely unplanned when Magnus set off, but he had a strategy. From his time in the US decades earlier, he had a keen sense of American mores. Americans loved celebrity and ostentatious displays of wealth, and behind their upright Puritan facades, they were as sex obsessed as any people on earth. Magnus splurged for a first-class ticket so he could debark on the Manhattan docks as a VIP. And he hired himself a press agent: George Sylvester Viereck, a gay German-born science writer who was the son of an old friend that had emigrated to New York in his youth.

Viereck went to work, pitching the American press on the upcoming arrival of the man behind the famed Pearls of Titus, the over-the-counter impotence drug Americans knew from their corner drugstores. A savvy PR man, Viereck brilliantly christened Magnus the "Einstein of Sex." Viereck had no interest in burdening the public with complex theoretical explications of how Hirschfeld's conceptions of gender as perspectival and nonbinary echoed Einstein's theories. All he meant was that, like Einstein, who had recently taken a visiting professorship at the California Institute of Technology, Hirschfeld was a brilliant German Jew whose increasing unease at home could be a boon to America. And unlike the Einstein of physics, with his inscrutable ideas that few ordinary minds could grasp, this other Einstein focused on everyone's favorite topic: sex. Knowing that America could never handle a theorist of niche kinks, queer love, and trans identity, Viereck pitched Hirschfeld as an expert on straight marriage, whose most controversial position was his support for accessible birth control.

The press ate it up. After docking in New York and going through passport control, Magnus was mobbed by reporters who, he later wrote, "turned their cameras and fountain pens" on him. The next day, *The New York Times* hailed his arrival: "Dr. Magnus Hirschfeld . . . has come here after an absence of twenty years [*sic*; actually 37 years] to study the marriage question in this country. . . . [H]e founded the Institute for Sex Science in Berlin and has written many books on the subject. Dr. Hirschfeld advocates birth control." Over the course of his trip, which eventually included a meeting with Albert Einstein himself, the American press would photograph Hirschfeld over a hundred times and live-action footage of him made the Hearst and Fox newsreels shown in movie theaters nationwide.

Keen to look flush for the Americans, in New York, Magnus took a room in the gargantuan New Yorker Hotel. The Art Deco pile had recently opened opposite Pennsylvania Station, a neoclassical structure modeled on the Baths of Caracalla in Rome. New York was already impressive the first time Magnus visited in 1893, but in the time since, it had boomed in a manner similar to Berlin. In the intervening years, the metropolis had unified and built a subway system that connected four of its five boroughs to Midtown Manhattan, which was now studded with innumerable skyscrapers, his hotel among them.

From his base on West Thirty-Fourth Street, Magnus moved about the city, lecturing to the American Society of Medical History, being fêted by a doctors' association, and meeting with leading writers and activists. Always drawn to those who blurred the line between artistic creativity and politics, Magnus was thrilled to meet the socially engaged novelists Theodore Dreiser and Upton Sinclair. He also called on America's leading birth control advocate, Margaret Sanger, who had first met Magnus on her visit to his Berlin institute in 1920. In public, however, Sanger kept her distance from Hirschfeld out of concern that his homosexuality would reflect poorly on her cause.

In his first lectures, Magnus stuck to his safest topic: the trials and tribulations of straight marriage. This safe focus brought in the most lecture invitations, ranging from well-heeled professional organizations to New York's Labor Temple, a hub of American leftism just off Union Square.

In New York, as in Berlin, Magnus couldn't help himself and was drawn to the margins. He explored the bathhouses and sat in on vice arraignments in night court. He found Harlem, the city's vast "colored" section uptown, the most magnetic of all. From his hotel, he could slip away unseen through a basement tunnel that connected directly to the city's subway system. Hopping on the Eighth Avenue express train, he could zip from Midtown to the heart of Harlem in minutes.

On his first trip in the 1890s, Magnus had been struck by America's cruel and bizarre racial system and returning now, with rising racism in his homeland, he gave it more focused attention. On December 29, a cold dreary day, Magnus went for a cozy get-together at the apartment of Carl Van Vechten, a writer, photographer, and self-appointed white ambassador to the Harlem Renaissance. Van Vechten, though married to a woman, had discreet affairs with men, and his connections to New York's gay scene rivaled his connections to its Black world (not that the two communities were mutually exclusive). Over tea, Magnus met Langston Hughes, a young queer African American poet already making a name for himself, and James Weldon Johnson, one of the nation's leading civil-rights leaders. After working as a State Department diplomat in Latin America, Johnson had recently been tapped to lead the National Association for the Advancement of Colored People, a position never before held by a person of color. More than a political activist, Johnson was a man of letters, publishing frequently in W. E. B. DuBois's journal, *The Crisis*, and penning the poem "Lift Ev'ry Voice and Sing," which became widely known after being set to music. Sipping tea with these brilliant African Americans, Magnus couldn't help but grow angry at the millions of white Americans who refused to break bread across the color line. But it was their loss really; he almost pitied them.

The economic divide between Midtown and Harlem was stark. White Americans typically pinned their wide racial disparities in wealth, health, and education on Black racial inferiority, but Magnus was skeptical, particularly after meeting luminaries such as Hughes and Johnson. He brought the same framework he'd applied to anti-gayness in Germany to anti-Blackness in America. Just as the prevalence of depression and suicide among gays in Germany was a reflection of anti-gay prejudice in society, not a reflection of anything inherently depressing about being gay, the sole source of the problems plaguing Black America, Magnus came to believe, was White America's oppression. Even as Magnus was keen to be a gracious guest abroad, needling but never lecturing his guests, he spoke in no uncertain terms about what he called in the American press, "the humiliations to which [African Americans] are condemned daily through no fault of their own."

Harlem was famous as a nightlife hub, renowned for evading America's Prohibition laws in jazz venues like the Cotton Club and at drag balls like those hosted at the Odd Fellows' Hamilton Lodge. Magnus was keen to take it all in. While many white Americans looked down on Black music and dance as hypersexualized or primitive, Magnus viewed it as a "safety valve for the repressed desires and ambitions of the Negro people" and "a dance of joy," in which the participants reveled in a taste of freedom that the wider America society denied. Ironically, it was in white dance clubs, where people of pallor could briefly escape the Puritanism that straitjacketed their lives, that Magnus saw sex as the main draw.

As Magnus spent more time in the United States, he grew ever more suspicious of its supposedly stark racial borderlines. Just as he had come to see sexual orientation and gender as continua after encountering so many individuals who didn't fit neatly into binary categories, now he came to see race as a continuum. Magnus marveled that the size of New York's Black population made it "the largest Negro city in the world." Yet for all of the Americans' insistence that there was a clear distinction between the "white" and "colored" races, the African Americans of New York encompassed the full color spectrum from, as Magnus put it in his journal, "the deepest black to the shade of Viennese coffee to the lightest mélange, indeed to the color of milk." Among the lightest complected, Magnus wrote, "one can barely notice their [African] ancestry." In his capacity leading the NAACP, James Weldon Johnson routinely sent his lieutenant Walter White south to document lynchings. Though defined as "colored" under the American one-drop rule, as he would explain in his autobiography, *A Man Called White*, he was so fair skinned, blond haired, and blue eyed that he could safely join the lynch mobs to secretly craft first-person reports on America's system of racial terror. Though the stakes were higher, the US situation was reminiscent of the "Slavs," "Balts," and "Semites" in Latvia who couldn't keep each other straight. Viewing America through foreign eyes, Magnus saw the irony and cruelty of a country that proudly called itself "the melting pot," where the freckled Irish lass could marry the bronzed Sicilian youth at the parish church with nary a complaint, but had created a pariah caste of Americans—almost all of whom were themselves of European ancestry—on account of their fateful "one-drop" of African blood.

In America, Magnus bravely defended relationships across the so-called color line, which were against the law in most American states despite the clear evidence of centuries of interracial sex walking the country's streets. In an interview he gave to Viereck—undoubtedly the pair collaborated closely on editing both the questions and the answers—

Magnus argued that attraction across the supposed racial borderlines was not a perversion and was, in fact, quite common. Institutionalized social inequality and power dynamics between an in-group and an out-group, Hirschfeld speculated, may even encourage sexual fantasies between members of the two groups. Against an American culture that viewed the children of such unions as "tragic mulattoes," fated to never be fully accepted by either white or Black society, Magnus explained that these children would likely be healthier on average because they'd be less likely to carry inherited diseases. In the interview, which was syndicated from coast to coast, mostly in African American newspapers, Magnus explained that human history was filled with remarkably accomplished multiracial individuals, proving that "miscegenation is not necessarily biologically objectionable." Hirschfeld noted that Alexandre Dumas, the French novelist, was of mixed Afro-European descent, to which Viereck added the Afro-Russian poet Alexander Pushkin and America's own Alexander Hamilton, a Founding Father believed to be of Afro-Caribbean descent.

Viereck's PR strategy proved a success. Positioning Hirschfeld as tame enough to be platformed but risqué enough to be interesting, lecture invitations poured in from many cities within easy reach of New York and Chicago, including Newark, Philadelphia, Milwaukee, and Detroit. Soon, others arrived from as far away as Los Angeles. (Unsurprisingly, this open advocate of "miscegenation" was not welcomed in any of the antebellum slave states, the District of Columbia included.)

After six weeks in New York, Magnus set off by train for Chicago, making a brief stop at the Canadian border to take in the natural wonder of Niagara Falls. As usual, Magnus traveled in style. Arriving in Chicago in January 1931, he lodged on the twenty-fifth floor of the Stevens Hotel, a new edifice fronting Grant Park that claimed the title of largest hotel in the world. The banquet hall kitchen could churn out 120 gallons of ice cream per hour—perhaps the reason why their diabetic guest's blood sugar spiked during his stay, sending him to a one-night stay in a hospital.

It wasn't only the size and grandeur of Chicago's buildings that had changed since Magnus's first visit in 1893. The queer scene, which was then one of nod-and-a-wink red ties, was now front and center. This change was indirectly a credit to Magnus himself.

In 1924, Henry Gerber, a German immigrant, founded America's first gay-rights organization, the Society for Human Rights. The Chicago-based group was explicitly modeled on Hirschfeld's Scientific Humanitarian Committee. In the aftermath of the Great War, Gerber had been stationed in his homeland by the US Army and soon learned of the Scientific Humanitarian Committee. Contacting the organization, Gerber was stunned and inspired to learn of Dr. Hirschfeld's theories and his campaign against Paragraph 175. As he later recounted, while on base in Koblenz he "subscribed to German homophile magazines and made several trips to Berlin." Gerber's taste of freedom in Germany underscored "the injustice with which my own American society accused the homosexual of 'immoral acts.'" For years, in the self-declared "land of the free," he had been hounded by the American medical establishment, persecuted for his sexual orientation, and even briefly committed to a mental institution. "I hated this society which allowed the majority, frequently corrupt itself, to persecute those who deviated from the established norms in sexual matters."

Returning to Chicago, the still fresh-faced Gerber took a day job with the postal service and founded his Society for Human Rights. Its innocuous name, Gerber later explained, was his attempt at an elegant translation of "the same name used by the homosexuals of Germany for their work." By being coy about its purpose, the group won an official charter from the State of Illinois. As its application form obliquely stated, the group's goal was "To promote and to protect the interests of people who by reasons of mental and physical abnormalities are abused and hindered in the legal pursuit of happiness which is guaranteed them by the Declaration of Independence, and to combat the public prejudices against them by dissemination of facts according to modern science among individuals of mature age." The group launched a newsletter, *Friendship and Freedom*, America's first gay-rights publication, and began planning a lecture series to enlighten the public.

Shortly after its founding, the wife of one member, a closeted man with two children, discovered his copy of *Friendship and Freedom*. She contacted a social worker who promptly called the cops. Shortly thereafter, at 2 a.m. one Saturday night, a police officer burst into Gerber's apartment with a tabloid reporter in tow. "Where's the boy?" the cop barked. A groggy Gerber was alone, confused, and terrified. The officer rampaged through his apartment seizing piles of the group's literature, Gerber's diaries, his typewriter, and his person. He was held overnight in the police station without charge. At dawn, a station house officer taunted Gerber with a copy of that day's *Examiner*, hot off the press. "Strange Sex Cult Exposed," the headline blared.

At arraignment, Gerber, a mailman himself, was charged with sending obscene material through the mail. It was a huge scandal. When the Postal Service bureaucracy in Washington heard the news, it demanded "the removal of Clerk Henry Gerber for conduct unbecoming a postal employee." In the public spotlight, the Society for Human Rights melted away, having survived six months on American soil. It managed to put out only two issues of *Friendship and Freedom* and never hosted a single lecture.

Even after the destruction of the organization, the principles for which it stood could still at least get a hearing in Chicago. With its massive German immigrant population, Chicago kept a closer eye on developments in Berlin than most other American cities did. As Hirschfeld's profile had grown in Germany, the *Chicago Tribune* covered his activism and published his writings in translation. A few months before his 1930s visit, the paper put out a story on the trans permits Hirschfeld was issuing in his homeland under the headline, "Berlin Youth, 22, Wins Right to Dress as a Girl; Herbert Is Now Hertha and Student Nurse." In this relatively progressive urban climate, Magnus was able to give a lecture in 1931 explicitly entitled "In Defense of Homosexuality." In New York, by contrast, the stated aim of Hirschfeld's talks had been straight marriage advice; to the extent he veered into queer issues, those digressions were mentioned only in the city's German language immigrant press and studiously ignored in its English-language papers.

On the appointed Sunday night, lured by an advertisement for a lecture with "Beautiful Revealing Pictures" by "Europe's Greatest Sex Authority," Chicagoans poured from the frigid streets into the Dil-Pickle Club, Hirschfeld's brave host organization. Located down a back alley in the bohemian neighborhood surrounding Chicago's historic Water Tower, visitors were instructed to "Step high, stoop low, and leave your dignity outside." A raucous debating society, the Dil-Pickle was founded in 1917 as the brainchild of three political radicals: Jack Archibald Jones, a veteran Industrial Workers of the World labor organizer; Jim Larkin, an Irish republican activist; and Ben Reitman, an anarchist medical doctor best known for his romantic attachment to the more prominent anarchist Emma Goldman. On debate nights, innuendo from the speakers and bawdy outbursts from the audience were assured. During a talk from an anti-smoking advocate, one audience member loudly asked for a light. In a debate between Reitman and a man of the cloth on the existence of God, the anarchist kept accidentally on purpose referring to the Old Testament as the "Old Testicle." The audience lapped it up, laughing down the reverend's screams of "blasphemy!"

Long before Magnus's talk, the venue had hosted queer-themed lectures, including one on "The Third Sex" and another on political lesbianism. Now, on his appointed Dil-Pickle night, Magnus laid out for the friendly audience his born-this-way hypothesis, explained his conception of human sexuality as a continuum, and detailed his gay-rights activism in Germany. In an accompanying essay in a local literary magazine, Magnus wrote, "We are fighting for the most precious possessions of men and women—justice, freedom, and love. Our enemies are powerful, but they are not invincible." Those enemies soon made their presence known. Leaving another lecture in the city, Magnus found the tires of the car that had brought him had been slashed. Writing of the incident, he attributed the attack to white supremacist "young people (almost certainly Ku-Klux-Klan people or German Hitler followers, who also exist in America in small groups)."

Back home, Hitler's movement kept growing. While Magnus had initially planned a brief sojourn abroad, now he decided to delay his return home and extended the trip with a swing through the West Coast. In February, he booked train passage to California with a stop en route to see the Grand Canyon and nearby Native American reservations.

Since landing in New York, the English words that had lay dormant in Magnus's mind from his 1890s visit had been slowly coming back. During the long train trip west, he focused on improving his mastery to the point where, on the West Coast, he would be able to deliver his standard talk in English. By the end of his trip, he would be able to banter in English with the press.

In California, the Einstein of Sex met the Einstein of everything else. As a social democrat and a signer of Magnus's petition to abolish Paragraph 175, Einstein had long been a political ally, but the two had never met in person. Whether they compared notes on their respective theories of relativity or just commiserated over the collective insanity sweeping their homeland is unknown. Magnus also took a meeting with the leaders of the Human Betterment League, a eugenicist group, in Pasadena. The potentially explosive face-to-face between Paul Popenoe, the avowedly racist leader of a group that sought to prevent race mixing, and Magnus, who explicitly supported it, seems to have ended without fireworks. One can only imagine what Popenoe might have said about Magnus behind his back.

Magnus then went north to San Francisco. Always keen to see the city outside his luxurious accommodations, he was drawn down from his hotel on Nob Hill to Chinatown and the working-class Mission District.

By American standards, San Francisco was a broad-minded place, and Magnus was more open about his criticisms of American society with the local press there. In his interviews with San Francisco newspapers and KFRC radio, he voiced his opposition to both capital punishment and Prohibition. As in Chicago, Magnus managed to give a lecture explicitly focused on queerness: a talk entitled "Homosexuality" at the San Francisco County Medical Society. It was his last scheduled lecture in America, so he may have felt more empowered to speak his mind on the way out the door. Still, small-town California took this provocation as their cue to rail against their cosmopolitan Sodom-by-the-Sea. Inland Modesto's local newspaper attacked Hirschfeld in an editorial headlined "Wild Sex Talk Has Not Been Helpful."

On the most remarkable day of his Bay Area visit, Magnus visited San Quentin, the state penitentiary a short ferry ride north of the city. Guided by San Quentin's warden and its medical director, Dr. Leo Stanley, Magnus met inmates who'd run afoul of California's draconian laws against consensual sex. At the time of his visit, California was even stricter than most American states in policing sex acts between consenting adults. The state legislature prohibited what it termed "oral copulation" within the bounds of the Golden State. Needless to say, most straight Californians could violate the law with impunity, while more femme-presenting men ("fairies" in the slang of the era) were likely to attract the attention of the police, especially if they were Black. At San Quentin, Hirschfeld met numerous queer inmates in the laundry room where they were typically sent for work detail. He wrote of seeing "hundreds of homosexuals—a third of them negros—who are isolated from the other prisoners and work in the prison laundry. Many were in women's clothing and were very feminine." He counseled these prisoners and advocated on their behalf to Dr. Stanley, a notorious homophobe, trying in vain to convince him to see their humanity.

Still nervous about a return to Berlin, Magnus deferred again. From San Francisco, he booked a ticket aboard the Japanese ship *Asamu Maru*, which would stop in Honolulu en route to Japan. Sailing out from what he called "the fabulously beautiful harbor of San Francisco"—the Americans had not yet decided that this natural vista needed a bright orange suspension bridge—Magnus had time to gather his complex, sometimes contradictory, thoughts about America. The country had been good to him. He'd been handsomely paid on his three-month-long lecture tour and had been treated warmly even as he often felt the queer and trans themes of his research were unwelcome. He loved that America was a nation of immigrants where in many city neighborhoods his halting, accented work-in-progress English was virtually the norm. But he hated Prohibition. He didn't only mean the nationwide ban on alcohol, though he did hate that. To Magnus, America's deranged crusade against drink was symptomatic of a spirit of puritanism lodged deep in the nation's psyche. As he would publish once he'd left American shores, the nation's sexual prohibitions—from California's blowjob ban to the laws all over the South that barred loving interracial couples from marrying—ensnared "thousands of people [who] have been stamped as criminals who are not criminals at all." In the vaunted "Land of the Free," Magnus smarted, "even to send articles on birth control through the mails [is] prohibited."

For all the underground gay culture he found, America was an officially homophobic society. Magnus railed against American immigration officials who attempted to weed out queer people from even entering the country. How was it possible, he demanded, that "homosexual men and women are barred from the land of Walt Whitman?" He saw these strictures as a betrayal of the truer spirit of America, a barrier to fully embracing its melting-pot destiny. On the nation's sidewalks, both "whites" and "coloreds" came in every skin tone. Yet America insisted the two groups were distinct—"separate but equal" in their high court's cynical turn of phrase. When African American men had love affairs with white women, they were lynched as "rapists"; when white men fathered children with African American women, everyone pretended not to see what was right before their eyes. With its criminalized speakeasies, *sotto voce* queer life, and Jim Crow railcars peppered with blue-eyed "Africans," America, Magnus wrote, was not "a sanely ordered society."

After a week at sea, Magnus debarked in Honolulu rather than continuing straight to Japan. Among his fellow layover-takers were a Colombian diplomat, a Japanese heir to the Mitsubishi industrial fortune, and a man described in the local press as a "prominent Long Beach dentist." Perhaps with the nasty editorial from Modesto on his mind, Magnus held his cards close, refusing to pontificate on his theories for the assembled media. Instead, he presented himself as a ho-hum marriage therapist and offered them an anodyne, heteronormative salute to the "trinity [of] father, mother, and child."

Magnus lodged at the Royal Hawaiian Hotel, a pink stucco fantasia set around a manicured garden of palms and banyan trees. Though the hotel was sited on a newly developed tourist hotspot, Waikiki Beach, the architects designed all the rooms to face the interior garden. The designers claimed that after spending a week at sea to reach Hawaii, guests would have no interest in seeing any more ocean. Magnus surely found their claims suspicious. Knowing the US quite well at this point, he understood that most Americans could never stomach the scene playing out on Waikiki Beach where, as he wrote, "the erotic fires [were] kindled by the fetich of racial attraction."

During the roaring twenties, Hawaii had become a *de rigueur* vacation destination for well-heeled young singles from the mainland. And central to the lure of Hawaii was hooking up with the Hawaiians. For young white males, whether navy enlisted men or Ivy League toffs, this typically meant fee-for-service sex in Honolulu's Chinatown. For proper white ladies, however, such behavior was forbidden. Instead, they could pick up a "beachboy." In Hawaii, exoticized as a primitive outpost in the Pacific, unaccompanied white women were believed to require a native guide. On Waikiki Beach, indigenous young men worked as these jack-of-all-trades servants, fetching drinks, setting up beach umbrellas, and giving surfing lessons. Under the plausible deniability of this mistress/servant relationship, anything could happen.

To ensure that his charge never got sunburned, a beachboy was duty bound to rub her hard-to-reach spots with coconut oil. Surfing lessons proved the ultimate alibi. Successfully mounting a board all but required a nearly naked expert to hold up a nearly naked newbie. As one client later reminisced, "Can you imagine what it was like for me, going to a Catholic school on the mainland, to have a man take me surfing? To sit on top of me, on the back of my legs? The thrill I had. Skin to skin. In the water."

Mainland Americans took in the scene on Waikiki and saw racial chaos. Black men had been lynched for less in the beach towns of Florida. The whole territory of Hawaii, officially an American possession but operating by its own racial rules, was viewed as out of control. Unlike most mainland states, interracial marriage was legal in the territory. Indeed, it had always been popular, from the moment Europeans and Asians began arriving on the remote archipelago. By the time of Magnus's visit, nearly one in four new marriages registered in Hawaii was interracial. It was enough to make the ordinarily staid journal of the California Bar Association rail apoplectically that, in Hawaii, "a mongrel race now threatens white supremacy."

Magnus saw no such threat. Ever the scientist, he examined the evidence. As he later recounted in his travelogue *World Journey of a Sex Researcher* (*Weltreise eines Sexualforschers*), "On my journey . . . I tried to investigate impartially the problem of mixed marriages . . . to determine whether and to what degree there is any justification for the contempt implicit in the word 'half-breed,' which is commonly intended and received as an insult." In Hawaii, he met with German expatriate medical doctors and others who "told me that its many nationalities . . . frequently produce children who in no way bear out the current theories of the supposed physical and mental inferiority of the descendants of mixed races, known to us as 'mixed breeds,' 'half-breeds,' 'half-castes' or 'Eurasians.' "

Magnus spent only a week in Hawaii but, after his months on the segregated mainland, it was a revelation. This American-run territory definitively proved Americans' fears of "miscegenation" to be unfounded. But rationality was in retreat. America clung tightly to its self-conception as a society divided between "whites" and "coloreds," while his native Germany moved increasingly toward a parallel racial division of "Aryans" and "Semites." As Magnus learned through telegraphs from allies in Berlin, for his own safety he needed to keep his distance. The pace of political murders was picking up. In the relatively calm years from 1924 to 1929, there had been around 170 deaths from paramilitary street brawls. Now, in the past twelve months alone, there had been 300. Lecturing wouldn't be as lucrative outside of America, but Magnus was still earning income from his impotence drugs. And if there was ever a time to tap a rainy-day fund, this was it. He resolved to remain abroad, taking his lecture and research tour to Japan and continuing onward through Asia and the Middle East to circumnavigate the globe.

Sailing out for Tokyo after his Hawaiian sojourn, Magnus wrote his partner, Karl, that he had no immediate plans to return to Germany. For Karl, it was a tragic situation. The love of his life needed to stay away for reasons everyone who loved him had to understand were valid. He also briefed Karl on his last wishes should his health not hold up on the journey. Upon his death, he specified, all of his property would become Karl's. His body, he instructed, should be cremated. If he were to die at sea, he wanted his ashes to be scattered in the ocean; if he passed away on land, he wanted them returned to his beloved hometown, Berlin.

Chapter 12

Full Circle

Magnus Hirschfeld posing with ancient phallus stones in Indonesia.

AS MAGNUS'S OCEAN liner pulled into Yokohama's harbor, the crowds and intensity hit him immediately. In Honolulu, he and a handful of well-heeled vacationers had debarked trailed by a scrum of society columnists. In Japan, after immigration protocols, hundreds of steerage passengers were disgorged into a chaotic nighttime traffic jam as taxis and rickshaws groped their way through the dark in the rain. With no one to meet him and not a word of Japanese in his repertoire, the sixty-two-year-old Magnus struggled to get a cab to the Imperial Hotel, Frank Lloyd Wright's acclaimed East-meets-West Tokyo landmark.

Still, Magnus was thrilled to be here. He'd ached to go to Asia for decades. In his *Annual of Sexual Intermediaries*, over the years, he'd published numerous articles on the cultures of the world's largest continent, highlighting their often less repressive attitudes toward queerness and gender nonconformity. Now he could finally experience it all firsthand.

Visiting the rising East seemed, to Magnus, a requirement for anyone who hoped to understand the modern world. Much as the driving force in world events had moved over the course of his lifetime across the Atlantic, from Europe to America, now it was pivoting to Asia. As he wrote in his travelogue, the "centre of gravity seems now to be shifting more and more toward the Pacific."

In gender and sexuality, Asian societies often stood in mind-expanding counterpoint to the West. On his journey, Magnus hoped to conduct on-site sexological research and turn it into an accessible book for a wide audience. He also planned to amass materials to bring back to his institute for display. On account of his remarkable access to the Berlin underworld, the collection had always leaned local, but his goal had always been to make it a truly global museum of sex.

Magnus soon got to work, taking in the full panorama of Japansese society. As in Berlin after dark, from its elegant champagne flute heights to its beer-and-schnapps dive bar depths, no space was too effete for Magnus and no space too dissolute.

The far-flung researcher's well-to-do hosts—mostly doctors and diplomats and their proper wives—did their best to steer him toward high culture. One group in Tokyo threw a geisha party in his honor at a traditional teahouse. As he took in the performance of ultrafemininity—all painted faces and perfect poise in meticulous kimonos—it struck him that geishas were Japanese culture's version of his "absolute woman," the most feminine in his conception of forty-three million gender possibilities.

Magnus was similarly captivated by kabuki theater, particularly the male actors who played the female roles in the marathon performances. As on the Elizabethan stage of Shakespeare's time, in traditional kabuki, certain male actors specialized in portraying women, wearing elaborate makeup and costumes and delivering their lines in falsetto voices. Bantering with them backstage, Magnus watched as many of Japan's leading female impersonators were "being metamorphosed into complete femininity." Several stars gave Magnus their femme publicity headshots, which he was eager to add to his Wall of Sexual Transitions in Berlin.

Confirming the theory he'd first formulated in his landmark *Transvestites* in 1910, Magnus discerned a wide range of sexual orientations among these actors. Some were straight men for whom this was simply a paid acting gig. Others felt psychologically drawn to dress in women's clothing. Yet even this later group ran the gamut between those who were happily married to women—some paired off with well-known geishas—and those who were solely attracted to men. Between the two extremes, Magnus reported, was the full panorama. "Naturally," he wrote, among the actors, "there are all the transitional forms of bisexuality."

Exploring gay life in Japan bolstered Magnus's long-held belief that the continuum of sexual orientation exists independent of race and ethnicity. "Every form of homosexuality, in tendency as well as expression," he wrote, "is precisely the same in Japan as in Europe." The cruising grounds Magnus observed in Tokyo's Hibiya Park reminded him of the Gay Way in Berlin's Tiergarten.

In Japan, Magnus found a refreshing openness about sex typified by the fact that homosexuality had never been criminalized. He hoped this could withstand the rampant Americanization he saw all around him on the archipelago. Japan was proud to be the only Asian country keeping pace in industrial development with Western Europe, but Magnus grew melancholy taking in the homogenization of the modern world. "Besides [American] automobiles and films," he lamented, "there are other things that . . . accompany you around the whole globe: the same song hits, the same hotel menus, the same travel bureaux and travel tours." How long could the tradition of coed naked bathing that he'd indulged in at the Atami hot springs endure? And what of the gender fluidity evident in traditional Japanese art? Magnus loved "the fusing of the male and female halves . . . embodied in the image of the Buddha." In rapidly industrializing Japan, would this come to be seen as a relic of a benighted past?

Concerned that Japan's unique sexual culture was under threat, Magnus resolved to do his part to document it for posterity. A Japanese psychiatrist, who'd visited his institute on a trip to Europe, loaded Magnus down with photographs from his collection of "flagellation and fettering" practices—Japanese rope bondage. Magnus grew excited brainstorming how these images could provide an Asian counterpart to his exhibit's photos of restraint tables in Berlin's massage parlors.

Less than two weeks into his explorations of Japan, a telegram arrived from China written in German inviting Magnus to lecture in Shanghai at Tongji University. Founded by expatriate German physicians in 1907, Tongji was part of a wave of foreign institutions popping up in China's most cosmopolitan city. American alumni of Harvard Medical School would soon open a branch of their alma mater in Shanghai as well.

On a spring day in 1931, Magnus made the twenty-four-hour boat journey from Japan to Asia's largest city, a proud crossroads of the world. His ship docked and he walked right out onto the Bund, the riverfront avenue built to look like the West, with the newest buildings done in the voguish Art Deco style. There was no immigration checkpoint to clear. Dedicated to international trade and exchange, Shanghai famously had an open-admissions policy, with neither passport nor visa required for entry.

The strangest thing about Shanghai was that it didn't just look like the West, in a very real sense, it was part of the West. Pried from China in the mid-nineteenth century, vast swaths of the city around its historic Chinese core were run by foreign powers and administered by expatriate "Shanghailanders," as they cheekily called themselves. The "unequal treaties" struck long ago with the beleaguered Chinese emperors exempted expats from obeying Chinese law, leaving them beholden, instead, to the laws of their home countries, in an arrangement known as "extraterritoriality."

By the 1930s, when Magnus arrived, Chinese nationalism was rising, and local authorities had managed to bind more and more foreigners to Chinese law. Only citizens of the world's leading powers—the United States, Great Britain, France, and Japan—still enjoyed extraterritorial privilege. Germany, the Great War's biggest loser, was not among them. But Magnus counted himself lucky to be bound by Chinese law rather than German since the Chinese legal code had no prohibitions on homosexuality. In Shanghai, he was free from the anti-gay laws that had stalked him across Germany and America.

Shanghai was excited to have him, with the newspaper of record, the English-language, *North China Herald*, hailing Magnus as "the world's foremost authority on sexual psychology." But the inequalities that plagued quasi-colonial Shanghai shocked him. On his first day in the city, during a rickshaw ride on the Bund, he was disturbed to see a policeman savagely beating a rickshaw puller for a minor traffic infraction—riding in the wrong lane. The officer only ceased the assault when the cabbie kowtowed to him, bowing so low that he scraped his forehead against the pavement, the act of utter submission historically performed only before the emperor of China himself. As Magnus would later write, the scene "filled [him] with deep pity for the fate of these enslaved and tortured human beings."

Hirschfeld gave his first lecture in early May to the Chinese Women's Club, a local feminist group whose membership was drawn from elite Chinese business and professional families. As the attendees took their seats in the China United Apartments, a luxurious Beaux-Arts complex fronting the Shanghai Race Club, Magnus took in the crowd. Some among the audience wore Western attire while others dressed in *qipao* dresses, a hybrid style that paired traditional silk fabrics with a scandalously high slit. Magnus lectured in English, befitting the location in the city's Anglo-American–run International Settlement.

As the talk let out, a trim, dapper young man approached. He introduced himself in flawless English as Li Shiu Tong, and he offered himself up not merely as a translator but as a "companion and protector." A native of British Hong Kong, where his father was a wealthy businessman and a justice of the peace, Li, twenty-three, was studying to be a doctor at St. John's University, the very first of the city's foreign-run medical schools, founded by American missionaries in 1879. Though nearly forty years Magnus's junior, Li shared his passion for both the sciences and the humanities. In college, back in Hong Kong, Li had majored in philosophy. As a worldly queer man of wide-ranging interests, Li had keenly tracked the clash between Freud and Hirschfeld on the origins of homosexuality. Now he was thrilled to meet his hero.

Magnus felt an immediate connection to Li, a young gay man fleeing to the cosmopolitan metropole from a proper bourgeois family. They seemed to be living parallel lives—just four decades and one continent apart. Magnus had long fretted that the lack of formal education of his partner, Karl, would bar him from carrying on the mission of the institute once Magnus grew old. In Li, Magnus saw a worthy mentee—and a comely one. Magnus took on Li as his assistant and translator, and the pair grew close as they began to explore first Shanghai, then China, and, ultimately, the world together.

In Shanghai, the most libertine city Magnus had encountered since leaving home, audiences were open to his most controversial ideas. In addition to lecturing in buttoned-down environments like Tongji University, Magnus also gave a talk at the Plum Blossom restaurant in the heart of Shanghai's red-light district. He was even invited to give a lecture on homosexuality at the Shanghai YMCA. Nearly three decades earlier, in his dishy book *Berlin's Third Sex*, Magnus had dropped the open secret that YMCAs skewed queer. Now he had the privilege of discussing this in an actual Y. His talk went so well—just one lone audience member, a strait-laced missionary, pushed back on his points—that Magnus was invited back to give a second lecture, this one on birth control.

By the end of their first jaunt beyond Shanghai, Magnus and Li had crossed the line from mentor and mentee to lovers. The pair traveled together to the ancient Chinese city of Hangzhou, just a day's journey from the bustling metropolis but a world away. In this beautiful spot, all rolling hills and charming lakeside teahouses, Li got to play local guide. Magnus was soon calling his beloved by the affectionate diminutive "Tao Li."

With Li at his side, Magnus reveled in Shanghai's nightlife. The all-hours city with its blissfully disreputable cast of expatriates and hinterland transplants was reminiscent of Berlin as was its metropolitan scale. Only five cities on earth were larger than Shanghai, Berlin among them. In the coming years, numerous café owners and cabaret impresarios driven from Berlin would take refuge and reopen in Shanghai.

But the anti-Chinese discrimination evident in foreign-dominated Shanghai stunned him. When one European "Shanghailander" invited Magnus to meet him in a private club, he arrived with Li in tow and was informed by the white manager that the club was racially restricted. No Chinese could enter. Magnus was enraged and berated the manager. "You seem to forget that you yourself are a guest in China," he yelled as they stormed out.

In his Shanghai lectures no less than his talks in segregated America, Magnus "made no secret of the fact that as a biologist I can never approve the drawing of the 'colour line.'" But now, shadowed by Li, racial bigotry was growing personal. And the contemporaneous rise of fascists in his homeland, who saw German society as inexorably divided between "Aryans" and "Semites," was making racism more than an academic issue for Magnus. Always thoroughly secular in his Jewish identity, the world was now focusing on it whether he liked it or not. His whole life, Magnus had traveled in circles made up disproportionately of secular Jewish physicians and professionals, but in Shanghai he began to reckon more deeply with his Jewishness.

For nearly a century, Shanghai had been renowned for its small but prominent Jewish community. By the time Magnus arrived, a handful of Sephardic families with roots in Baghdad—the Sophers, the Sassoons, and the Kadoories, among them—were some of the leading landholders in Shanghai's foreign-run concessions. These families welcomed Magnus into their palatial estates and showed interest in his research. The Sopher siblings, Arthur, Theodore, and Rachel, keenly followed the latest scientific developments, and they had Magnus's sexual orientation questionnaire translated into English so the Shanghai community could understand the science behind his continuum of queerness and place themselves in the sexual panorama.

Returning the compliment, Magnus read Arthur Sopher's new book, *Chinese Jews*, which detailed the history of the small, ancient Jewish community that had existed for centuries in the Middle Kingdom. Magnus saw that Chinese Jews had cultural and religious similarities to Jewish communities in Europe and the Middle East, but in their "physiognomy"—skin color and eye shape—they resembled the Han Chinese majority. Indeed, for all the claims of the far right in his homeland that Jews constituted a single "Semitic" race, it was becoming clear to Magnus that all over the world Jews resembled their non-Jewish neighbors. Certainly German Jews looked more like German Christians, Moroccan Jews more like Moroccan Muslims, and Chinese Jews more like Chinese Confucians than members from any of these Jewish communities looked like each other.

Leaving the comfortable cosmopolitan confines of Shanghai, Magnus crisscrossed China, giving thirty-five lectures as Li ran the slide projector. With Li along as his guide and translator, Magnus glimpsed beyond the expatriate bubble. Parting with his usual love of creature comforts, sometimes out of cultural interest and sometimes because racially restricted hotels required it while travelling with a Chinese partner, Magnus stayed in Chinese-owned and -operated lodgings even though they tended to be less luxurious (and, he complained, noisier) than accommodations built for foreigners.

All over the country, Chinese youth clamored to hear Magnus speak. In Beijing, he lectured to an overflow college crowd; at Sun Yat-Sen University in Canton (now known as Guangzhou), a thousand students packed the hall. In Nanjing, then China's capital, Magnus met the minister of health and frankly discussed sexual issues including birth control, sex work, and homosexuality. But the country he took in between speaking gigs proved to be the highlight. In the northern port city of Tianjin, Magnus toured the red-light district that catered to sailors onshore from Korea, Russia, and Japan. Then he got a look at the city's queer subculture on the putting greens of a miniature golf course, likely keyed in by a local who had informed Li. Mini golf, an American fad that had gone global—much like jazz music, Magnus noted—was all the rage among Tianjin's lesbians and transmen. As Magnus recorded, on the course, "we watched gay Chinese women in men's clothes courting other ladies."

Magnus's sexuality research continued in Canton, where a German immigrant who ran a silk industry research center was eager to show Magnus his discovery: gay silkworm moths. Magnus had been cataloguing queerness in the animal kingdom for decades, but he initially thought this man's claim about invert invertebrates must be a joke. When he visited the facility, however, he found male silkworm moths exhibiting sexual interest in other males: sniffing, pursuing, and mounting them. The gay proportion in this silkworm population turned out to be roughly 3 percent.

Experiencing the wonders of China and the brilliance of the Chinese, coupled with seeing Europeans so dismissive of Li, pushed Magnus to embrace a humanistic egalitarianism. Even at twenty-three, Li had already endured a lifetime of racial slights growing up in British-colonized Hong Kong and living in foreigner-dominated Shanghai. Now Magnus witnessed them too.

Yet China's chauvinistic belief that it was the world's only true civilization struck Magnus as equally absurd as Eurocentrism. Magnus found humor in the European and Chinese pseudoscientific stories about their own supremacy, with each side packaging the same physical characteristics as evidence of superiority or inferiority depending on their preconceived notions. With the fact that the average European had more body hair than the average Chinese, the Europeans argued that they were hairier because they were more evolved, much like adults were hairier than children. The Chinese gloss on this same fact was that *they* were more evolved, much like humans are less hairy than animals. Magnus concluded that no single society had a monopoly on progress. He believed the West was more technologically advanced while China was more ethically advanced, in part swayed by China's more accepting views on homosexuality.

Spending ten weeks seeing China through Li's eyes and those in his circles pushed Magnus to embrace anti-imperialism. He was, he wrote, "one who fundamentally stands on the side of the unjustly oppressed, whether that oppression is the result of national, racial, religious, social or sexually antagonistic instincts and causes." Before leaving the mainland for Li's native Hong Kong, Magnus gave a final press interview in which he openly opposed imperialism. The anti-colonial tongue-lashing he had given privately to the racist maître d' at the restricted club was now offered to all Western chauvinists in the city. "Foreigners in China are guests of the country and not its masters," Hirschfeld told the paper. The "existence of foreign-controlled areas in [Shanghai] appears not only anomalous [but] not right to me." The article was headlined "Hirschfeld Hits Foreigners Idea of Superiority."

Moving on to the full-fledged colonies of Portuguese Macau and British Hong Kong, Magnus found the haughtiness of their European residents even more shameful. In Macau, a citywide gambling den, Magnus wrote, the "hypocrisy of the . . . European colonizers unmasks itself so nakedly." In Hong Kong, an expatriate merchant told Magnus about a Chinese sedan-chair porter who made his meager living hauling wealthy foreigners up to their posh hillside abodes on Victoria Peak.

The merchant concluded with a chuckle that "the coolie" said he hoped in his next life he'd return as a rich Englishman's dog since "they have it so good."

"How can you laugh about it?" Magnus asked the merchant. "It's a tragic story."

It wasn't only the assumption of European superiority that bothered Magnus but how unmerited it was. Nowhere in China was homosexuality more restricted than in the British spheres of influence. In Hong Kong, Magnus found the worst of British prudery transported halfway around the world. Lecturing to the uptight English women at Hong Kong's Helena May Institute for Women left Magnus yearning for the open discussions he'd been able to host on the mainland. Only after interminable discussions and negotiations was Magnus permitted to give the signature lecture he'd delivered in Shanghai and Canton—"Is Homosexuality Inherent or Acquired?"—in Hong Kong.

Setting professional frustrations aside, Magnus viewed visiting Hong Kong as a personal requirement. In the colonial city-state, Li introduced Magnus to his family, who welcomed him as an honored guest and treated him to all the luxuries their wealthy clan could provide. Li's father proved surprisingly supportive of his son moving to Berlin to work and study at the Institute for Sexual Science. After taking Magnus to a traditional Chinese puppet theater, the old man told him he hoped his son "might some day become the Dr. Hirschfeld of China." Magnus was unsure whether Li's parents realized that the relationship between him and their son went beyond that of teacher and student.

On July 4, 1931, fourteen members of Li's family sent the couple off aboard the *President Cleveland*, an American ship bound for Manila. Sailing out of Hong Kong for the Philippines, Magnus had the strange feeling that he was going backwards. He'd left the United States weeks before, but now, in a sense, he was returning. The Philippines was the closest thing America had to a full-fledged European-style colony. On board the ship that evening, American passengers monopolized the dining room to "noisily celebrate . . . their Independence Day," Magnus wrote in his travelogue, while he "retired to a quiet bench on the upper deck." The American passengers were particularly raucous on account of the Supreme Court's 1923 "booze cruise" decision, a seven-to-two ruling that exempted US vessels more than three nautical miles offshore from Prohibition.

While Magnus took in the South China Sea vista from the upper-deck bench, his mixed feelings about America came flooding back. The US had seized the Philippines from Spain under bizarre circumstances in the Spanish-American War, a brief struggle that had broken out half a world away, in Cuba, in 1898. Following a global debate that included anti-imperialist author Mark Twain squaring off against Bombay-born Briton Rudyard Kipling, who penned his "White Man's Burden" to encourage America to join the scramble for colonies, the US annexed the Philippines and went to work creating an Asian society in its image. The president at the time, William McKinley, reportedly couldn't even find the archipelago on a map.

Soon a steady stream of haughty, mustachioed white men began arriving in the Philippines from America. William Howard Taft, a federal judge from Ohio, was lugged in to run the colony. Then Chicago city planner Daniel Burnham was dispatched to redesign its capital. The architect of the "White City," which Magnus had taken in decades before at the Chicago world's fair, was tapped to build a whole white world in Manila. In his 1905 urban plan, Burnham bragged, his Southeast Asian metropolis would be "equal to the greatest of the Western world." In quick succession, Washington, DC–style neoclassical government buildings, Floridaesque beach clubs, and Adirondack-y mountain resorts began incongruously dotting the Filipino landscape.

Colonial and condescending, Governor-General Taft referred to Filipinos as "our little brown brothers," while hewing closely to the American racial system to ensure that Americans and Filipinos never actually became one family. Careful to avert another Hawaii, Americans brought their "miscegenation" phobias with them to the Philippines. Burnham and his team erected segregated institutions all over Manila. The YMCA had separate "white" and "colored" entrances. Americans who married locals found themselves blackballed from elite clubs and banished from society. Filipinos sometimes quip that their history was "three centuries in a Catholic convent and fifty years in Hollywood," but, as Magnus learned, sexual mores were far looser in the Spanish "convent" period than in the American "Hollywood" era.

On July 6, the *President Cleveland* entered Manila harbor. Members of the local press were so impatient to meet the Einstein of Sex that they hitched a ride on a harbor pilot's boat to snag an interview with the sexologist before he even docked. But when the ocean liner came into port and Magnus and Li touched dry land on their first trip together outside China, the border guards stopped Li in his tracks. Assuming in their bigoted ignorance that Hirschfeld spoke English and Li did not, they sternly informed Magnus that "American territory is closed to the yellow race."

Since the passage of the Chinese Exclusion Act in 1882, America had been closed to Chinese manual laborers (derisively dubbed "coolies") and its more recent Johnson-Reed Act of 1924 barred immigration from anywhere in Asia. But Li was neither a "coolie" nor a would-be immigrant. Despite Li's perfect English, Magnus, with the gravitas bestowed by his skin tone, did the talking. Li, he explained, was not Chinese at all but rather a native of the British colony of Hong Kong and therefore a subject of his majesty George V, the king of England. Rifling through his papers, Magnus produced a transit-visa that had been prepared for Li by the American vice-consul in Hong Kong, likely in an effort to head off this very situation.

The border agent looked back incredulously. The idea that Li was British rather than Chinese was absurd. After all, just look at him.

To Magnus, the notion that Americans could retroactively ban Chinese people from the Philippines was madness. The Philippines, like most of Southeast Asia, had been home to a Chinese diaspora community for centuries. Manila hosted an enormous Chinatown and a historic Chinese cemetery.

But with two long trips to America under his belt, Magnus knew he wasn't going to win an argument about race with a bunch of Americans, so he opted for a pragmatic approach. Magnus would entertain the Americans' notion that Li was Chinese, not British, and approach the Chinese embassy in Manila for help. The Chinese consul proved sympathetic and ironed out a deal with the American authorities that allowed Magnus and Li to enter Manila on condition that they surrender their passports and leave the Philippines when the next international ship left port four days later. The effete, accomplished medical student entered Manila as if it were a provincial American "sundown town."

On his forcibly brief visit, Magnus delivered two lectures—one for a white American audience at the Rotary Club and another for thousands of Filipino students on the lawn of the Philippine Government University. Several local students befriended Magnus after the lecture and gave him a tour of the historic Spanish settlement in the center of Manila while recruiting him to their anti-imperialist cause. When one student gave the apocryphal Abraham Lincoln quote that "no nation stands high enough to rule another nation," Magnus grew outraged at America's unique hypocrisy: the former British colony was now aping Britain in amassing colonies. At the end of his journey through Asia he would write, "There is . . . no doubt about it: future generations will regard the holding of colonies just as we regard the holding of slaves."

In Japan, Magnus had found expatriate Germans who had married locals—often his German-born hosts and their local spouses—and confirmed that mixed-race children were generally happy and healthy. None of it squared with the calumnies against "miscegenation" so common in America and, increasingly, in his native Germany. Now, in Manila, he found yet more evidence that the prejudice against race-mixing had no scientific basis. "The cross-breeds resulting from [interracial] unions . . . bring forth well-built, mentally well-endowed offspring," he wrote. "One hears over and over again . . . that these half-breeds are sterile, but this assertion, though frequently used to frighten people away from such unions, is without foundation in fact [and is] no more than [a] fear-inspiring device." It was, in fact, the opposite reproductive course—inbreeding—that led to unhealthy children.

With the trip limited to four days on account of the Chinese exclusion laws, Magnus had become a victim of America's anti-Chinese racism by proxy. "Full of regret that my schedule did not permit me to remain any longer in this far too little-known archipelago," Magnus was forced to rely on other Philippines-based researchers for his understanding of gender and queer life on the islands. Dr. Margarete Hasselmann, a well-traveled German physician, enlightened him about a mountain tribe in a remote part of Luzon, north of Manila, that raised its youth communally. A Dutch ethnographer told Magnus of numerous tribes in which some members wear gender-nonconforming clothing and, as Magnus recounted, "the entire village knows and respects these hermaphrodites."

On the appointed date, Magnus and Li boarded a Dutch steamship bound for that nation's East Indies colony, modern-day Indonesia. Despite common conceptions of the region as sexually repressed on account of fanatical Muslim missionaries and proper Dutch Protestant colonial administrators, upon landing, Magnus found a remarkably open sexual environment. A local group welcomed him to speak on the sometimes-touchy subject of sex education for adolescents. And interracial marriage was widespread and accepted in the archipelago. Indeed, most people considered to be "Europeans" on the most populous island, Java, had some indigenous ancestry. This mixed-race community even had its own activist newspaper, *Onze Stem* (Our Voice).

For a collector of sexual paraphernalia, Indonesia proved a treasure trove. For his museum, Magnus obtained a hundred-pound stone phallus and had it shipped back to Berlin. One doctor's wife told Magnus that if she'd known in advance that he'd be visiting Indonesia she would have purchased a special item for his collection. In the local market, an old woman had offered to sell her a life-sized polished carved-stone erection as a love amulet. Of course, she told him with a laugh, it would do no good under glass; the vendor was emphatic that it only worked if you kept it on your person at all times.

In the colonial capital, Batavia (now Jakarta), Magnus found the most open trans community he had ever encountered. For decades, Magnus had been publishing on trans communities beyond the West, largely relying on first-hand accounts sent by his global network of informants. He'd long known that Indonesia, like many societies in Oceania, was home to individuals assigned male at birth who, from early childhood, took on the clothing and social role of women. Neither the coming of Islam nor Dutch colonialism had stamped out the practice. Now, however, in the urbanizing capitalist world, many had left their ancestral villages and had moved to the metropolis, and some found themselves adrift.

When Magnus showed up in the summer of 1931, he met an expatriate European psychiatrist who had worked with members of the community and gave Magnus tips on where to meet them. In Batavia, these individuals, who are today known as *waria*, often lived together in group homes in certain neighborhoods. On his final night in town, Magnus visited the Moldenfliet red-light district and stayed out till dawn. Around midnight—still steamy in the tropical metropolis—transwomen poured out and congregated by a bridge. Some were sex workers seeking clients, but most were just seeking the company of others like themselves. Conversations that night, in Javanese with German translation, were dominated by talk of one community member who had suffered a nervous breakdown. Magnus noted sadly, the "pent-up emotions" of trans individuals who face barriers to acceptance in their wider society, led to elevated levels of mental illness. As always, he believed, there was nothing inherently depressing about being trans, only about living in a society where one felt out of place. In Germany, the basis was anti-trans prejudice; in Indonesia, it was the experience of losing their traditional social role in the village and feeling lost in the city.

After the all-night outing on the streets of Batavia, Magnus and Li headed to the airport. For any traveler who hoped to explore both China and India on the same trip in that era, a stop in Singapore, the port city at the tip of the Malaysian peninsula, was inevitable. Commercial flight was a novelty at the time and Magnus sat spellbound on his first airborne journey looking out the window. Craving an even better view, he talked the Dutch flight crew into giving him a cockpit tour mid-flight.

Singapore was a sailor town, and Magnus was familiar with its contours. The crowded streets contained visitors seeking adventure, immigrants hoping to get rich, and poverty and wealth cheek-by-jowl. "Singapore's renown for exotic pleasures is especially linked with Raffles Hotel for the élite and Malay Street for those of less refined tastes," Magnus wrote. While he and Li holed up in luxury at the whitewashed, palm-bedecked Raffles, they were soon drawn to seedier surroundings. Two years earlier, the British colonial authorities who ran Singapore had passed their Women and Girls' Protection Ordinance, which banned brothels in the city while still permitting cash-for-sex transactions one-on-one. But when Magnus finally arrived in Singapore's notorious Malay Street red-light district, it seemed unchanged. Women of every age and color were soliciting men from all over the world from buildings that were blatantly houses of prostitution. The sight proved too debased even for Magnus who later wrote of "the barred windows of their wretched cages."

Alma Sundquist, the head of the League of Nation's commission on human trafficking, happened to be in town to examine the city's poorly executed experiment with brothel prohibition. A medical doctor by training and a veteran suffragist in her native Sweden, Sundquist was a global advocate for sex education. Magnus had long hoped to meet her, and he called on her at her hotel. Discussing trafficking and sex work, he urged her to consider prostitution in its broadest context. It could only be reduced, Magnus argued, by addressing its root causes—the economic desperation of working-class women, the taboo against premarital sex imposed on well-to-do women, and the larger racial and economic inequalities of the world system. These savage inequalities were on vivid display in Singapore where, Magnus wrote, "there [are] only a handful of Europeans, but they are all powerful."

This was his mindset as he sailed for India, Britain's most prized colonial possession. India's nearly 300 million souls were ruled by a few thousand white men, soldiers and civil servants shipped in from—and answering to—London. Making landfall in Madras (now Chennai), Magnus boarded a train for Calcutta, the first capital of the British Raj. Even en route, Magnus found India's human pageantry, on display at the station stops, intoxicating. On the platforms, sari-clad women dripped with jewelry, "laden with anklets and bracelets, necklaces and stomachers, finger and toe rings—their nostrils, ear-lobes and frequently even their lips pierced by ornaments." And then there were the men, in pointed shoes and elaborate headdresses, their foreheads painted with markings of various religious and caste affiliations.

Calcutta awed Magnus. In the center of town sat the landscaped Dalhousie Square. Its central water feature was flanked by stately government buildings and reflected the domed, whitewashed neoclassical central post office and the redbrick Victorian-style civil service headquarters. Magnus stayed steps away at the Great Eastern Hotel. From a gracious, block-long verandah on the second floor, guests enjoyed their tea while taking in the chaotic bustle of the metropolis below. As Magnus would recount, "Shanghai has been called the Paris of the East [but] Calcutta is its London." It wasn't just "the style of the parks and public buildings" that were so "very reminiscent of the city on the Thames," he explained. It was that Calcutta, like London, was a cultural and intellectual hub of global import.

India embraced Magnus. While in America, he had been dubbed the Einstein of Sex, in India, they called him the "Vatsayana of the West" after the author of the Kama Sutra. He was flattered by the comparison, noting that the ancient Sanskrit text had included homosexuality in its encyclopedic catalogue of human desire under the term "the third natural sex" (*Tritia Prakriti*). With so many Indian students reverently approaching him, he began to feel like "a kind of Yogi." The rumor in Indian society that yogis, with their renunciation of sex with women, were frequently gay may have played a role in Magnus being associated with them.

The renowned intellectual Rabindranath Tagore invited Magnus to meet him at his country estate. The poet Tagore, the first non-European to win the Nobel Prize for Literature, had been knighted by King George V but renounced the honor to protest British imperialism after a horrific massacre of peaceful demonstrators in Punjab in 1919. On Indian soil, Magnus felt required to take a position on the independence question. People kept asking him his opinion, especially since so many of the debates over the progressive or malign influence of the British in India had to do with his area of expertise: sex. The British maintained that they had a "civilizing mission" in their colonies, and in India, they took pride in having wiped out *sati*, the ritualized suicide of widowed women who threw themselves on their husband's funeral pyres. In certain factions of the Western women's movement, British imperialism in India was seen as advancing humanitarian aims.

Magnus was skeptical of these apologists for empire. As he knew better than most, anyone writing about the sexual life of any society could create a slanderous polemic by cherry picking the most scandalous facts. Having toured Western colonies in Asia, Magnus now found the British defense hollow. The Dutch rulers of Indonesia, hardly selfless themselves, had all but wiped out tropical diseases on the main island of Java. Meanwhile, Magnus noted, in India, cholera, dysentery, tuberculosis, and malaria still ran rampant. The British bragged about the rail system they built in India as if it were a gift to the local populace and a mere coincidence that it helped them to extract the subcontinent's bounty. Tellingly, Magnus noted, after nearly two centuries of imperialism, the British had never built a public school system and roughly 90 percent of the Indian population remained illiterate.

The real impetus for reforming Indian society, Magnus came to see, was coming from Indians themselves. The leader of the independence movement, Mohandas K. Gandhi, was "among the bitterest opponents of child-marriage," Magnus pointed out. And Indian feminists were agitating to end the tradition of *purdah*, which kept women hidden at home, cut off from a public sphere they could observe only through latticework-covered windows overlooking the street. After a lecture in Calcutta, several local women approached Magnus to urge him to take up their anti-*purdah* cause in his global campaign for sex reform. He later described *purdah* in India as "deplorable" and an insult to the intelligence of Indian women.

The deeply ingrained caste system was also being criticized by indigenous leaders, Gandhi among them. Indians pointed out that their system was not as unique as Westerners liked to portray it. Until the French Revolution, European societies had had similar hereditary divides between nobles and commoners. And Magnus himself was now in Asia in part to seek refuge from the second-class citizenship threatening him from a resurgent European antisemitism. Meanwhile, in America, Magnus wrote, "the Negroes are just as untouchable as the [Dalits] in India." Magnus opposed the caste system in India as he opposed Jim Crow in America and fascism in Germany. The caste system, he wrote, is "a deep disgrace, not only to the Indian nation but also to the whole of humanity." He remained confident that progress was possible. On his trip to Japan, which had only abolished its caste system in the wake of the Meiji Restoration of 1868, Magnus met Japanese people who never knew it had ever existed. He found hope in the rising rate of intercaste marriages in India.

British rule, Magnus came to believe, relied on a self-serving system of bait and switch through which they left certain regressive practices in place to justify continued colonial domination. The British, he noted, had stamped out *sati* suicide but had never banned child marriage. Now they held up child marriage as a barbaric practice that justified their enduring rule. Similarly, the British ginned up communal tensions between Hindus and Muslims and then justified foreign rule as the only way to prevent mass slaughter. To Magnus, for all of their theological differences, the Hindus and Muslims of India shared a common subcontinental culture. They were comparable, he thought, to the Protestants and Catholics in Germany, who had warred for centuries but now got along fine.

Being outside East Asia with Li for the first time brought them closer. They were both equally out of their element and India had an undeniable romance. To Magnus, the Taj Mahal, the world's greatest monument to love, more than lived up to its reputation. "Just to look at it is worth a trip around the world," Magnus declared of Agra's wonder. "It is unquestionably the most sublime work of art ever created by human hands. In comparison to the Taj Mahal, the Milan cathedral . . . appears clumsy, and the Cologne cathedral stiff." That the complex was dedicated to human love rather than a distant deity greatly appealed to him.

Shortly before they arrived in Agra, Magnus had confided to his diary that Li was the mentee who could carry on his mission after his death. "I . . . have found in him the student I have sought for so long," Magnus wrote. Now he changed his will. Rather than leaving his estate to Karl, he would leave "my manuscripts and money" to Li. The will instructed Li to bring Magnus's ashes to Berlin and give them to Karl.

In the shadow of the Taj, this new love was tested. Urged by Indian friends and his growing anti-colonial convictions, Magnus opted to stay in an Indian-run hotel built for locals rather than a British-run establishment catering to foreigners. When Magnus and Li returned to their room, they found it swarming with mosquitos. Li ran out to buy incense sticks, a natural insect repellent, but by the time he returned, Magnus had been bitten over forty times. A week later, the sixty-three-year-old came down with malaria, a testament to imperial Britain's lackadaisical public health efforts. Though Li nursed his partner back to health, Magnus would suffer flare-ups for the rest of his life.

Even with new health challenges, Magnus was able to conduct fieldwork on sex and gender. In Agra, he watched a religious festival celebrating the life of the Hindu god Ram. Devotees paraded dressed as the deities of Hindu myth. As Magnus recounted, "Many men were dressed as women. Two youths, who depicted Indian goddesses, looked especially gorgeous." When Magnus told his Indian hosts that he believed this phenomenon to be related to his research in Germany on the urge to wear gender-nonconforming clothing, they grew defensive. Cross-dressing, they maintained, was a requirement of the gods, not a personal sex kink.

In Delhi, Magnus met members of the indigenous trans community he had read so much about. As with the *waria* of Indonesia, the members of this group, *hijras*, had a traditional social role—it was auspicious when they blessed newborn babies and wedding couples—but in modern society, they often lived together in urban red-light districts. Each evening, trans sex workers sat out on lamp-lit balconies, while touts in the street below pitched "eunuch" services to potential johns, taking a commission from every sale. *Hijras*, Magnus learned, were divided into two categories—those who needed to shave and those who did not—but he speculated that there were relatively few intersex individuals among them. The majority, he thought, were experiencing the same type of gender dysphoria he had studied back home in Berlin. Britain's laws against wearing gender-nonconforming clothing were binding in its colonies, but they were rarely enforced against indigenous *hijras* in India. Similarly, prosecutions under Section 377, the British colonial law against same-sex intercourse, were rare on the subcontinent.

For decades, Magnus had been reading about matriarchal societies and now he could finally observe one. "To . . . the sex ethnologist," he wrote, "there is hardly any sight more interesting than the weekly market of Darjeeling," a Himalayan hill station near the border with Tibet. Magnus wandered the city market as polyandrous women strode in trailed by their "three to five husbands . . . who, bearing burdens, trot behind her like slaves." In an inversion of the society from which Magnus came, here the husbands did the scut work while the matriarch calmly smoked her pipe and desultorily attended to business affairs. Magnus had heard about similar matriarchal societies on the island of Formosa and in a remote part of the Indonesian archipelago where husbands took their wife's name, lived outside the family home, and were brought in only to service her sexually. But this was the first time he was able to observe a matriarchal culture firsthand.

Magnus concluded his journey through India with a three-week stay in Bombay, the cosmopolitan entrepôt, where he gave half a dozen lectures in the English he had honed in America. Lodged at the luxurious harborside Taj Mahal Hotel, his malaria symptoms came and went, but they didn't stop him from getting around town. The locals couldn't get enough of him. As his reputation grew, a line began forming daily outside his hotel room made up of individuals hoping to confide in him about their sexual orientation, secret kinks, or ambiguous genitalia. Magnus relished the irony of the religious Muslim women who eagerly asked him their most outré sexual questions while refusing to let him see their face out of modesty.

As in Shanghai, Bombay's Jewish community tried to adopt Magnus as one of their own. Sir David Esra, who had attended one of Magnus's lectures, and his wife, Lady Esra (née Sassoon), invited him to their spacious home. In their gardens where David, an amateur ornithologist, kept his collection of rare birds, the family celebrated the fall harvest festival of Sukkot. Magnus had never marked it before in his life; it was among the numerous rites that had been pushed aside by secular German Jews in favor of holidays like Christmas and the kaiser's birthday.

Magnus was pleased to learn that the Jews of Bombay, like those of Berlin, were well integrated with their non-Jewish neighbors. Many local Jews were in mixed marriages, most typically with Muslims. The adage of a European Jewish woman Magnus knew who'd met and married a Muslim in Berlin that "the Mohammedans are three-quarters Jewish" rang particularly true in this polytheistic part of the world.

By contrast, the small local Parsi community, descendants of Zoroastrian refugees who had fled Islamic fundamentalism in medieval Persia, strictly forbade intermarriage. Children without two Parsi parents got excommunicated. Magnus warmed to the Parsi community of Bombay as they played a disproportionate role in the cultural life of the city. But as a sexual scientist, he worried for their future. "As a consequence of inbreeding," he wrote, "quite a few have weak lungs and eyes [or] are tubercular and short-sighted."

In India, Magnus began to receive explicit warnings from allies in Germany not to return home. The situation was getting even worse. Far-right street violence had become a regrettable fact of life in Berlin, and he would undoubtedly be a prime target were he to resurface there. Buying more time, Magnus decided to head to Egypt and monitor the situation in tinderbox Europe from the more stable Middle East. One of his last nights in Bombay happened to be Diwali, the Hindu festival of lights. True to form, he eschewed the city's lavish Britified celebrations, many held downstairs in his hotel, and took in the festivities in Kamatipura, the red-light district, among the working-class betel-nut-chewing "ground floor girls."

From Bombay, Magnus and Li crossed the Red Sea and sailed through the Suez Canal, a French-designed shortcut between Asia and Europe now in British hands. In the Egyptian city at the canal's northern end, Port Said, they went through British immigration and customs, a grueling but now familiar exercise in racial humiliation for Li. For four hours, their luggage was picked over and their health checked while their paperwork was languorously processed. Traveling with Li, Magnus witnessed Western authorities' blatant double standards. "Travellers from Asia are more closely inspected than those from Europe," he wrote. When Gandhi passed through the canal on the way home from London a few weeks later, the authorities refused to even let him debark in Egypt, depriving Magnus of his best chance to meet the Mahatma.

The absurdity of the binary between "white" and "colored" struck hard in the multicultural panorama of Egypt. Port Said was a sailor town with crews arriving from all over the world. And traveling the length of the Nile to Upper Egypt, Magnus came to see that Egyptians came in "every shade." The historic beachfront city of Alexandria was fully part of the mixed-up Mediterranean world. Founded by the ancient Greeks, it had always been home to myriad communities. In the modern era, its populations had grown even more diverse. Layered in with the Greeks and Jews and Egyptians who had been present for centuries, there were now Lebanese, Turks, and Armenians as well as Europeans from nearby Mediterranean countries like Italy and faraway ones like Russia. Together, it formed what Magnus called "an almost inextricable racial mixture. It is hardly possible now to separate and recognize all these inherited component parts. Even those, who, like some of my acquaintances there, asserted that they could do this, made more mistakes than correct guesses."

Alexandria also hosted a sizeable German expatriate community, so when Magnus grew homesick during the holiday season, he traveled there with Li to get a taste of Central Europe. "I'd like to see a Christmas tree," he wrote in his journal, "so I'm taking Tao Li to the Bavarian Beer Hall, a sailors' bar in Alexandria." Cosmopolitan Alexandria was the kind of place a German-Jewish refugee and his Chinese-British gay lover could enjoy some Christmas cheer together in a Muslim country.

During his winter in Egypt, Cairo cast its spell over Magnus. From the bazaars to the mosques to the pyramids to the incomparable archeology museum, he took it all in. As a European, he expressed shame over the colonial looting of the country. Berlin's most prized museum piece—the iconic 3000-year-old bust of Queen Nefertiti—Magnus declared, should be given back. "Germany ought to return it to Egypt," he wrote. "It belongs [in] the Egyptian Museum in Cairo."

Another flare-up of malaria put a damper on New Year's Eve celebrations, and Magnus took this portion of his journey at an uncharacteristically slow pace. He and Li cruised down the Nile to take in the ruins at Luxor. The tombs of the ancient pharaohs, with their towering sculptures, paintings, and bas-reliefs, Magnus believed, outshone those of the Forum in Rome. With this break from his relentless lecture schedule, Magnus and Li, now more than half a year into their relationship, were able to enjoy some down time together. In a bid to entertain tourists, the hotels of Upper Egypt ran camel, horse, and donkey races and allowed their braver guests to participate. On a whim, Li entered as a donkey jockey, and Magnus, being a good boyfriend, bet on him to win. When Li crossed the finish line first, Magnus took in quite a sum. The German doctor was, unsurprisingly, the only guest who'd bet on the Hong Kong medical student to win the desert donkey race.

Even while trying to relax, when it came to being a sex researcher, Magnus could never really turn it off. He was fascinated by the rumors that the Upper Egyptians who touted their services to tourists as guides at archaeological sites and the men who offered them donkey rides turned tricks on the side. Whether or not the rumors were true, the authorities took them seriously. The vice squad kept a close watch on the guides and the "donkey-boys," regarding them all as potential hustlers.

In Egypt as in India, Magnus was heartened to find women leading the push for sex reform and gender equality. Powerful women had, of course, been a fixture in ancient Egypt. Queen Hatshepsut and Cleopatra, Magnus knew, were frequently shown in sculptural portrayals wearing men's clothing and a strap-on beard. Now, Magnus met the leader of the Egyptian Feminist Union and saw firsthand that the *purdah* system was collapsing. He also discerned a laudable sex positivity, at least within the bounds of marriage.

Even as a guest speaker, he was keen not to lecture the locals from a condescending position of European superiority. In his "Love in the Light of Science" series at the University of Egypt, his local host introduced him to the audience with the explicit disclaimer that his lectures were not meant to put local customs on trial. Still, few were shy about asking Magnus to opine on these very matters. Many clamored to know his position on the controversial local practice of female circumcision (now called female genital mutilation). Here he parted with his usual reticence to criticize his hosts' sexual practices and openly condemned the cutting of girls' genitals as "senseless, heartless cruelty." He tempered the harshness of his judgment by voicing skepticism of male circumcision, historically a practice among Jews as well as Muslims and not uncommon in the West. During his time in America, he'd met a Detroit medical doctor who was harshly critical of foreskin removal, and Magnus had been convinced by his arguments. "As an objective student of sex," Magnus wrote, "surely Nature creates no organs for the purpose of their being cut off."

Magnus also met quietly with Egypt's minister of health and advocated for queer tolerance. The official, a medical doctor by training and the primary care physician to the king, was firmly convinced that homosexuality was a curable disease. He fretted that societal tolerance would lead to rising rates of homosexuality. Having encountered over ten thousand cases of homosexuality in his medical practice, Magnus told the official, he could assure him that there were neither "cures" nor "contagion" through "recruitment."

Magnus resisted the urge to attribute the minister's benighted views to aspects of his identity: non-Western, Muslim, African, etc. Magnus had met enough powerful men in the West with similarly misguided ideas about homosexuality—Sigmund Freud among them—to chalk up this health minister's ignorance to his origins. The problem Magnus had come to see was not Arab ignorance or Indian ignorance, Muslim ignorance or Catholic ignorance, German ignorance or American ignorance—but human ignorance.

Despite his anger at imperialism, even Magnus had to concede that British global domination had certain conveniences for the international traveler. Going from Cairo to Tel Aviv was just a matter of buying a train ticket. After a few hours' journey peacefully gliding through the Sinai Peninsula and Gaza, Magnus and Li arrived at the Lydda rail junction midway between Tel Aviv and Jerusalem. Chaim Berlin, a physician who'd worked with Magnus at the institute in Germany before departing for Palestine, met the couple at the station and drove them to the San Remo Hotel near the beach in Tel Aviv. It was Valentine's Day 1932.

Magnus enjoyed Tel Aviv, the largest of the new secular Jewish settlements in the British colony. He'd grown up in a beach town, albeit one that was saddled with prim, buttoned-up Northern European mores and no swimming days in February. The raucous Mediterranean scene in Tel Aviv, with prudery thrown to the wind, was reminiscent of Honolulu. Under pressure from Orthodox rabbis and others worried about their city's image in the West, skinny-dipping had been officially banned by the Tel Aviv city council. Still unsatisfied, the religious right pushed for the beach to be segregated by gender. But out on the actual seafront, without a rabbi in sight, all rules went blissfully unenforced. "The prohibition of undressing on the beach was far more honoured in the breach than in the observance," a British colonial official had recently lamented, and "many persons habitually bathed without costume." As Magnus delighted in his journal, "swimmers of both sexes, tanned athletes male and female . . . cheerfully crowd[ed] between the vast rows of beach chairs." Li and Magnus happily "loitered" at the shoreline, admiring the sunbathers.

Knowing that, for the time being, at least, he couldn't return to Berlin, Magnus took his time exploring Palestine. He had few fixed appointments beyond his series of lectures in Tel Aviv. He delivered them in his native tongue despite Palestine being a British colony. Already, Tel Aviv was filling up with German exiles, and German was largely intelligible to any European transplant who knew Yiddish. For those who could not follow along, a translator rendered Magnus's words in Modern Hebrew, an updated version of Biblical Hebrew that used Latinate neologisms to fill in the concepts and technologies that had arisen since ancient times.

Even for a secular man of science, the Holy Land felt magical. Bible stories Magnus had learned in childhood came flooding back as he drove by the walls of Jericho and visited the Tomb of the Patriarchs. Unsurprisingly, his favorite biblical site was Sodom and Gomorrah.

Magnus saw the roots of religion as psychological, not theological. To him, the religious ecstasy of the young men at Jerusalem's Wailing Wall "throw[ing] themselves hither and thither" was obviously sublimated sexuality. As he recounted, "I repeatedly saw pale youths whose movements grew more and more violent, whose groans and shrieks grew louder and louder, until they rose to the point of passionate frenzy; and then they gradually declined and faded away as their strength finally became exhausted."

Magnus was far more interested in the modern experiments in sex and gender underway among the secular socialist settlements. At the Beit Alfa kibbutz, a collective farm, Magnus lectured, at the residents' request, on his experience in revolutionary Moscow and Leningrad. His talk was entitled "Sexual Enlightenment and the Soviet Solution of Sexual Questions." The kibbutzniks, Magnus found, were more Soviet than the Soviets, though he noted they never called themselves "communists" for fear of alarming their bourgeois donors in the West. Even in its most radical early revolutionary phase, the Soviet Union had built only small-scale prototype "kitchen factories" to free women from the drudgery of housework. But on the Jewish collective farms in Palestine, as his hosts proudly showed him, every meal was taken communally in the vast mess hall and prepared by kibbutz members on kitchen duty. Even more radical were the children's dormitories. In the baby room, mothers would drop in, nurse their infants, and then leave while trained nurses, typically older women, kept a constant watch over their collective charges. In another building, older children lived away from their parents in coed dormitories grouped by age. Abolishing the nuclear family had long been a central feature of schemes for communistic utopias from Plato's *Republic* through Marx and Engels's *Manifesto*. While the Soviets balked at this radical measure, the kibbutzniks did not.

Under these collectivist conditions, Magnus found, love relationships could truly flourish. With all property held in common, the for-richer-or-for-poorer question was removed from marriage decisions, and couples could pair off purely on grounds of love and sexual compatibility. And with the children raised communally, couples that had fallen out of love could separate or divorce without disrupting their children's home life. The kibbutz system, he later wrote, was "unquestionably an experiment of great value."

As he toured the children's home at Beit Alfa, the youngsters largely ignored Magnus and flocked to Li; the kids had never seen an East Asian person before. But while the children looked in slack-jawed amazement at this racial other, Magnus noted that they themselves didn't all look the same. The more time Magnus spent in Palestine, the more suspicious he became of the ethnonationalist concept that Jews—or any group for that matter—constituted a distinct race. It was reminiscent of Harlem, the neighborhood Americans insisted was all Black even as Magnus had plainly seen the full gamut of skin tones among its inhabitants.

Like any German Jew of his era, Magnus felt he had some ability to pick out a fellow *landsman* in a crowd. But now on the streets of Tel Aviv and in the kibbutzim of Palestine, in these all-Jewish environments, he second-guessed himself. In a kindergarten for Jewish children, Magnus counted thirty-two blondes among the fifty-four children—a solid majority. Had he observed the very same group of fair-haired and dark-haired children in Germany, he would have guessed that the dark-haired children were Jews and the blondes Christians. According to racists in Germany, hair color and eye color were telltale signs of who was an "Aryan" and who was a "Semite." But now it became clear that these traits didn't actually reveal a person's ethnicity. Among the crowds in Tel Aviv, Magnus found that the stereotypical "so-called 'Jewish nose' [was] hardly more frequent than the pug nose." He began to realize that his sense of who was Jewish in Germany was built more on class clues than on physical ones.

In urban Germany, secular Jews were vastly overrepresented in the learned professions. Given their 2,000-year head start on mass literacy,

Germans of Jewish descent made up nearly half of Berlin's doctors and most of the city's lawyers, even though they constituted less than 4 percent of the city's population. Meeting a random attorney on the streets back home and venturing that he was Jewish was math, not prejudice. But this meant that in Berlin, the exact same person with the exact same hair color, eye color, and nose would seem more Jewish if he were dressed in a physician's lab coat than if he wore the overalls of an automobile technician. By contrast, in Tel Aviv, everyone—every doctor and every mechanic—was Jewish. At the San Remo Hotel where he was staying, "all the employees, from the director to the bootblack, are Jewish," Magnus marveled. In Tel Aviv, "from the municipal government to the working-class, from the police to the streetcleaners and chimneysweeps, all are Jews."

Faced with the puzzle of this ostensibly ethnically pure settlement whose residents looked anything but pure, Magnus concluded that everyone must be mixed. "Not pure, but mixed, races are a matter of course biologically," he would write. In hindsight, it seemed obvious. How could it be otherwise since "every individual possesses and unites in himself a line of paternal and maternal ancestors embracing thousands, perhaps even hundreds of thousands of generations." For Magnus, the greatest value of the ethnonationalist Zionist experiment was an ironic one: it proved to him that ethnic purity didn't exist. Having grown up in a multiethnic society, Magnus had not recognized this fact. But in a society that claimed to be ethnically pure, the concept of ethnic purity itself was debunked.

Magnus politely ignored the entreaties of European Jews who had relocated to Palestine that he join them in their state-building efforts. Meir Dizengoff, the retired founding mayor of Tel Aviv, urged Magnus to turn from his global humanitarian mission to a particularist Jewish one. "May Dr. Hirschfeld, who has dedicated his life to the benefit of the human race, help us in the regeneration of our nation," the elder statesman wrote in Magnus's notebook. But the scientist looked askance at the Zionists' withdrawal from the wider world, their de-cosmopolitanizing of themselves. He was particularly critical of the creation of the Modern Hebrew language. Why not use English, the global lingua franca, he wondered? To Magnus, after centuries of medieval oppression and segregation, self-ghettoization seemed a daft response. And he fretted that it would have increasingly corrosive impacts the more entrenched it became. "Experience has shown that linguistic isolation noticeably increases every nationalistic and chauvinistic instinct," he wrote.

Despite his wonder at the kibbutzim, Magnus harbored reservations about the Zionist project. In his exile from Nazism, he would take the position that "Zionism and the assimilation of Jews in the lands where they have been settled for centuries are not mutually exclusive." Healthy Jewish communities could exist both in the diaspora and in Palestine, he believed, if a just peace could be reached with the Arabs. But he worried that only "the highest diplomacy" could resolve tensions with local Muslims and Christians, who also had legitimate claims on the land. When Nazi persecution made life in Germany impossible, he urged his own family members to move to America rather than Palestine, having seen both firsthand.

At the root of the racial and ethnic conflicts of the modern world—racial segregation in America, haughty Shanghailanders in China, British imperialists lording it over Indians on the subcontinent, Zionists clashing with Arabs in Palestine—Magnus saw sex. After all, sex was the means by which race and ethnicity were transmitted. One's "race" was a record of all the reproductive sex one's ancestors had had over the generations. In a sense, race *was* sex and sex *was* race. The "racists," as Magnus would soon dub them, had already figured this out. Racist societies could only perpetuate themselves through the regulation of sex. The "racial chaos" they railed against was a puritanical way of saying "sexual chaos"—sex unbound by racial lines. Without strict regulations on who could reproduce with whom, racial lines would grow blurry—even blurrier than they already were. At the end of his trip, Magnus summarized, "sex is the basic principle around which all the rest of human life, with all its institutions, is pivoted."

Shortly after leaving Palestine, where he felt foreign even as locals like Dizengoff insisted that he was "home" and unable to return to his homeland where fascists insisted that he was and had always been a "foreigner," Magnus mulled his predicament in his travel diary. "The questions: where do you belong? What are you really? [These] give me no peace," he wrote. "I formulate this question: Are you a German, a Jew, or a citizen of the world? and my answer is, 'world citizen,' or 'all three.'" Human identity could be multiplicitous. Indeed, in the modern world, it had to be.

Chapter 13

Exile

Li Shiu Tong and Karl Giese in front of the Institute for Sexual Science in Berlin.

REENTERING EUROPE IN March 1932, Magnus knew he could not return to Germany, at least not yet. He hoped to find a neighboring country where he could settle until the fascist tide receded in his homeland.

It had now been over five hundred days since he'd bid farewell to his partner, Karl Giese. What was supposed to have been a brief jaunt across the Atlantic had turned into a nearly two-year circumnavigation of the globe. Corresponding by post and telegram, the pair planned to reunite in Athens. There, Karl, long Magnus's eyes and ears at the institute, could bring the long-gone founder up to date on the situation at home. Beyond that practical matter, there was now the personal one. After thirteen years as Magnus's life partner, there was no telling how

Karl would react to Magnus's new love, Li Shiu Tong, who was also now Magnus's heir, both personal and professional.

From British-occupied Palestine, Magnus and Li passed into French-dominated Lebanon and caught a boat from Beirut to Athens. On March 16, 1932, the couple landed at Piraeus, the seaport on the edge of the Greek capital, where Magnus's hero Socrates had once sketched his vision of the ideal state, run by its most rational citizens irrespective of gender.

The Greece Magnus arrived in was ominously reminiscent of the Germany he had left. Though still officially a republic, the pain of the Great Depression had emboldened extremists. The country that had birthed democracy was now threatened from the right by militants who idolized Mussolini's Fascist Italy.

The first weekend, Magnus gave a seemingly successful lecture at the Medical Society of Athens. But the following week, he found himself attacked in the press. An ultranationalist newspaper tarred him as "a German so-called Professor [smuggling in] strange kinds of depravity . . . hidden under the transparent veil of the so-called sexual science and the Institute for sexual research, established by this 'Professor' in Berlin."

Local allies rose to defend Magnus. For decades, they noted, he'd bravely published research on the laudable tolerance of homosexuality in ancient Greece. Magnus himself flagged Greek traditions, writing that, "I am certain [my enemies] would have an entirely different opinion had [they] read just one of my works, or . . . visited my Institute. I regret having to make these explanations . . . in Greece, whose great civilization . . . I have always held in high esteem." The paper ran Magnus's letter but printed it alongside an editorial endorsing the antisemitic conspiracy theory that his scientific research and gay-rights activism were "Jewish propaganda [designed] to shake . . . the pillars of Christian morality."

The situation would have been even more dangerous had Magnus's local critics been aware of his personal life. Locals seemed to take at face value the news reports that Li, Karl, and Magnus were just colleagues. Hirschfeld "arrived to our city in [the] company of his assistant, Dr. Giese, and of Chinese psychiatrist Tao Li," one paper stated, inflating both men's credentials. Whatever the dynamics of their relationship, all three did their part to keep matters private.

Over their years together, Karl and Magnus had had plenty of sex outside of their relationship. In addition to Karl's preauthorized masochistic escapades, Magnus was rumored to have had affairs with at least two institute staffers besides Karl. Still, this was the first time either had introduced a full-fledged life partner.

Working-class Karl may have resented Li's wealth and status and perhaps his youth as well. Li's medical education made him, not Karl, the obvious heir apparent to Magnus's institute in Berlin, no matter Karl's years of service there. Neither Karl nor Li ever voiced any misgivings about the situation and long-term relationships are famously opaque to outsiders, but observers claimed to see tensions. As one German acquaintance who spotted the three together gossiped, "Aunt Magnesia has once again arranged [a] glorious nuisance. . . . He's living now with both flames (Tao and Karlchen). And the best part is, both of them are soooo jealous about the old geezer. Now if that's not true love?!"

It fell to Karl to give Magnus the bleak update from Berlin. Under the canopy of the liberal Weimar constitution, the Institute for Sexual Science remained free to operate—educating visitors, offering psychotherapy and gender-affirming care, and publishing research—but it could no longer guarantee the day-to-day safety of the staff. The Nazis, now the second-largest party in the Reichstag, were routinely to siccing their thugs on opponents in the streets. There was simply no way Magnus could safely return to Berlin.

The best of the bad options, Magnus decided, would be to settle in a German-speaking city outside Germany—either Vienna or Zurich. From there, he could turn the voluminous research notes from his world tour into an accessible book on gender beyond the West. After two weeks in Greece, Karl, Li, and Magnus set off for Vienna together.

Magnus found Vienna scarier than it had ever been—and that was saying something. A 1923 lecture he'd given in the Austrian capital had been interrupted by stink bombs and gunfire. The fascist mindset, being "race"-based, paid no heed to the Germany–Austria border. Hitler was Austrian by birth, and his Nazi Party saw all German-speaking lands as a single entity destined to be unified into a grand Germanic ethnostate with vast imperial holdings. Austria's German National Socialist Workers Party (DNSAP) was indistinguishable from Germany's National Socialist German Workers Party (NSDAP); both flew the same swastika flag. The key difference was that Austria's party still had few followers. Polling less than 5 percent in the most recent election, it held no seats in the Austrian parliament.

Immediately upon his arrival, far-right newspapers flagged Hirschfeld's presence in the country, endangering his life. In Graz, Austria's second city, DNSAP thugs protested a screening of *Mystery of Gender*, the documentary film on Hirschfeld's theories with Dora, Charlotte, and Toni, who had surgically transitioned at the institute, showing the results of their vaginoplasties. Soon death threats were pouring in—"his time has run out"; "we'll take care of him"—though indications were that most had been sent over the border from Germany.

Magnus dispatched Karl to check on the institute—a big ask given the political climate in Germany and their all-too-brief reunion. Li went along for a short visit, taking in the vaunted institute before returning to Magnus in Vienna and continuing his medical studies at a local university. Magnus got to work in his hotel room drafting the travelogue of his sexual science research in Hawaii, Japan, China, Southeast Asia, India, and the Middle East.

From Vienna, Magnus followed the gay-Nazis scandal roiling German politics from afar. It had begun the previous year while he was still in Asia. Magnus learned that the *Munich Post*, a left-leaning newspaper aligned with the Social Democrats, had published an exposé on gay Nazis, tarring the NSDAP as a hypocritical party of "175ers" (violators of Paragraph 175). Focusing on Ernst Röhm, the leader of the Nazi Party's paramilitary wing, the *Sturmabteilung* (SA), which also oversaw the Hitler Youth, the paper condemned the "abhorrent hypocrisy" of a far-right party that in public fights "a battle against sodomy" while, in private, "shameless[ly tolerates] sodomy in its own ranks."

Magnus had always known that there were gay Nazis. His rivals in Adolf Brand's masculinist wing of the German gay movement had long been sympathetic to this flavor of misogynistic, antisemitic, queer ultranationalism. And Röhm was a classic case, with his rants that "the Germans have forgotten how to hate [as] feminine complaining has taken the place of masculine hatred." But Magnus and his allies in the Scientific Humanitarian Committee had always taken a firm moral stance against outing closeted critics for political gain. The Social Democratic Party, growing increasingly desperate, did not feel it could afford to maintain such lofty principles.

Röhm's gayness was an open secret among the Nazi elite. Hitler knew of Röhm's sexual orientation and had long chosen to ignore it. The two went way back. Both were disgruntled veterans of the Great War—Röhm bore the face scar to prove it. After organizing "German Day" in the summer of 1923, a unite-the-right extravaganza held in Nuremberg, Röhm had stood at Hitler's side during the Beer Hall Putsch.

When the *Munich Post* articles first came out in 1931, Hitler's party dismissed them. Berlin regional party chief Joseph Goebbels took the lead, calling it, predictably, a conspiracy engineered by Marxists and Jews. Now, in the spring of 1932, the Social Democrats showed the receipts. Helmuth Klotz, a former rightist who had defected to the Social Democrats, published a series of love letters Röhm had penned to a gay German doctor. In one, sent when Röhm was working as a mercenary for the Bolivian army, Hitler's right-hand man pined for the rollicking queer nightlife of Berlin. This letter and others were compiled into a pamphlet, printed three hundred thousand times, and sent as a mailer to German voters just after Hitler announced his intention to become chancellor. The Social Democrats highlighted Röhm's sexual orientation in their campaign posters as well.

To Hirschfeld's old associates, it was becoming a bitter inside joke to see which individuals who'd come to the institute to discuss their gay desires or gender dysphoria had embraced the far right. It was well known within Berlin's gay circles, for example, that Karl Ernst, the SA chief in the capital, had been a regular at the Eldorado and that one of his key Nazi underlings had been a drag performer there. As more and more Germans went Nazi, former patients who'd placed themselves on Hirschfeld's continuum of queerness were pledging their allegiance to Hitler even as their now-incriminating files sat in the institute archive. As Li would later recount, the Institute for Sexual Science "had the record of sexual type of [certain] Nazi leaders."

On May 12, Helmuth Klotz, the leaker of Röhm's love letters, showed up in the Reichstag cafeteria to take a meeting with a Social Democratic MP. When the legislator was called away for a vote, Klotz remained behind sipping his coffee. A moment later, three Nazi members materialized and cornered him. They were led by Edmund Heines, Röhm's deputy and, reputedly, his lover as well. The trio pounced, first slapping Klotz, then punching him, and finally beating him with a chair. A waiter jumped in to shield Klotz as several MPs tried to help. When the capitol police arrived, the Nazis turned their furor on the cops.

As news of the cafeteria riot reached the floor of parliament, police arrived to ensure order. Nazi MPs responded with shouts of "Heil Hitler!" and antisemitic slurs directed at the force's leader, Bernhard Weiss, who was Berlin's deputy police chief and the department's highest-ranking Jewish officer. In print, Goebbels relentlessly referred to Weiss as "Isidor," which was not his name, purely because Goebbels thought it sounded more Jewish than "Bernhard." As fascist MPs heckled him with cries of "Isidor!" and "Jew!" Weiss restored order.

For all the mailers and posters and newspaper exposés, German voters mostly shrugged off the scandal. What Röhm did in his private life, most Germans concluded, was his own business. Ironically, the German public, prepared by decades of activism and advocacy by Hirschfeld and his comrades, was now quite tolerant of homosexuality. The progressive left had unwittingly inoculated its enemies against morals charges even if charges of hypocrisy were still fully merited.

Hitler himself argued that what happens in Röhm's bedroom should stay in Röhm's bedroom. The SA "is not an institute for the moral education of genteel young ladies, but a formation of seasoned fighters," Hitler wrote in his official statement. "The sole purpose of any inquiry must be to ascertain whether or not [an] SA officer . . . is performing his official duties. . . . His private life cannot be an object of scrutiny unless it conflicts with basic principles of National Socialist ideology." Needless to say, this was further hypocrisy from a party that, in principle, opposed not only gay sex but queer desire itself.

Magnus could take little solace in having convinced so many of his fellow citizens that homosexuality was a normal part of the human sexual panorama. His country was collapsing. The rule of law was giving way to the rule of fists even in the Reichstag, the citadel of German democracy. What pained Magnus most was that his country no longer recognized him. According to Nazi ideology, on racial grounds, he himself was not German and never had been. Writing to an American friend three days after the Reichstag riot, Magnus expressed that not only was it unsafe to return to Germany "with its 13 million Hitler backers,"—he no longer even wanted to return. "I consider it beneath my dignity to live among a people who regard me as a 'foreigner,'" he wrote in his diary, even as he still referred to Germany as his "homeland" (*Heimat*).

Magnus's estimate that Hitler had thirteen million backers may have sounded hysterical to the American recipient of the letter, but elections that summer proved him right. When German voters went to the polls on July 31, 1932, nearly fourteen million of them voted Nazi—more than twice as many as had voted for the party two years earlier. In the new parliament, Hitler's party would be the largest by far.

In August, after receiving a particularly terrifying death threat—this one with a higher degree of specificity than usual and, likely, a local Austrian origin—Magnus decided to leave for Switzerland. According to Li's recollections, Magnus fled Vienna like a stowaway, lying flat on the floor of a hired car to escape detection.

In the climate back home, even the Berlin police force, long famous for its tolerance, was turning reactionary. Over the summer, under a new Berlin chief, Kurt Melcher, the force launched an "extensive campaign against Berlin's depraved nightlife," and, in October, ordered a "cessation of dancing of a homosexual nature" in public. Gay dance spots scrambled to skirt the new regulations by declaring themselves private clubs. A final grand ball was held down the street from the institute on December 2, 1932, hosted by the Hollandais Club, known for throwing lavish costume parties open to both gay men and lesbians. It was the ultimate "dance on the volcano"—the turn of phrase contemporary Germans use to refer to their Weimar era.

Over the border in Switzerland, Li and Magnus initially settled in Zurich, the country's German-speaking hub, and lost themselves in their work. As regulars at the University of Zurich library, Magnus continued writing his travelogue, *World Journey of a Sex Researcher*, with Li, now severed from his medical school in Vienna, serving as research assistant. Magnus was thankful to find a Swiss publisher willing to put the book out since the chance was close to nil in Germany. The book would be, in the words of one contemporary scholar, "Hirschfeld's account of embracing the world while losing his homeland." In September, Magnus and Li traveled to Czechoslovakia to attend the International Convention for Sexual Reform on a Scientific Basis, the organization Magnus had founded to take his activism global. Together mentor and mentee jointly delivered a paper on the continuum of human sexuality, presumably hoping it would be the beginning of a decades-long intellectual collaboration.

Back in Zurich, Magnus was constantly on edge. Absolutely anyone in the German-speaking world could be a Nazi spy. That winter, Magnus and Li decamped to Ascona, in the Italian-speaking south of the country. The lakeside resort town was becoming a magnet for exiled German leftists. Women's movement leader Helene Stöcker, who fled when the Nazis shuttered her organization, overlapped with her longtime ally in Ascona.

From this idyllic setting on the shores of Lake Maggiore, Magnus watched helplessly as the Weimar Republic he had done so much to birth and serve offed itself. The elections that November began as a minor setback for the Nazis, whose vote total dipped below twelve million. But in the political horse trading that ensued to create a coalition government, Hitler was made chancellor of Germany. He took office on January 30, 1933. Even with the Weimar constitution technically still in effect—and even with a gay man, Ernst Röhm, as arguably the second-most powerful man in the NSDAP—the Nazis launched an anti-gay "Campaign for a Clean Reich." Under the rule of law, gay publications still had a clear right to publish. But in the streets, as in the Reichstag, it was now the rule of fists. Publishers were too intimidated to print queer publications and newsstand owners too terrified to stock them. Squads of Nazi thugs began roaming the streets around Nollendorfplatz, the center of the city's trans nightlife, beating anyone whose gender presentation they disapproved of. Through threats and violence, over a dozen of the capital's most prominent queer gathering spaces were shuttered. Despite the constitution, all gay-rights organizations were banned.

On February 27, a fire engulfed the Reichstag. Hitler claimed it to be the launch event for a communist coup and used the fire as an excuse to request—and be granted—emergency powers. The ostensibly temporary emergency abrogated free speech rights, freedom of the press, the right to protest, the right to privacy in written and telephonic communications, the presumption of innocence, and the right of the accused to a public trial. On March 23, parliament voted away its powers to make Germany's laws and gave Hitler the authority to rule by decree. Only the beleaguered Social Democrats voted against it, the Communists having already been banned as a party and expelled from parliament. That very day, the leader of the Scientific Humanitarian Committee, Kurt Hiller, Magnus's protégé turned rival, was swept up in one of the Nazis' first roundups. Hiller was imprisoned in a series of slapdash prisons, including an abandoned brewery outside Berlin that had been requisitioned by Röhm's SA and hastily outfitted with holding pens and torture chambers. In the coming months, with increased funding and formalization, this site would be turned over to a rival Nazi paramilitary group, the SS (*Schutzstaffel*), and become one of the first concentration camps.

A few weeks into the dictatorship, life in the capital had been turned upside down. Anyone walking past what had been the Eldorado bar that spring would find it had been turned into the local SA headquarters. The murals of genderqueer cabaret performers had been expunged. In their place were swastikas and election campaign posters exhorting passersby to vote for Hitler and the Nazi Party—a big lie, since they would never hold another free and fair election. The overnight transformation of Berlin was too much for many. On March 30, a leading cabaret emcee and comedian killed himself. "For once, no joke," he wrote in his suicide note, "I am taking my own life [because] I cannot live in these times."

All over the city and beyond, Jewish-owned businesses were marked with crude graffiti instructing "Aryans" that it was racial treason to patronize "Semites." On April 7, any government employee who had even a single Jewish grandparent was abruptly fired (Great War veterans were, for a time, exempted). Civil society organizations soon drummed out their Jewish members. Painter Max Liebermann, an old ally of Hirschfeld's, was, at age eighty-six, expelled from the Prussian Academy of Arts despite years serving as honorary president in its headquarters by the Brandenburg Gate. Asked how this indignity felt, he quipped that it was particularly sad at his advanced age since "One can't gobble as much up as one would like to puke." The reports shocked even Magnus despite the innumerable forms of racial degradation he had witnessed on his world tour. As he wrote after hearing reports from Berlin, "the humiliation and debasement of the Jews grows by leaps and bounds day to day and is today almost worse than that of the negros in America."

Along with leftists, Social Democrats, and trade unionists, members of the queer community soon began disappearing from the streets of Berlin and other German locales—especially those whom the Nazis considered Jews by "race." Some of the disappeared, like Hiller, were clearly opponents of the regime, but others appeared to have been picked up at random—just friends, lovers, or exes whose names had happened to show up in the little black book of a regime target.

"Aryan" gays could avoid suspicion only by actively collaborating with the dictatorship. There was no shortage of collaborators. In the first three months of Hitler's rule, 1.6 million Germans of all sexual orientations joined the Nazi Party, dwarfing its pretakeover membership rolls. By summer, the size of the paramilitary SA had more than doubled under Ernst Röhm's new rule allowing any "patriotically-minded" German man to join up.

As one contemporary queer German historian explains, there were initially "many homosexuals who believed they could come to an arrangement with the Nazis." In the spring of 1933, Christopher Isherwood was stunned to recognize one of the uniformed youths enforcing the boycott of Jewish family businesses at the Nathan Israel Department Store. The young Nazi was one of the teenage hustlers he'd known at the Cozy Corner bar. Making the situation even more surreal and horrifying, Isherwood was also friends with Wilfrid Israel, the gay scion of the family that had built the store. Even more shocking, Ruth Roellig, who had written the lesbian guide to Berlin in league with Magnus, began penning an antisemitic novel, cozying up to the regime that had banned her guidebook and destroyed the queer Berlin it celebrated.

At the Institute for Sexual Science, SA stormtroopers were soon making regular visits. Answering directly to Röhm, they'd been sent on a search-and-destroy mission to cull from the archives questionnaires completed by prominent Nazis. The stormtroopers also sought Hirschfeld himself, demanding to know his whereabouts. In their efforts, Hitler's henchmen were aided by a small clique of "Aryan" institute staffers who began collaborating with the new regime, in particular one administrator who now came to work each day wearing a swastika lapel pin. Most were motivated by self-preservation, but some sympathized with the masculinist wing of the gay movement. Dr. Erwin Gohrbandt, who had worked with Dr. Levy-Lenz on gender-affirmation surgeries at the institute, became a Luftwaffe staff doctor and is alleged to have been a participant in sadistic medical experiments at Dachau. Luckily for Magnus, none of these turncoat employees knew his precise location in Switzerland. Staffers who remained loyal to the institute's mission began secretly smuggling key museum holdings out of the country.

In despair, Magnus admitted to himself that he'd be in exile forever. As he wrote that April, "For a freedom-loving person of Jewish descent it seems to me that life in Germany, if one is not utterly forced into it, is a moral impossibility. I have personally resigned myself to the idea of never seeing Germany, my homeland, again, as much as I suffer from it emotionally."

On May 7, less than three weeks after Magnus penned this letter, Karl Giese showed up in Switzerland. He was distraught. The previous day, he told Magnus, the institute had been "raped." There was really no other way to put it.

In hindsight, Karl told him, the attack had really begun on the night of May 5 when the Nazis posted a guard in front of the institute. Early the next morning, the *Berliner Lokal-Anzeiger*, a Nazi-aligned newspaper, announced that this would be the day the libraries would be cleansed of "books of un-German spirit." This nationwide campaign, it explained, would begin with the most reviled trove of all: the archive of the Institute for Sexual Science.

Before the republic imploded, news that took place during the day would be reported in the following day's newspapers. Now, increasingly, future events got reported in advance. In the top-down society that Hitler ruled by decree, major events were preplanned. Tipped off by the newspaper coverage that the institute was about to be raided, at dawn staffers hastily gathered unpublished manuscripts and other irreplaceable items. They planned to spirit them out only to find themselves stopped at the front door by the Nazi guard.

At 9:30 a.m., a line of trucks drove down the edge of the Tiergarten. Each was filled with young men and strung with banners: "German Students March Against Un-German Spirit" and "Fight Against Un-German Trash and Smut." The trucks stopped in front of the institute and roughly a hundred teens emerged lining up with military precision. Each wore an identical white short-sleeved shirt, dark slacks, and Hitler Youth haircut—buzzed on the sides, longer on top, meticulously combed.

As the brass band which accompanied them struck up a march, the mob approached the stately building's entrance. The institute hadn't opened yet for the day, and a terrified housekeeper nervously cracked the door. She was met with a barrage of abuse and demands to hand over Hirschfeld.

"Dr. Magnus Hirschfeld is not home," she insisted. "You can search the whole house, from top to bottom." Then the teens, all students from the Nazi's Institute for Physical Fitness, stormed the building and the rape of the institute commenced.

Smashing through locked doors, they rampaged from room to room, knocking over bookshelves and ransacking filing cabinets. In the clinic, marauders smashed medical equipment with a mop handle. In the archive, invaders poured ink over manuscripts, rendering them unreadable. They dumped so many files and photographs on the floors that they rose waist-high in some corners.

Among the plunder was Hirschfeld's prized German/English/French Wall of Sexual Transitions exhibition display. With its multilingual cosmopolitanism and scientific claims that sexual orientation and gender were continua, the display was a show-and-tell refutation of the student's fascist politics of us and them. It stood in silent rebuke to the marauders, as well, suggesting that even this butch all-male revue of strapping paramilitary youths in their matching get-ups, fastidiously coiffed hair, and brass backup band was, maybe, if you squinted, just a little bit queer.

Most indelible in the minds of the institute staffers who witnessed the attack was the broken glass. It was everywhere. Cases holding rare finds—the sexual amulets and artifacts Magnus had painstakingly collected from all over the world—were smashed to pieces. Framed photographs of trans clinic patients, with their sheepish "before" and proud "after" photographs, were ripped from the walls. Exterior windows shattered as students inside the building tossed pillaged items to peers outside waiting below. With Hirschfeld absent, the raiders seized the next best thing: a large bronze bust of his head crafted by German-Jewish sculptor Harald Isenstein for his sixtieth birthday. They carted it off as a trophy.

At noon, the teens reassembled in front of the ransacked institute, glass crunching under their boots, and unfurled a huge swastika flag as the band played on. In unison, they screamed slogans against the "un-German spirit" in front of a museum that people from all over the world had long considered so quintessentially German that no visit to Germany was complete without taking it in.

That afternoon, more trucks arrived, this time ominously empty. A small detachment of SA stormtroopers emerged, experts tasked to sort through the plunder and seize the most valuable items. Proceeding methodically from room to room, from the piles on the floor, the group culled banned books on the blacklist—works by Hirschfeld, Freud, Oscar Wilde, August Bebel, Margaret Sanger, and others. They cast a wide net, presuming books guilty unless proven innocent, and seizing over ten thousand volumes, more than half of the institute's holdings. Photographs of patients, staffers, and institute allies were taken as were some completed sexuality questionnaires and medical files.

By the time the stormtroopers finished loading their trucks, they had seized, according to *The New York Times*'s report, "about half a ton of books, pamphlets, photographs, charts and . . . slides" from an institution "which has long been a place of interest for some tourists as well as a centre for scientific research."

As the vehicles pulled away, Karl and the other institute staffers wondered what the hoodlums were going to do with it all. The next edition of *Der Angriff* (*The Attack*), the Berlin Nazi Party newspaper edited by the new propaganda minister, Joseph Goebbels, explained it—as was now typical—in advance. The article, "Energetic Action Against a Poison Shop; German Students Fumigate the 'Sexual Science Institute,'" read:

> Detachment X of the German student organization yesterday occupied the "Sexual Science Institute," which was controlled by

> the Jew Magnus Hirschfeld. This institute, which tried to shelter behind a scientific cloak and was always protected during the fourteen years of Marxist rule by the authorities of that period, was an unparalleled breeding-ground of dirt and filth, as the results of the search have proved beyond question. A whole lorry-load of pornographic pictures and writings as well as documents and registers have been confiscated. . . . The criminal police will have to deal with a part of the material found; another part of it will be publicly burnt.

In hindsight, all of it had been preplanned. A month before, on April 6, the German Students' Press and Propaganda Office announced that "In view of the shameless horror stories being propagated by Judaism abroad"—a reference to German-Jewish refugees in free countries telling the media why they had left their homeland—"Germany's students are planning a four-week . . . campaign against the subversive Jewish spirit to promote nationally conscious thought and action in German writing. The campaign will begin on 12 April, when twelve Theses Against Un-German Ideas will be pinned to public boards, and it will end on 10 May with public rallies in all German university towns."

In keeping with the new system, the prophesies that appeared in the official party press all came to pass. As announced, on May 10, four days after the raid, an assembly of SA stormtroopers, accompanied by a crowd of forty thousand, gathered in the drizzly chill on Opernplatz, the square between Berlin's oldest opera theater and the columned library of Frederick Wilhelm University. In the center of the plaza, where crowds once gathered after lectures by luminaries and Nobel laureates, the Nazis had erected a wooden pyre where over ten thousand volumes from the institute's library would be burned as the seized bronze bust was paraded around to cries of "Burn Now, Magnus Hirschfeld!" Smaller book burnings were held in college towns all over Germany that night, thirty-four in all.

In the coming days, Giese's firsthand rendering of the rape was seconded in press accounts all over the world on the book-burning barbarism in Berlin. Later that week, Magnus wrote to his allies from Switzerland:

> My dear friends . . .
>
> I don't know how much you already know about the terrible fate which has struck its blows against our Institute, my collaborators and myself. You have probably read something about it in your newspapers, as I can see from your letters to me.
>
> In the last week the government has dissolved our Institute, has taken by force the greatest part of our library and many other items, and willfully destroyed them. Most of the books, including foreign literature, were removed with violence, and four days later everything was thrown onto an auto-da-fé and burnt to cinders . . .
>
> Karl Giese, who saw with his own eyes everything which went on in the Institute, has come to me partly because he wanted to inform me of the tragedy, and partly for his own safety.

Magnus, like so many other writers, reached for historical metaphors to describe what had befallen modern Germany. Magnus, called it an "auto-da-fé," the ritualized burning at the stake of Jews, gays, "witches," and other heretics in Spain under the Inquisition. Gifted German-Jewish newspaperman Joseph Roth, in exile in Paris, chose the same metaphor, calling the book-burning "The Auto-da-Fé of the Mind." To other left-wing refugees, the events back home reminded them of Old Russia lost in medieval fog under the tsars. Some dubbed the book burning a "pogrom against advanced literature," using the Russian word for an antisemitic riot.

But to the editors of *Time* magazine in the US, the book burning appeared not as some return to a wretched past but as something out of an unprecedented and even more frightening future. They told their readers that the "pride of the book burners was the seizure and destruction of the files of famed Sexologist Dr. Magnus Hirschfeld, who has analyzed many an abnormal Nazi leader in his Institute for Sex Science." Of course, Magnus didn't consider queer Nazis to be "abnormal" in their sexuality at all, only barbaric in their politics. *Time* headlined its story on the Berlin book burning, "Bibliocaust," a neologism built from a then-obscure word for complete destruction by fire: "holocaust."

Reeling from the destruction of his institute, Magnus, in Switzerland, confronted another crisis: his passport was about to expire. When he'd set off for New York in 1930, its expiration date, May 18, 1933, had seemed far off, all but irrelevant. But now, with the Nazi takeover, he knew the German authorities would never renew his travel permit. They wanted him home for a show trial.

He had just one more week to choose his permanent place of exile, and he hastily weighed his options. Paris was becoming the default destination for anti-Nazi German exiles, and Magnus decided to join them. With a few days to spare before the deadline, Li, Karl, and Magnus drove to the French-Swiss frontier. Fearing the border guards might comply with a German extradition request—the Nazis had demanded Magnus be returned to Germany to answer for amorphous "corruption" charges—he decided on the spur of the moment to sneak across the border with a Swiss friend even though his passport was still valid. Li crossed legally at the official checkpoint and once safely in France, the couple reunited, and Li drove them on to Paris. Karl remained behind in Switzerland for the rest of the month, hoping the natural beauty of the lakes and mountains would help him overcome the trauma of the raid. Then he would move on to Paris to reconstitute the partnership.

In the French capital, Magnus initially stayed in a hotel by the Quai d'Orsay and then got an apartment fronting the Champs de Mars near the Eiffel Tower. As more and more leftists, liberals, avant-garde artists, and Jews of all levels of observance—including none at all—fled Germany, Paris became the center of the German émigré world. Between the Nazi takeover in January 1933 and that summer, 25,000 Germans moved to France. Yet even there, Magnus worried about his safety. He told friends not to send him mail at his hotel but instead to reach him through a neighbor, a French-Jewish gynecologist and activist for the legalization of birth control.

Not long after moving to Paris, Magnus slipped away to the cinema seeking some escapism. As usual, before the feature presentation, a newsreel briefly chronicled world events. Running through the latest developments over the border in Germany, a reporter rattled off the news in French, a language Hirschfeld couldn't comprehend. On screen, the grainy black-and-white celluloid struggled to depict the sharp contrast between the dark, drizzly Berlin night and the hot white of the flames. But Magnus immediately understood what he was seeing. His heart sank with recognition. As students and paramilitary troops enthusiastically hurled volumes into the pyre, Hirschfeld watched his archive immolated. He even spotted the bronze bust of his head, his sixtieth-birthday gift, as it was paraded around on a pike.

The camera panned Opernplatz and then cut to a close-up of Joseph Goebbels overseeing the proceedings. Dressed in a trench coat that swallowed his thin frame, the gaunt 35-year-old propaganda minister, who held a PhD in German studies, stood at a lectern, draped in a swastika flag and set with microphones.

"The age of effete Jewish intellectualism has come to an end," the spectral Nazi intoned in Hirschfeld's native tongue, with superfluous French newsreel subtitles below. "In the last fourteen years, comrades, as you have been forced in silent shame to suffer the humiliations of the [Weimar] Republic, the libraries became filled with trash and filth. [Now] the past is lying in flames."

In the darkened theater, Hirschfeld wept, descending into what he termed "the deepest psychic shock." His life's work was burned to ashes before his eyes. And he could never go home.

Following the Opernplatz bibliocaust, the authorities seized the Institute for Sexual Science without compensation. Over the course of the Third Reich, the former institute building would house several fascist organizations, thinktanks, and government departments including the Institute of Studies Relating to the Jewish Question, the General Association of German Anti-Communist Organizations, and the State Academy of the Public Health Service, which used the institute lecture hall for public "racial hygiene" talks on the dangers of "miscegenation."

Jarringly, becoming a public enemy in his homeland made Magnus even more of a celebrity in Paris. That summer, the glossy weekly *Voilà* put him on the cover. For the photo shoot, Magnus, seated in a dark suit and natty cravat, pored over an illustrated scientific volume while Li, in a shimmering silk *changshan*, a modern take on the formalwear of Imperial China, stood at his side. In the staged scene, Li points to a photograph in the pages of the book with one hand while his other remains coyly hidden in shadow, perhaps touching the back of Magnus's arm. The resulting *Voilà* tableau and its headline—"Love and Science"—perfectly captured the hidden-in-plain-sight nature of their relationship.

In exile, German intellectuals did their best to resurrect the life of the mind the Nazis had burned out of Berlin. Magnus hoped to found a new iteration of the Institute for Sexual Science in Paris and tasked Karl Giese with leading this effort. But the institute's mission had always relied on Magnus's vast global collection of materials. It was the sex toys that brought the crowds through the door; they were the lure for the tourists who, once inside, could be pushed to reconsider their positions on gay rights, trans rights, birth control, abortion, indeed the whole nature of human sexuality. With enough time, effort, and funding, Karl and Magnus might be able to rebuild the research center and the clinic. But the institute had always been more than that. The meager remnants of the collection that Giese salvaged and the few pieces that Magnus managed to buy back at auction through friendly straw buyers weren't enough. Their makeshift *Institut des Sciences Sexologiques* drew few visitors and closed its doors soon after opening.

A more successful endeavor was the Library of Burnt Books, whose opening Magnus led on the one-year anniversary of the Opernplatz book burning, May 10, 1934, in the heart of Paris's Left Bank. The library stocked copies of the volumes consigned to the flames all over Germany and made them available to the reading public in German, French, and other languages. The text on the library wall detailed the level of thought control now being imposed in Germany. "May 10 [1933] was merely a symbolic act," it explained.

> It was about ten days later that the great cleansing of the public and of some private libraries took place, when over 2,000,000 volumes were taken away as waste paper. A large number of books, though not officially on the index, are no longer available at many German public libraries, and are not easily bought. A few copies of the prohibited books are still kept at the main public libraries, but only in what is called the *Giftschrank* (the poison chest), and those, who wish to consult them must produce evidence that they 'intend to write against them.' "

On Nazi Germany's official blacklist of banned books, the *List of Harmful and Undesirable Literature*, the entry for Magnus Hirschfeld was devastatingly succinct: "all writings."

Knowing his travelogue, *World Journey of a Sex Researcher*, issued in German in 1933 by a Swiss publisher near Zurich, could no longer be accessed in Germany, except perhaps in a "poison chest," Magnus worked to get it published in English translation. Fortuitously, he found publishers in both London and New York. Magnus was unsurprised to learn that the English translations would be issued under alternate titles befitting the puritanical Anglosphere. The British edition would be primly called *Women East and West* and the American, simply, *Men and Women*, pushing the very binary Magnus was trying to question. A subsequent US edition would be called *Curious Sex Customs of the Far East*, a title that fully contradicted the open-minded attitude of the text within.

Even knowing that his future writings could be published only abroad, Magnus kept at it. Making the most of his freedom in France, Magnus began writing a book-length refutation of Nazi race theory. He would call his book *Racismus* (*Racism*). Much as he had two decades before in *Die Transvestiten* (*Transvestites*), he now coined a new vocabulary (*racism*, *racist*, *anti-racist*) in a groundbreaking study.

Like so much of Magnus's output over his career, *Racism* would grow directly from his life. While *World Journey of a Sex Researcher* had sprung from his research on his trip, *Racism* would be the product of his personal experiences of being in an interracial relationship and being exiled from his homeland on racial grounds. He'd set out on his world tour to study gender, but it had unintentionally become a study of race.

It began in America where Magnus, zipping up to Harlem on the subway, was confronted for the first time in four decades by the country's adherence to what it called the "color line." Then in Honolulu, he discovered a much more honest and enlightened racial system only to learn that educated mainland Americans dismissed it as "racial chaos." In the foreign concessions of Shanghai, a chance meeting and romance with Li Shiu Tong led Magnus to witness the discrimination that tormented people with non-European roots all over the globe. Just a short walk from Li's medical school, Magnus watched him get thrown out of a club for being Chinese in, of all places, China. By the end of his trip, something similar was happening to Magnus. He was being excluded from his homeland on racial grounds, told that on account of his Jewish ethnicity he had never been German and never could be.

In *Racism*, for the first time, Magnus would have to write openly as a member of a minority group. His Jewish background was common knowledge even as he continued to keep his homosexuality quiet. Now he would write explicitly against the absurd assumption that had dogged him his entire career: that a member of a minority group cannot write credibly about their own oppression. He engaged the issue head-on, writing, "It is hard to be dispassionate when one is oneself numbered among the many thousands who have fallen victim to the practical realization of this [racial] theory; but I am sure that an objective exposition and study are indispensable, and I trust that my readers will find me fair and unprejudiced." He'd surely formulated this thought decades ago when penning his first gay-rights pamphlet but never before voiced it publicly.

Hirschfeld's conception of race naturally echoed his theories of sexual orientation and gender since he had formulated them all through the same process: moving from individual cases to an overarching concept. Early in his career, Magnus had attempted to divide people by sexual orientation into three categories—straight, gay, and bisexual—but as he discovered a panorama of gradations, the divisions collapsed. He'd found the same spectrum in looking at masculinity and femininity. Now he applied these insights to race.

As he examined the history of racial theory, he looked askance at various attempts to discern and define some supposedly fixed number of races. The number kept growing. In the eighteenth century, German philosopher Immanuel Kant claimed there were four races—the White, the Black, the Hindu, and the Mongolian. But as more corners of the world were explored, more peoples were discovered who did not neatly fit into the Kantian categories. Despite mounting evidence, scientists remained wedded to the idea that humans belonged to distinct, often gradable, groups. Less than a century later, German scientist Ernst Haeckel proposed that Kant had been grossly mistaken; there were, in fact, thirty-six races.

Scholars sparred over where the borders between these races lay. As race theorists went from seeing Europe as a unified continent of

"Whites" to seeing it as a balkanized continent of "Nordics," "Alpines," and "Mediterraneans," the question of where one race ended and the next began—and which trait was the giveaway—confounded experts. Race science began to resemble physics before Einstein, when scientists were convinced that there must be some unmoving substance in the universe—ether—and puzzled over why it was so hard to find.

What if instead of searching for the correct number of races, Magnus proposed, we admit that race is a continuum? As Magnus wrote, "From a biologist's outlook, all human being are hybrids, persons of 'mixed' descent from forbears endowed with differing qualities. We are none of us the fruit of what [botanists call] a 'pure line,' sprung from creatures propagated by self-fertilisation." Despite the protests of racists who claimed that mixed-race "mulattos" were sterile, "all human stocks can interbreed freely and produce fertile offspring," Magnus wrote. Recapitulating the prophetic (now DNA-backed) claim he'd first made in his 1919 pamphlet "What Unites and Divides the Human Race," Magnus explained that all humans are "alike in respect of ninety-nine per cent of their attributes; and that, as regards the residual one percent of differences and contrasts, these are far more individual than racial. . . . Especially are the qualities we esteem or dislike, individual rather than racial."

Faced with this continuum, only by picking out some random hereditary trait and deeming it important can humans be categorized into various races—"as many varieties as you please," Magnus noted. Choosing the border between the two chosen categories was itself an arbitrary decision—a one-drop rule or a one-grandparent rule? Hair color or eye color or skin color? Head shape or shoe size? A brown paper bag test? Well, then, which brown paper bag? The binary itself was created by an arbitrary decision. As with sexuality, the categories tell us more about the categorizer than the categorized.

When Nazi race theorist Alfred Rosenberg, in a speech to the party faithful at Nuremberg, declared racial science to be the greatest discovery of the age, Magnus countered that Rosenberg "was confusing invention with discovery." For Magnus, race was an invention—a manufactured human concept forcefully grafted onto a natural world on which it can never fit. The racists had not discovered race; they had invented race.

Fortuitously—and ironically—perhaps the clearest evidence that "no people constitutes a racial unit" was Hirschfeld's native Germany. Located in the heart of Europe, it had few natural boundaries. This accessibility to outsiders had rendered Germany's population remarkably mixed. Anyone walking the streets of a German city would encounter locals with hair ranging from jet black to ice blond, eyes of every shade, and skin ranging from so fair that it burns in even the mildest sun to so dark as to be impervious. As Magnus observed, "perhaps no race on the European continent is more of a hotch-potch than that which is called the German." The Nazis' Third Reich is a "mishmash . . . thanks to its central position and to its having been repeatedly overrun by its neighbours."

By the same token, among Germany's Jews, one found the same phenotypic range, including plenty of individuals with the ostensibly telltale "Aryan" blond hair and blue eyes. Magnus's medical school faculty mentor, Rudolf Virchow, had conducted a study of German Jews and found that nearly a third had fair hair and nearly half had light-colored eyes. The reasons for this were no mystery. Jews had been dispersed out of the Middle East in ancient times and had lived in the German lands for more than a millennium and a half.

Since the French Revolution and the coming of Napoleon, Jewish and non-Jewish Germans had been free to intermarry and had done so often. In Berlin, early-twentieth-century records showed that one third of Jews married non-Jews. The ratio was similar in Düsseldorf. Data from Hamburg just before the Nazi takeover showed that most local Jews—over 70 percent—were marrying non-Jews. But even before that, Magnus believed, the mixing—both acknowledged and unacknowledged—had been common. In the supposedly racially pure Middle Ages, German rabbinical authorities permitted Jewish women traveling outside their communities to don nun's habits if they feared being raped by Christian mobs—an indication of how common such sexual violence must have been. Indeed, in the face of so many pregnancies of unclear paternity, Judaism flipped from a religion based on patrilineal descent to one based on matrilineal descent. Anti-Jewish persecution also led to forced conversions of Jews as well as Jews converting to Christianity to escape prejudice in a bigoted society. And even before the arrival of Napoleon, not every German city was equally strict about keeping Jews and Christians segregated. Berlin, notably, never had a ghetto. Instead, Berlin's Jews sorted themselves by class, with wealthier Jewish families living in wealthy neighborhoods among wealthy Christian neighbors and poorer Jewish families living in poor neighborhoods among Christians of modest means.

Having some fractional Jewish ancestry, Magnus speculated, was nearly universal among German Christians. As he wondered aloud in *Racism*, anticipating twenty-first-century genetic tests and the ensuing family freakouts, "Should a trustworthy blood-test ever be devised for the recognition of racial origins . . . the Antisemites would not be gratified with the results."

All over the world, Magnus had found the same phenomenon—rampant and evident mixing being denied to construct a fictitious and pernicious racial binary, between a majoritarian in-group and a minority pariah community. In their frantic attempt to halt centuries of mixing, Magnus observed, Americans had famously invented the "one-drop rule." As he wrote, "in the southern States of the American Union, where colour prejudice is exceedingly strong among the Whites, intermarriage between Whites and persons with even a trace of Negro blood (betrayed by a violet tinge beneath the finger-nails and blue circles round the eyes) is persistently discountenanced." In South Africa, too, Magnus noted in *Racism*, this prohibition was written into the legal code. In 1927, the Union of South Africa made consensual relationships across the color line punishable by five years in prison for the man and four years for the woman.

In Hitler's new Germany, the Reich began taking American-inspired measures to prohibit marriages between "Aryans" and "non-Aryans." But even the Nazis lamented that this policy had come too late, admitting that after generations of mixing, there was little "racial integrity" left. As Nazi geneticist Fritz Lenz had conceded in his 1931 book *Human Selection and Racial Hygiene*, "our main practical problem is that of marriage between Germans and Jews. Neither of these groups is racially pure."

Since Nazi ideology viewed race mixing as a plague of liberalism's baseless belief in human equality, the new regime declared that there had never been any race mixing in Germany before Napoleon and his French invaders imposed liberalism on Germany in the early nineteenth century. Defining race mixing as a relatively recent phenomenon, the Nazis decreed that anyone who could trace their Aryan racial purity back to New Year's Day, 1800, would be assumed to be purely Aryan. Every German was ordered to create an Ancestry Passport, a genealogical table tracing their roots. As an official from the Racial Office of the Ministry for Home Affairs explained in the *Racial Observer*, "The burden of proof is not ours. We regard as non-Aryan all persons who cannot show satisfactory evidence of pure Aryan ancestry as far back as January 1, 1800. That date was chosen because prior to it there were no mixed relationships."

What the Nazis could not deny was that, in their own time, interracial relationships—which they dubbed "racial defilements" (*Rassenschanden*)—were common. To halt the open mixing that had swept Germany, the Nazis not only banned mixed marriages, they broke up many marriages already on the books through a vast national program of forced annulments. The Nazis were surprisingly lenient with Christians who had entered into such unions. In *Racism*, Magnus quotes extensively from one of the many court decisions annulling the marriages of "Aryans" who'd wed Jews before 1933. In this case, the husband was a card-carrying member of the Nazi Party. "We [must] assume that the petitioner, when he entered into this marriage, did not realize the essential significance of the fact that the woman he was marrying was a Jewess," the court explained. "Like the great majority of our people at that date, he considered that when a German married a Jewess this meant no more than that husband and wife professed different religions [since in] the liberal system of thought, whose eradication has only become possible since the rise of National Socialism to power, it was usual to insist upon the equality of all races, and to point to racial chaos as the ideal."

Going forward, there would be zero tolerance for relationships between "Aryans" and "Semites." In the city of Dortmund, the police launched a dating crackdown on "girls of Aryan blood [who] have danced with Jewish partners." Even this fanatical police force conceded that their effort came over a century too late, but they still vowed to do their best to prevent "any further mingling of German blood with Jewish elements." Even the Prussian justice minister himself admitted that German Christians and German Jews were already so thoroughly mixed that the two could not always be distinguished by sight. Facing this difficulty, the justice minister declared it an "aggravating circumstance" when "racial treason is attended by willful concealment that one of the persons concerned is of alien blood or race, or when it has been achieved under false pretences."

German Jews often had a bitter laugh at the race-based state's inability to distinguish the supposed "races." A Jewish student leafing through an illustrated Nazi "racial science" textbook that touted perfect specimens of each race stumbled across a photo that looked just like his cousin Selma. Underneath, it was labeled "Nordic."

In modern Germany, it sometimes appeared that the physical stereotypes had been fully flipped. In a high-profile murder trial Magnus had attended before his exile, he realized that the thirty-two Germans in the courtroom were evenly split: sixteen Christians and sixteen Jews. Ironically, Magnus noted, on the whole, it was the Christians who were shorter and darker haired, despite stereotypes to the contrary. In the courtroom, the Christians comprised the three defendants and the witnesses while the Jews constituted the attorneys and the media. The distinction between the two groups, if one was to be drawn, was a class distinction, not a racial distinction.

Nazism, with its fascist alchemy, transformed class tensions into racial tensions. To turn a social democracy into a fascist dictatorship, Magnus explained, the Nazis needed race. How else to replace a politics of universal rights with a politics of us and them? Anger that in the depths of the Depression might have been directed against conservative industrial oligarchs and the independently wealthy descendants of medieval noblemen was deflected by convincing the German masses that their society was not controlled by these wealthy heirs but by shadowy racial Others who had taken over their professions and cultural institutions. It was all quite explicit. "Race war instead of class war" ("*Rassenkampf statt Klassenkampf*") was an official Nazi slogan. Magnus called it their "pithy formula [and] momentous watchword."

As Magnus crafted his manuscript in exile, he knew that trying to publish an openly anti-racist text in German would be fruitless. No publisher in Nazi Germany could issue it and even German language publishers in Austria and Switzerland were now too nervous to take on such a project. To add to these troubles, there was now a personal crisis with Karl: that summer, he got arrested for having sex in a bathhouse. Even in France, where consensual gay sex had been legal since the Revolution, public sex remained a crime, and bathhouses were considered public. Karl was sentenced to three months in prison and then, as a criminal alien, his visa was revoked. Magnus, who had always tolerated, even encouraged, Karl's sexual explorations outside of their relationship, didn't blame Karl for what he called "an unlucky circumstance." Instead, he railed against "the most acute injustice [that] Karl was expelled [over] a meaningless trifle," a victimless crime. While Magnus had been growing ever closer to Li—the pair had gone to London together in 1933 and to Venice in early 1934—all three had been making a life together in Paris. Now this was no longer an option. Released from prison in October and expelled from France, Karl opted for Vienna. On the day of Karl's exile, Li, looking characteristically sharp in a Parisian beret, and Magnus, looking characteristically rumpled in an ill-fitting topcoat, saw him off.

By the time of Karl's sendoff, Germany had become less safe for queer people than at any time since the Middle Ages. As Hitler worked to consolidate his power, he'd come to view the gay leader of the SA paramilitary, Ernst Röhm, as a rival and a threat. Now that the party had taken over the state and commanded the nation's army, there was no longer a need for an armed wing of the party.

Hitler initially planned to merge the SA into the German army, but the military was resistant. Under the Treaty of Versailles, Germany's army was capped at one hundred thousand troops while SA membership had now ballooned to over two million. Who exactly would be merging with whom, the army brass wondered nervously. To push back against the merger proposal, they ingratiated themselves with Hitler by incorporating the swastika into the army's official insignia and dismissing their Jewish soldiers. Some also smeared Röhm for his sexual orientation. As one general, Walther von Brauchitsch, sneered, "Re-armament is too serious and militarily important to be left to hoodlums and homosexuals like Captain Röhm." Hitler had long tolerated Röhm's gayness, often chalking it up to his time spent working overseas in South America. (The *Führer* believed the tropics could turn you gay.) But now, facing the resistance from his new generals, Hitler changed plans. Rather than merge the two forces, he would sideline the SA and have the German army swear loyalty to him personally.

On the night of July 2, 1934, the leaders of the SA, including Ernst Röhm and his deputy, Edmund Heines, were targeted in a series of overnight raids by the rival SS paramilitary force. Initially formed to serve as Hitler's personal bodyguards, the vicious expanded force rather unsubtly used the skull and crossbones as its official insignia. Numerous SA officials, perhaps eighty-five in all, were arrested and executed in short order including twelve who were sitting Nazi members of parliament. According to Hitler's driver, who dished after the war on what had become known as the Night of the Long Knives, the *Führer*, whip in hand, personally arrested Röhm. As for Heines, Hitler ordered him to put his clothes on and come out, which he did with "an 18-year-old fair-haired boy mincing in front of him."

After the killings, Hitler highlighted his victims' sexuality, presenting the raid as a war on groomers and the purge of a lavender menace that had reached the highest levels of the Nazi Party. Hitler's agents spread rumors that Röhm and his associates had been discovered in the raids on their homes in bed with men, boys ("catamites"), even each other. In the wake of the executions, Hitler scolded, "I expect all SA leaders to help to preserve . . . its capacity as a pure and cleanly institution. In particular, I should like every mother to be able to allow her son to join the SA, [the] Party, and Hitler Youth without fear that he may become morally corrupted in their ranks. I therefore require all SA commanders to take the utmost pains to ensure that offenses under Paragraph 175 are met by immediate expulsion of the culprit from the SA and the Party."

Homophobia was mere pretext for the Night of the Long Knives, a convenient cover for a power grab. But in the raids' aftermath, it became official policy. With Ernst Röhm dead, his rival, Heinrich Himmler, the fanatically homophobic SS leader and chief of the Racial Office, was unleashed. Himmler saw homosexuality as a grave threat to society, "a symptom of dying races [that caused] every achievement . . . in a state, to collapse." He pinned the Weimar Republic's weakness, chaos, and inability to restore Germany to global dominance on its vast openly gay population. Some gays, Himmler believed, could be cured through reeducation in a concentration camp but others, some of his own SS men and Hitler Youth leaders among them, were lost causes, best "shot while trying to escape," the Nazis's bureaucratic euphemism for murdered in custody.

Soon Himmler was scheming to make Paragraph 175 more draconian. The new Nazi version enacted the following year lengthened prison sentences and criminalized gay sexual intent even when no contact had taken place. Under this new decree, unconsummated desire—thoughtcrime as expressed in love letters or tapped phone calls—was deemed a violation of the law. Under Himmler's watch, forty-eight men who had been previously arrested under Paragraph 175, convicted, punished, and released were rearrested and deported to Dachau. In December 1934, newspapers reported two thousand arrests in a series of raids on gay bars and clubs. Shortly thereafter, Himmler launched the Reich Central Office for the Combating of Homosexuality and Abortion to help enforce the new Paragraph 175. Under the regime, fifty thousand men would be arrested for violations.

With homophobic propaganda increasing under Himmler's influence, Hirschfeld was yet again trotted out in conspiracy theories about the left-wing Jewish plot to undermine Germany from within by blurring traditional gender roles and turning the Fatherland queer. Shortly after the Night of the Long Knives, Hitler publicly raged that Weimar-era women's liberation had been an invention of "Jewish intellectuals" and was fundamentally un-German. A Nazi pamphlet featured a grotesque caricature of Magnus with the caption: "He introduced the oriental vice [homosexuality] into Germany." (The reference to the orient flagged his "Semitic" origins in the Middle East, where none of his forebears had lived for the previous two millennia.) Magnus responded with bitter humor to the charges: "But for [me], I gather, there would have been no homosexual scandal at [Kaiser Wilhelm II's] court . . . and no Röhm, Hitler's chief of staff and oldest friend, whose [execution] was excused by the chancellor . . . on the ground of Röhm's 'notorious sexual perversion.' "

With the Nazis adding virulent homophobia to their fanatical antisemitism, Magnus hunkered down for permanent exile. He had limited options. The Nazi government had revoked his citizenship rendering him a stateless person. Attempting to cross any international border was now a risk. Even entering a sympathetic country would entail a rigamarole of calling and writing diplomats, visiting embassies and consulates, and waiting for bespoke documents to be drawn up in lieu of a valid passport. Facing these realities, Magnus gave a final Paris lecture, at the Sorbonne, and went with Li to Nice on the French Riviera.

The couple took a hotel room facing the sea over the palm-lined promenade, as Magnus considered a few possibilities. The couple could return to Shanghai, where neither passport nor visa was required for entry, and no one could be turned away. The cosmopolitan Chinese port city was already becoming a haven for Germans rendered stateless by their "race" and/or their politics. From Shanghai, Magnus surmised, he could likely get authorization to move to British-run Hong Kong, Li's hometown. But tensions were rising between Li and his father, who resented his move to Europe and, possibly, his gayness. Li was not eager to return to China.

Joining the Zionist community in British-controlled Palestine held little appeal. Magnus's intellectual opposition to the construction of ostensibly pure ethnic communities was now reinforced by his personal life. He was partnered with two gentiles, neither of whom could ever be full-fledged members of any future Jewish state no matter how secular or queer friendly.

Moving to the United States posed other challenges. Li liked the idea. He wanted to continue his medical studies but not in French—he'd learned enough foreign languages for one lifetime. Both Harvard and Columbia medical schools looked good to him. But, for Magnus, money would be an issue. Given Li's strained relationship with his father, living off his partner's family wealth sounded as uncertain as it was unappetizing. And when Magnus inquired about arranging another US lecture tour, he found little interest. On his first trip, he could plausibly be packaged as an anodyne "marriage therapist." But after the headlines in *Time* magazine and the newsreel coverage of the raid on his institute, that was no longer possible. He had been outed as, if not necessarily gay himself, at the very least, a controversial champion of queer rights. No American speaking agent would touch him. And George Sylvester

Viereck, the gay German-born New Yorker who had so savvily represented and booked Magnus on his earlier tour as the "Einstein of Sex," was dead to him. Viereck, long an admirer of Hitler, was now a hardcore Nazi. He'd recently addressed a fascist rally of twenty thousand "friends of the New Germany" in Madison Square Garden.

Facing these options, the couple decided that Magnus would settle in Nice while Li would study medicine in German-speaking Zurich, visiting France on school breaks. In February 1935, Magnus leased a seaside apartment.

The Riviera in this era was enlivened by an influx of German-Jewish exiles. Theodor Wolff, the erstwhile editor of the German capital's leading liberal newspaper, the *Berliner Tageblatt*, fled Berlin on the night of the Reichstag fire and now lived in the very same building as Magnus. In Nice, Magnus was visited by numerous luminaries including the Eastern European–born artist Marc Chagall, the acclaimed German-Jewish novelist Alfred Döblin, and Emma Goldman, the anarchist and sometime habitué of Chicago's Dil-Pickle Club, who had been deported from the United States for her radical politics.

The exiled sexologist's greatest hope, he wrote in his diary, was to "live to see this Hitler-spook disappear." How long that would take, he couldn't say. And he worried his health wouldn't hold out. Magnus was a man living in an Eden of endless sun and sea who would have given anything to return to the smog and drizzle of a Berlin that no longer existed.

With Karl in Vienna and Li in Zurich, Magnus made modest plans for his sixty-seventh birthday. He spent the morning of May 14, 1935, reading birthday cards from well-wishers all over the world. Then, accompanied by his twenty-year-old first cousin once removed Ernst Maass, who'd been living in Milan, he walked to the Café de France to celebrate with some friends, many of them fellow German exiles. Without Karl and Li there to restrain his worst impulses and remind him to take the precautions warranted for a sixty-seven-year-old diabetic surrounded by pastries, Magnus likely hit the sweets hard in this Gallic gourmand's paradise. On the walk home, he began feeling dizzy. He collapsed in his building's garden in a coma. By the end of the day, Magnus was dead.

On hearing of their partner's sudden death, Li rushed back from Zurich. Karl, despite his criminal record, was given a two-week visa by

French authorities to attend Magnus's funeral. He arrived after a madcap journey by train, plane, and motorcycle.

Magnus had planned for this moment. In the final version of his last will and testament, drawn up two months before his death, he'd left his assets to both Karl and Li and asked that they devote them to furthering his justice-through-science crusade. As for his funeral, he wanted it German, thoroughly secular, and low-key. As his demands read, "My wishes regarding my burial: cremation—music of Mendelssohn and Schubert—no words from any clergy—remarks of friends, etc." At the ceremony, held in Nice's Israelite Cemetery, his wishes were ignored as a rabbi offered brief remarks.

Magnus's body was cremated and his remains moved to Nice's Caucade Cemetery, where a black monolith simply inscribed "Magnus Hirschfeld 1868 1935" was erected over his grave. The sole decoration was a bronze bas-relief of the deceased in profile crafted by sculptor Arnold Zadikow, like Magnus a German-Jewish native of Kolberg, then living in exile in Prague.

Dying of natural causes in 1935, Magnus likely escaped a much worse fate. For many of his compatriots still in Berlin, suicide was the best way out. In the twelve years of Nazi rule, eight thousand Berlin Jews took their own lives—fully 5 percent of the city's Jewish population. The brave Berlin-born German-Jewish cabaret-world figure who had published *Transvestites* in 1910 persevered only to be murdered in Auschwitz in 1943.

Even many of Magnus's fellow exiles, who thought they had cheated death, had done no such thing. After the Nazi seizure of Czechoslovakia, Zadikow the sculptor was imprisoned. He died in Theresienstadt. After Paris fell, Hirschfeld's neighbor in Nice, newspaper editor Theodor Wolff, got deported. He died in the Sachsenhausen concentration camp outside his hometown of Berlin.

In 1936, Karl Giese went into exile in Brno, Czechoslovakia. Because of the difficulty of transferring funds across international borders in a fracturing continent, Giese never received Magnus's bequest. In Brno, he found a new partner, Karl Fein, a Jewish lawyer. In 1938, three days after the Nazis annexed Austria and shortly before they annexed much of Czechoslovakia, Giese took his own life. While Magnus's death made headlines around the world, Karl died in obscurity. Today, on the site of the Institute for Sexual Sciences at the edge of the Tiergarten in Berlin, a "stumbling stone" (*Stolperstein*) memorializes Karl, recording that he "fled into death" ("*flucht in den Tod*"). His attorney partner perished in 1942 in the Lodz Ghetto in Nazi-occupied Poland.

Li, for his part, insulated by family money, studied at Harvard during the war and returned to Zurich after it. He ultimately settled in Canada, where he lived a quiet life in Vancouver safeguarding a trove of Hirschfeld documents that now reside at the Magnus Hirschfeld Society archive in Berlin.

Magnus's cousin Ernst Maass made it to safety in New York. He worked as a librarian at the United Nations, a position one can imagine Magnus would have been very proud of.

Epilogue

A Life's Work, Interrupted

"The Empty Library" on the site of the 1933 book burning in Berlin.

IN THE MONTHS before he died, Magnus had grown increasingly worried about finding a publisher for the book he was writing, *Racism*. With fascist thugs now running the largest German language book market, even publishers in Austria and Switzerland were growing intimidated. But as the Nazis' archenemy, Magnus felt duty bound to warn the world about the dangers of their ideology, to rally the allies he called "we anti-racists" before it was too late. "Racism," he wrote with chilling prescience, was "an invention [like] poison gas, which can only minister to death, to conflict, and to destruction, can only foster hatred instead of love."

"Poison gas" was meant to be a metaphor. Even Magnus, literally writing the book on the Nazis' nightmarish racial theories, couldn't imagine they would undertake a global campaign of industrialized mass murder. At the very worst, Magnus wrote, "under the Hitlerite regime, there is considerable probability of castration and milder methods of sterilisation being applied wholesale to Jews, should other methods of 'keeping Aryan blood pure' prove ineffective."

As he feared, no German language publisher would touch *Racism*. After Hirschfeld's death, two progressive British friends, Eden and Cedar Paul, a married couple, translated his work-in-progress into English, finalized his manuscript, and continued the search. In 1938, fully three years after Magnus's passing, they found success when book publisher Victor Gollancz, the London-born son of German-Jewish immigrants, agreed to put out the work.

As the Pauls explained in their introduction to *Racism*, "This posthumous work, of which the present is the first complete publication in any language, was planned by the author, in his native tongue, toward the end of 1933 and the beginning of 1934, as an exile from Nazi Germany." Their late friend, they wrote, was a man of "character," a scientific "pioneer," and a "genius," and they insisted that it was not too late for the world to heed his final call. "Is it not fitting," they wrote, "that Magnus should arise from the tomb with a work which is intended to dispel the poison gas of racism?"

Tragically, Magnus's posthumous warning to the world was ignored. And soon his memory was as well. While his death made international headlines, as the decades passed, Hirschfeld himself disappeared from history.

When postwar historians began analyzing democratic Germany's shocking descent into fascism, many came to blame the libertine sexual environment of Weimar Berlin for triggering a violent backlash. In 1948, a leading West German thinker argued that prewar "cultural decay . . . and moral nihilism" had left ordinary Germans craving authority and the country's elites with no standard of morality for resisting evil. The 1972 film version of the Broadway musical *Cabaret* implicitly bought into this argument. It grossly exaggerated the degree to which Berlin's underground art scenesters turned Nazi and it sneered at queer life, playing a drag queen at a urinal for laughs, and even straightening the protagonist. Seeing his writings bastardized onscreen, Christopher Isherwood disavowed the homophobia, transphobia, and retrograde politics of Hollywood's rendering of his work. But the film found a mass audience—and bagged eight Oscars—while Isherwood's objections were largely ignored.

In this era, highbrow American historians and public intellectuals also worked to downplay, even cover up, the stunning extent of queer liberation in prewar Germany fearing that if Middle Americans learned of it, they might think the Nazis had a point. In Berlin-born Holocaust refugee Peter Gay's 1968 *Weimar Culture*, queerness goes entirely unmentioned as does Hirschfeld. The erudite Yale historian undoubtedly knew of the Einstein of Sex and his achievements—indeed, the book's subtitle, *The Outsider as Insider*, sounds like a perfect description of Magnus himself—but in postwar America, even tenured defenders of Weimar dare not speak Hirschfeld's name. In a more popular take, *Before the Deluge: A Portrait of Berlin in the 1920s*, by *Time* magazine journalist Otto Friedrich, Hirschfeld is briefly flagged only to be dismissed as a "celebrity" producer of "pseudo-scientific pornography." With a stunning sense of finality, Friedrich informed his 1970s readers that "Hirschfeld's work [n]ever accomplished any notable goal, and nobody takes it very seriously today." In the 1995 reissue of the book, the slander remains, but Magnus has now been so thoroughly forgotten that he's referred to in the index as "Max."

Hirschfeld's absence in our time is even stranger since his concepts and coinages have come flooding back without him. Though Hirschfeld's term "transvestite," coined in his eponymous 1910 book, is no longer current, his injunction to believe people when they state their gender identity certainly is, as is his instruction to physicians to help patients align their bodies with their gender identity.

Hirschfeld's concept of sexual orientation as a continuum has never been better known, but it is still called the "Kinsey Scale" and associated with the man who filched it decades after Hirschfeld first conceived of it. Where exactly the anxiety of influence ends and the shame of plagiarism begins in Alfred Kinsey's Cold War–era work is difficult to pinpoint. What is clear is that Kinsey was well-versed in Hirschfeld's theories. At his institute in Indiana, Kinsey quietly amassed thousands of pages of original German language documents, handwritten letters, and period newspaper clippings by and about Hirschfeld and kept a Berlin-born German language professor on staff as a translator.

Today, Hirschfeld's concept that race is a social construction not a biological reality is also back, and, of late, even his term "anti-racist" has experienced a renaissance, repopularized by scholar Ibram X. Kendi. The key insight that racial groups are formed through power, often wielded for nefarious divide-and-conquer purposes of conjuring a majoritarian "us" to stand over an outnumbered "them," feels fresh almost a hundred years after Magnus first advanced it. As Ta-Nehisi Coates recently put it, eloquently, if unknowingly, waxing Hirschfeldian: "race is the child of racism, not the father."

IN BERLIN TODAY, a small memorial sits hidden in plain sight on the spot where the infamous 1933 book burning took place. On the square, now called Bebelplatz in honor of Hirschfeld's Social Democratic ally August Bebel, a metal marker sits flush with the cobblestones beside a small window anchored into the ground. The plaque is embossed with a quote from German-Jewish poet Heinrich Heine—"Where they burn books, they will ultimately burn people as well"—and explains curtly: "In the middle of this square on May 10, 1933, Nazi students burned the works of hundreds of free[-thinking] writers, journalists, philosophers, and scientists." The text does not mention where the books came from or to whom they had belonged.

Peering through the window reveals a room hidden beneath the square. The space is spartan, whitewashed, and lined on all sides with empty bookshelves. Entitled "The Empty Library," it is the work of sculptor Micha Ullman, the Tel Aviv–born son of German-Jewish refugees. The conceptual artwork is a monument to all the knowledge lost forever on this spot—the books and manuscripts burned that night but also those that would have been written by the individuals the Nazis murdered as well as by their descendants never born. Facing this memorial to books burned and to books unwritten where Magnus's name somehow goes unmentioned, the sense that his greatest work was never penned feels overwhelming. Exhausted by his exile and despondent over the state of his homeland, he'd died before he could write it.

With the "Einstein of Sex" dead and his warnings about "the poison gas of racism" unheeded, it fell to the exiled Einstein of physics to envision a weapon powerful enough to defeat fascism. Ultimately, of course, Nazi Germany surrendered before the atomic bomb was operational.

Even in peacetime, Albert Einstein declined to return home. Instead, he remained in the United States working on an overarching theory of the physical sciences—the so-called Grand Unified Theory of Everything—that could elegantly explain the forces of the universe. He died before completing it.

In hindsight, Einstein's weapon, for all its power, has proven impotent to stop forces of fascism from threatening the world again. Indeed, in the wrong hands, it could be the ultimate tool of genocide. Perhaps it was the Einstein of Sex who had come up with the true antidote to fascism.

Though Hirschfeld did not live long enough to survey the long arc of his thought and publish an overarching theory of the social sciences—a Grand Unified Theory of Everyone—he'd all but conceived of one. Beginning with sexual orientation, then moving to gender and, finally, to race, he had discerned that all social science categories are relative.

Our world is made up of billions of unique humans. Each of us occupies our own point on the continuum of sexual orientation, a sexual minority of one. Each of us is our own distinct mix of masculinity and femininity, a gender unto ourselves. And each of us is a racial mosaic of all of our ancestors, a race shared by none but our biological siblings, should we have any. Those who divide this seamless continuum of humanity into groups can only do so arbitrarily. The categorizations speak volumes about the social scientist or the party or the demagogue imposing the categories but say precious little about those being categorized. Embracing a category, as Hirschfeld himself did in coining "transvestites," can only be justified as a means to win an equality that never should have been denied to begin with.

The power of this theory is ultimately why Magnus Hirschfeld had to be the Nazis' public enemy number one. His threat to Nazism went beyond his particular identity as a gay Jew to his ideas about identity itself. It wasn't the boxes he checked but his thinking outside of all boxes. If the divisions that the Nazis put so much stock in—heterosexual and homosexual, Aryan and Semite, masculine and feminine—were themselves human creations, not independently existing scientific categories, then the hierarchical system they were building stood upon a faulty foundation.

The Einstein of physics held the secret to a bomb that could level Berlin in an instant, but the Einstein of sex had an even more powerful weapon in his arsenal: the Grand Unified Theory of Everyone. With its democratic politics of universal equality through universal diversity, it could break the fascist politics of us and them.

It still can.

ACKNOWLEDGMENTS

As with all book projects, I embarked on this one without fully comprehending what I was taking on. I'm grateful to my agent, Larry Weissman, and his partner in life and letters, Sascha Alper, for their excitement about this project from the start. My editor, Brendan Curry, perhaps on account of our many lunches together, had faith that I could ultimately chew all that I'd bitten off. Without Brendan's steadfast appreciation for my wide-ranging interests, I know I would have a far less stimulating and fulfilling professional life. Assistant editor Caroline Adams engaged deeply with the project and shepherded it through the organizational maze at Norton. Anna Oler and the design team put up with my micromanaging and created a thoughtfully designed and handsome book worthy of the stylish era it recounts.

The legendary editor Bob Silvers told me to study German years ago. I should have listened to him. Stuck at home during the pandemic, I finally began learning the language, first online and then in person. I was fortunate to end up in the class of native speaker (and accomplished jazz musician) Susanne Ortner at the New Orleans Deutsches Haus. I cannot *danken* her enough.

The Jewish Federation of Greater New Orleans saw the significance of the project from the start and offered helpful early grants. When domestic travel reopened, I was able to make it to Honolulu as a visiting scholar at the Center for Biographical Research at the University of Hawaiʻi at Mānoa. Craig Howes and Paige Rasmussen helped me secure campus housing and were wonderful guides to their community of scholars and writers. Librarian Jodie Mattos was an extraordinary help in directing me toward sources that helped me understand the new world of race and gender that Hirschfeld encountered and found so revelatory on Waikiki Beach in 1931.

I finally made it to Berlin in 2023, thanks to a Robert and Ina Caro Research/Travel Fellowship from the Biographers International Organization. German language classmate Rachel Gibbs connected me with choreographer Teo Vlad's charming sublet as well as some of the best clubs in Berlin. Scholar Noah Isenberg gave excellent tips of where to research in the city and where to just enjoy. Berlin's Magnus Hirschfeld Society and its leader, Ralf Dose, and archivist, Raimund Wolfert, graciously welcomed me and aided me in my research. Tour guides Brendan Nash, Nickolai Todorov, Hani Porter, and Jake Schneider allowed me to see the 1920s city hiding behind its 2020s avatar. Journalism and publishing colleagues including Sophie Duvernoy, Rob Madole, Alexander Wells, and Florian Beckerhoff made my time in Berlin more interesting and more fun.

In the time I was at work on the manuscript, the tight-knit world of scholars that had long been interested in Hirschfeld attracted increasing amounts of attention from curators, writers, and filmmakers. It is a credit to them that they had embarked on this important work in a time when few others were interested and when some of Hirschfeld's patients and colleagues were still alive. Veteran scholar James Steakley was particularly generous with his time and connected me to many others in the field including Rainer Herrn.

Librarians at libraries in New Orleans (Tulane University Libraries, New Orleans Public Library), Manhattan (the New York Public Library), and Berlin (the Grimm Centre at Humboldt University, the Library of the Deutsches Historisches Museum) guided me to primary and secondary sources. Friend and scholar Tom Wooten graciously made the resources of America's second-best university available to me upon request. Local New Orleans coffeeshops including Fatma's Cozy Corner, Café Tremé, Petite

Clouet Café, The Station, Mojo Coffee House, and The Orange Couch provided the spaces where much of the book was drafted and edited.

Informal chats with friends and colleagues have helped as I've crafted the manuscript. Kristi Magner had the brilliant idea to call Magnus by his mellifluous first name rather than by his cacophonous last name. Andrea Rubin decided (correctly) that the book title had to be *The Einstein of Sex*. Novelist Yuri Herrera helped me approach the historical material in new ways.

Several friends and colleagues agreed to read sections of the manuscript and give feedback based on their expertise. Freud scholar T. R. Johnson of Tulane University gamely volunteered to read the material on the Hirschfeld-Freud frenemyship and helped add nuance to that discussion. Loren Goldman of the University of Pennsylvania reviewed the sections of the manuscript on German political and intellectual history, and his advice helped me strengthen them. Rabbi Margot Meitner, psychotherapist and consultant on trans issues (as well as my friend for decades), kindly read relevant sections and offered feedback. The problems that remain fall squarely on me.

To my permanent astonishment, two of the most successful biographers working today, Walter Isaacson and Kai Bird, took the time to offer me advice on this project. I only wish I had the talent to implement all of their sage suggestions.

This work is the product of five years of research and writing but really half a lifetime of learning. The Pulitzer Center for Crisis Reporting funded my first trip to Germany in 2009 where, on an unrelated project, I stumbled upon Hirschfeld for the first time. The influence of the teachers who first exposed me to history, philosophy, and urbanism is evident throughout. Material I first studied with Frank Batemarco and Norman Wheeler at Great Neck South High School on Long Island and with Tamar Gendler, Bettina Drew, Corey Robin, and Vincent Scully at Yale College in Connecticut shaped this book immensely.

Beginning psychotherapy myself while writing about a psychotherapist was useful for the project and for me as a person. I only wish I had started earlier. Thank you: RG, RR, and GLR.

My parents have always been supportive of this project and all of my projects. I am thankful to have inherited from my mother, Judith

Marie Tholfsen Brook, M.D., a sometimes handy case of the perfectionist "Tholfsen Curse." The insight of my father, Helman Robert Brook, Esq., that a creation can be "serious but not somber" is reflected on every page of this book.

My life partner, Rachel Riezman, was a true intellectual partner in this project. Her encouragement to examine my blind spots and get out of my ruts vastly improved the manuscript. Her taste is impeccable and her editorial talents are fierce. Our cats, Elijah Chipster Brozman and the late great Princess Smokey Bear, were always there when I needed them.

Finally, I want to thank my niece Eliora Hansonbrook who put her significant German language skills at my disposal during a week of research in Berlin and read relevant sections of the manuscript. Watching her commune with the transcestors in the archives was pure magic. This book is dedicated to her and her generation.

BIBLIOGRAPHIC NOTE

In writing a biography for a general audience, I'm indebted to the scholars who did the heavy lifting to document the facts of Magnus Hirschfeld's life. I would never have known where to start without the work of earlier biographers, including Ralf Dose and Manfred Herzer in German and Charlotte Wolff and Elena Mancini in English. Historian Laurie Marhoefer of the University of Washington has done and continues to do groundbreaking archival work on Hirschfeld and his circle. While our interpretations of the unearthed material frequently diverge, Marhoefer's research finds have tremendously enriched this book.

Working primarily in English, I am deeply indebted to Hirschfeld's translators. By the early 1930s, the Einstein of Sex was so famous that his work was being published in the German original and in English translation simultaneously. All of the translators of that era are, of course, deceased, but that does not diminish my gratitude to them. Only in recent decades have Hirschfeld's earlier works been translated into English as scholars and activists in the Anglosphere have come to understand his accomplishments and breadth of thought. Michael Lombardi-Nash began translating Hirschfeld's major early writings into English in the 1980s. He continues to do so and was kind enough to translate several works into English for the first time specifically to aid me in my book project, most crucially the 1896 pamphlet, "Sappho and Socrates." James Conway, whose compelling translation of *Berlin's Third Sex* is quoted at length in the book, was kind enough to meet me in Berlin and offer tips for my stay there as well. Both Michael and James were exceedingly generous in granting me permission to quote extensively from their translations.

NOTES

Introduction: *O Magnus Mysterium*

1 **"the sex of a person":** Magnus Hirschfeld, epilogue to N. O. Body, *Memoirs of a Man's Maiden Years*, trans. Deborah Simon (Philadelphia: University of Pennsylvania Press, 2006), 110.

2 **"we anti-racists [. . .] poison gas":** Hirschfeld, *Racism*, 292, 264.

2 **"Einstein of Sex":** Ralf Dose, *Magnus Hirschfeld and the Origins of the Gay Liberation Movement*, trans. Edward Willis (New York: Monthly Review Press, 2014), 59.

2 **"I have always protested":** Quoted in Panayiotis Vyras, "Magnus Hirschfeld in Greece," *Journal of Homosexuality* 34, no. 1 (1997): 17–29.

2 **"Whether you like it or not":** E. K. Moy, "Happy Marriages Can Be Made in Laboratory, Says Dr. Hirschfeld," *China Press*, May 18, 1931; subsequent quotations from Moy are from "Happy Marriages" (italics in original).

3 **"the sex of a person":** Quoted in N. O. Body, *Memoirs*, 110.

3 **encountered over ten thousand volumes:** Eden Paul and Cedar Paul, biographical introduction to Hirschfeld, *Racism*, 26.

4 **"string him up or beat him":** Quoted in Richard J. Evans, *The Coming of the Third Reich* (New York: Penguin Press, 2004), 376.

4 **"the most repulsive of all":** Hans Diebow quoted in Dose, *Hirschfeld and the Gay Liberation Movement*, 13.

5 **"images and inscriptions":** Magnus Hirschfeld, *The Homosexuality of Men and Women*, trans. Michael Lombardi-Nash (Amherst, NY: Prometheus Books, 2000), 535.

Chapter 1: Born This Way

8 **"had gone far":** David Vital, *A People Apart: The Jews in Europe, 1789–1939* (New York: Oxford University Press, 1999), 275.

9 **"liberalism and Judaism":** Yuri Slezkine, *The Jewish Century* (Princeton, NJ: Princeton University Press, 2004), 64.

12 **nearly three hundred thousand:** Vital, *A People Apart*, 267.

14 **"family bathing area":** Map in the Museum of the City of Kołobrzeg, standing exhibition (2023), Kołobrzeg, Poland.

15 **"The shape of each human":** Plato, *Symposium*, trans. Alexander Nehamas and Paul Woodruff, in *Plato: Complete Works*, ed. John M. Cooper (Indianapolis, IN: Hackett Publishing Co., 1997), 190a; subsequent quotations from *Symposium* appear on 191a, 191e, 192a.

16 **"differ only in this respect":** Plato, *Republic*, trans. G. M. A. Grube, rev. C. D. C. Reeve, in *Plato: Complete Works*, ed. John M. Cooper (Indianapolis, IN: Hackett Publishing Co., 1997), 454d, 190a.

18 **"usually called 'politics'":** Magnus Hirschfeld, *Von einst bis jetzt* (memoir), trans. Michael Lombardi-Nash (Jacksonville, FL: Urania Manuscripts, 2019), 215.

19 **"dissident":** Ralf Dose, *Magnus Hirschfeld and the Origins of the Gay Liberation Movement*, trans. Edward H. Willis (New York: Monthly Review Press, 2014), 22.

19 **"I hardly ever heard":** Hirschfeld, *Von einst bis jetzt*, 228.

20 **"reasons why sex between men":** Quoted in Robert Beachy, *Gay Berlin: Birthplace of a Modern Identity* (New York: Alfred A. Knopf, 2014), 30.

20 **"felt more closely and essentially connected":** Quoted in Dose, *Hirschfeld and Gay Liberation*, 22–23.

Chapter 2: In Don't-Ask, Don't-Tell America

24 **most densely populated neighborhoods:** "Housing Density: From Tenements to Towers" (online exhibition), Skyscraper Museum, New York (accessed June 27, 2024).

25 **"appearance, language, dress":** Magnus Hirschfeld, *Women East and West: Impressions of a Sex Expert* (London: William Heinemann, 1935), 274.

25 **"Life kneads the dough":** Hirschfeld, *Women East and West*, 274.

25 **"MALES WHO BLEACH":** "Dives Closing Up," *World* (New York), Jan. 7, 1892, evening ed.

25 **"a youth, whose face was painted":** Charles W. Gardner quoted in Richard Zacks, *Island of Vice: Theodore Roosevelt's Quest to Clean Up Sin-Loving New York* (New York: Anchor Books, 2012), 19.

26 **"a great deal goes on":** Magnus Hirschfeld, *The Homosexuality of Men and Women*, trans. Michael Lombardi-Nash (Amherst, NY: Prometheus Books, 2000), 623.

26 **"queen of drag":** Gerard Joseph Channing, "The First Drag Queen?," *The Nation*, Feb. 17, 2020.

26 **"the infamous crime":** St. Sukie de la Croix, *Chicago Whispers: A History of LGBT Chicago Before Stonewall* (Madison: University of Wisconsin Press, 2012), 25; subsequent quotations from *Chicago Whispers* appear on pp. 20, 21, 24.

27 **"a young Negro woman":** Hirschfeld, *Homosexuality of Men and Women*, 624.

27 **"amazingly open display":** Donald L. Miller, *City of the Century: The Epic of Chicago and the Making of America* (New York: Simon & Schuster, 1996), 508.

28 **over twenty-seven million:** David Blight, *Frederick Douglass: Prophet of Freedom* (New York: Simon & Schuster, 2018), 725.

28 **"Never before in civilization":** Jane Addams quoted in Erik Larson, *The Devil in the White City: Murder, Magic, and Madness at the Fair That Changed America* (New York: Crown, 2003), 11.

29 **hundred thousand electric lightbulbs:** Deirdre Mask, *The Address Book: What Street Addresses Reveal About Identity, Race, Wealth, and Power* (New York: St. Martin's Press, 2020), 255.

29 **"ethnological villages":** Blight, *Frederick Douglass*, 726.

30 **"whole Indian circus [. . .] Barnum & Bailey Circus":** Quoted in Larson, *Devil in the White City*, 141.

30 **"I had a gold mine":** Quoted in Reid Badger, *The Great American Fair: The World's Columbian Exposition & American Culture* (Chicago: Nelson-Hall, 1979), 108.

30 **admission fee: twenty-five cents:** John J. Flinn, comp., *Official Guide to the World's Columbian Exposition* (Chicago: The Columbian Guide Co., 1893), 25.

30 **one hundred imported natives:** Badger, *The Great American Fair*, 108.

31 **"Mrs. Potter Palmer":** Flinn, *Official Guide*, 187.

31 **"Women's Work in Savagery":** Gayle Gullett, "'Our Great Opportunity': Organized Women Advance Women's Work at the World's Columbian Exposition of 1893," *Illinois Historical Journal* 87, no. 4 (winter 1994), 259–76.

31 **"As if to shame the Negro":** Frederick Douglass, introduction to *The Reason Why the Colored American Is Not in the World's Columbian Exposition* (Chicago: Ida B. Wells, 1893), 9.

31 **"In these wild people":** Quoted in Robert W. Rydell, "The World's Columbian Exposition of 1893: Racist Underpinnings of a Utopian Artifact," *Journal of American Culture* 1, no. 2 (1978): 269.

32 **"Haiti is herself French":** Frederick Douglass, *Lecture on Haiti: The Haitian Pavilion Dedication Ceremonies Delivered at the World's Fair, in Jackson Park, Chicago, Jan. 2d, 1893* (Chicago: Violet Agents Supply Co., 1893), Daniel Murray Pamphlet Collection, Library of Congress (online collection).

32 **Haitian coffee for ten cents:** Blight, *Frederick Douglass*, 728.

32 **"liable to be overlooked":** *World's Columbian Exposition Illustrated* quoted in Charles King, *Gods of the Upper Air* (Doubleday: New York, 2019), 71.

33 **"My father was a white man":** Quoted in Blight, *Frederick Douglass*, 13.

33 **"Anglo-African [. . .] I am identified":** Blight, *Frederick Douglass*, 731, 727.

34 **"In every other country":** Douglass, "Lecture on Haiti."

Chapter 3: The Hirschfeld Scale

36 **"apaches":** Magnus Hirschfeld, *The Homosexuality of Men and Women*, trans. Michael Lombardi-Nash (Amherst, NY: Prometheus Books, 2000), 643; subsequent quotations from *Homosexuality* appear on pp. 642, 643, 644, 645, 809.

40 **"grandfather of gay liberation":** Vern Bullough, introduction to Karl Heinrich Ulrichs, *The Riddle of "Man-Manly" Love*, trans. Michael Lombardi-Nash (Buffalo, NY: Prometheus Books, 1994), 1:21.

42 **"half the night in the lowest harbor pubs":** Magnus Hirschfeld, *Sappho and Socrates*, trans. Michael Lombardi-Nash (Jacksonville, FL: Urania Manuscripts, 2019), 5–6.

42 **"deep mental depression":** Magnus Hirschfeld, *Von einst bis jetzt* (memoir), trans. Michael Lombardi-Nash (Jacksonville, FL: Urania Manuscripts, 2019), 64.

42 **"invigorating alcohol":** Ralf Dose, *Magnus Hirschfeld and the Origins of the Gay Liberation Movement*, trans. Edward Willis (New York: Monthly Review Press, 2014), 25.

43 **"When I moved":** Hirschfeld, *Von einst bis jetzt*, 56–57; subsequent quotations from *Von einst bis jetzt* appear on p. 57.

44 **"I could not object":** Hirschfeld, *Sappho and Socrates*, 5.

44 **"abnormal":** Quoted in Norman Page, *Auden and Isherwood: The Berlin Years* (New York: St. Martin's Press, 1998), 103.

44 **"the thought that it could":** Hirschfeld, *Sappho and Socrates*, 5; subsequent quotes from *Sappho and Socrates* appear on pp. 9, 10, 11, 23–25, 27, 30, 32.

Chapter 4: The Coming-Out Party

52 **"not a vice or a crime":** Magnus Hirschfeld, *Von einst bis jetzt* (memoir), trans. Michael Lombardi-Nash (Jacksonville, FL: Urania Manuscripts, 2019), 62; subsequent quotations from *Von einst bis jetzt* appear on pp. 63, 67.

53 **"divided into three parts:":** Magnus Hirschfeld, *Annual Reports of the Scientific Humanitarian Committee (1900–1903)*, trans. Michael Lombardi-Nash (Jacksonville, FL: Urania Manuscripts, 2021), 19.

54 **"homosexual women in Germany":** Hirschfeld, *Annual Reports (1900–1903)*, 35.

54 **"according to the principle":** Magnus Hirschfeld, *Annual Reports of the Scientific Humanitarian Committee (1906–1908)*, trans. Michael Lombardi-Nash (Jacksonville, FL: Urania Manuscripts, 2022), 9.

54 **"Then we vowed":** Hirschfeld, *Von einst bis jetzt*, 73.

54 **"To the legislative bodies":** Quoted in Magnus Hirschfeld, *Berlin's Third Sex*, trans. James J. Conway (Berlin: Rixdorf Editions, 2017), 114; subsequent quotations from *Berlin's Third Sex* appear on pp. 114, 116.

55 **"entrusted them to the mailboxes":** Hirschfeld, *Von einst bis jetzt*, 74.

56 **"because I myself am contrary-sexed":** Hirschfeld, *Von einst bis jetzt*, 74–75.

56 **"Only after the death":** Quoted in Hirschfeld, *Homosexuality of Men and Women*, 971; subsequent quotations from *Homosexuality* appear on pp. 1091, 1092, 1093.

57 **nine hundred signatures:** Elena Mancini, *Magnus Hirschfeld and the Quest for Sexual Freedom: A History of the First Sexual Freedom Movement* (New York: Palgrave MacMillan, 2010), 92.

58 **"We have a printed petition":** Quoted in Hirschfeld, *Homosexuality of Men and Women*, 1095; subsequent quotations from *Homosexuality* appear on pp. 1094, 1095.

59 **"Only he who has crucified":** Hirschfeld, *Von einst bis jetzt*, 222.

60 **"an affair of men for men":** Charlotte Wolff, *Magnus Hirschfeld: A Portrait of a Pioneer in Sexology* (London: Quartet Books, 1986), 42.

60 **"In the course of the year":** Hirschfeld, *Annual Reports (1900–1903)*, 33.

60 **leadership remained overwhelmingly male:** Wolff, *Magnus Hirschfeld*, 148.

61 **"path over corpses":** Ralf Dose, *Magnus Hirschfeld and the Origins of the Gay Liberation Movement*, trans. Edward H. Willis (New York: Monthly Review Press, 2014), 45.

61 **"sentenced to death":** Magnus Hirschfeld, *Paragraph 175 of the Imperial Penal Code Book: The Homosexual Question Judged by Contemporaries,* trans. Michael Lombardi-Nash (Jacksonville, FL: Urania Manuscripts, 2020), 19; subsequent quotations from *Paragraph 175* appear on pp. 14, 26.

62 **"Does your sex drive extend":** Magnus Hirschfeld, *Annual of Sexual Intermediaries with Special Focus on Homosexuality (1899)*, trans. Michael Lombardi-Nash (Jacksonville, FL: Urania Manuscripts, 2023), 1:24.

63 **"In the case of the most disparate":** Quoted in Hirschfeld, *Homosexuality of Men and Women*, 720–21 (italics added).

64 **"their sons to wear women's clothing":** Hirschfeld, *Berlin's Third Sex*,107.

64 **equivalent of two postage stamps:** James J. Conway, afterword to Hirschfeld, *Berlin's Third Sex*, 135; subsequent quotations from *Berlin's Third Sex* appear on pp. 10, 107, 109.

65 **"There are only two sexes":** *Wiesbadener Volksblatt* [Wiesbaden People's News], Sept. 19, 1904, quoted in Magnus Hirschfeld, *Annual Reports of the Scientific Humanitarian Committee (1904–1905)*, trans. Michael Lombardi-Nash (Jacksonville, FL: Urania Manuscripts, 2022), 65.

65 **"How many a mother is unable":** Hirschfeld, "What People Should Know About the Third Sex" in *Berlin's Third Sex*, 106.

65 **"The reasons that led me":** Magnus Hirschfeld, foreword to the 2nd ed., *Sappho and Socrates*, trans. Michael Lombardi-Nash (Jacksonville, FL: Urania Manuscripts, 2019), 7.

66 **"I happily give you this":** Quoted in Michael Thomas Taylor, Annette F. Timm, and Rainer Herrn, eds., *Not Straight from Germany: Sexual Publics and Sexual Citizenship Since Magnus Hirschfeld* (Ann Arbor: University of Michigan Press, 2017), 40.

66 **"People continuously bring dogs":** Hirschfeld, *Homosexuality of Men and Women*, 722.

66 **"If a human right is withheld":** Quoted in Hirschfeld, *Von einst bis jetzt*, 222.

Chapter 5: Big Data

67 **"estimating the percentage":** Magnus Hirschfeld, *Paragraph 175 of the Imperial Penal Code Book,* trans. Michael Lombardi-Nash (Jacksonville, FL: Urania Manuscripts, 2020), 26.

67 **"external assimilation":** Magnus Hirschfeld, *The Homosexuality of Men and Women*, trans. Michael Lombardi-Nash (Amherst, NY: Prometheus Books, 2000), 531; subsequent quotations from *Homosexuality* appear on pp. 531, 534.

69 **"the relative number of Urnings":** Karl Heinrich Ulrichs, *The Riddle of "Man-Manly" Love*, trans. Michael Lombardi-Nash (Buffalo, NY: Prometheus Books, 1994), 2:629.

69 **"Doctor, twenty-five years of age":** Quoted in Hirschfeld, *Homosexuality of Men and Women*, 535; subsequent quotations from *Homosexuality* appear on pp. 535, 538, 539–43, 542.

71 **"Do you have feelings?":** Quoted in Hirschfeld, *Homosexuality of Men and Women*, 551–52.

72 **"Have you suffered":** Hirschfeld, *Annual of Sexual Intermediaries (1899)*, 1:25.

72 **"When polling":** Hirschfeld, *Homosexuality of Men and Women*, 538–39; subsequent quotations from *Homosexuality* appear on pp. 544, 545, 546, 548.

74 **"attack on student honor":** Magnus Hirschfeld, *My Obscenity Trial* (1904), trans. Michael Lombardi-Nash (Jacksonville, FL: Urania Manuscripts, 2021), 36.

74 **"As you probably already know":** Hirschfeld, *Homosexuality of Men and Women*, 553–56; subsequent quotations from *Homosexuality* appear on pp. 553–54, 555–56.

76 **"morals of dogs":** Quoted in Elena Mancini, *Magnus Hirschfeld and the Quest for Sexual Freedom: A History of the First Sexual Freedom Movement* (New York: Palgrave MacMillan, 2010), 100.

76 **"disseminated obscene writings [. . .] shame and morality":** Hirschfeld, *My Obscenity Trial*, 6, 22–23.

77 **"Just at the beginning":** Hirschfeld, *Homosexuality of Men and Women*, 546–47.

77 **"I believe I would be blameworthy":** Hirschfeld, *Homosexuality of Men and Women*, 546.

77 **"Through such inquiries":** Hirschfeld, *My Obscenity Trial*, 30–31.

77 **"The defendant had acted":** Quoted in Hirschfeld, *Homosexuality of Men and Women*, 547.

78 **fined 200 marks:** Charlotte Wolff, *Magnus Hirschfeld: A Portrait of a Pioneer in Sexology* (London: Quartet Books, 1986), 58.

78 **"such a judgment [. . .] possible in Germany":** Hirschfeld, *My Obscenity Trial*, 32, 34.

78 **"League of Perverts":** *Staatsbürgerzeitung* [Citizens News], June 29, 1905, quoted in Magnus Hirschfeld, *Annual Reports of the Scientific Humanitarian Committee (1904–1905)*, trans. Michael Lombardi-Nash (Jacksonville, FL: Urania Manuscripts, 2022), 65.

78 **4.3 percent self-identified:** Hirschfeld, *Homosexuality of Men and Women*, 559; subsequent references to *Homosexuality* appear on pp. 551, 556, 557, 560.

Chapter 6: Unpoliceable City

81 **"foolishness [. . .] exile for forty years":** Magnus Hirschfeld, *The Homosexuality of Men and Women*, trans. Michael Lombardi-Nash (Amherst, NY: Prometheus Books, 2000), 603.

82 **roughly four to one:** Robert Beachy, *Gay Berlin: Birthplace of a Modern Identity* (New York: Random House, 2014), 82.

82 **"I do not see why":** Hirschfeld, *Homosexuality of Men and Women*, 67.

82 **"champion of light":** Quoted in Alex Bakker, Rainer Herrn, Michael Thomas Taylor, and Annette F. Timm, *Others of My Kind: Transatlantic Transgender Histories* (Calgary: University of Calgary Press, 2020), 85.

82 **"extraordinarily lenient":** Magnus Hirschfeld, *Paragraph 175 of the Imperial Penal Code Book: The Homosexual Question Judged* by Contemporaries, trans. Michael Lombardi-Nash (Jacksonville, FL: Urania Manuscripts, 2020), 16.

83 **six thousand souls:** Michael Sontheimer, "The Rise, Fall and Rebirth of Germany's Capital," *Der Spiegel*, Nov. 21, 2012.

83 **Berlin's population increased:** James J. Conway, afterword to Magnus Hirschfeld, *Berlin's Third Sex*, trans. James J. Conway (Berlin: Rixdorf Editions, 2017), 139.

83 **most Berliners were transplants:** Eva-Marie Schnurr, "Berlin's Turn of the Century Growing Pains," *Der Spiegel*, Nov. 11, 2012.

83 **the third-largest city:** Peter Frizsche, "Fugitive City: Hans Ostwald, Imperial Berlin and the Grossstadt-Dokumente," *Journal of Contemporary History* 29, no. 3 (July 1994): 385–402.

83 **"The buildings are garish":** August Endell, *The Beauty of the Metropolis*, trans. James J. Conway (Berlin: Rixdorf Editions, 2018), 51–52.

84 **"the European Chicago":** Mark Twain, "The Chicago of Europe," *Chicago Daily Tribune*, Apr. 3, 1892.

84 **"has no traditions":** Twain, "The Chicago of Europe."

84 **three-quarters of the migrants:** Sontheimer, "The Rise, Fall and Rebirth."

84 **the *Berliner Tempo*:** Sontheimer, "The Rise, Fall and Rebirth."

85 **"let alone what the inhabitants get up to":** Hirschfeld, *Berlin's Third Sex*, 14.

86 **"aqueducts of Rome":** Schnurr, "Berlin's Growing Pains."

87 **"this woeful ugliness":** Endell, *Beauty of the Metropolis*, 52; subsequent quotations from *Beauty* appear on pp. 23–25.

88 **women in their twenties [. . .] "pointillist":** Frizsche, "Fugitive City," 386, 396.

88 **"bleary-eyed":** Quoted in Schnurr, "Berlin's Growing Pains."

88 **"actors, dramatists, painters":** Quoted in Iain Boyd Whyte and David Frisby, eds. *Metropolis Berlin, 1880–1940* (Berkeley: University of California Press, 2012), 186.

89 **"depict everything exactly":** Hirschfeld, *Berlin's Third Sex*, 10; subsequent quotations from *Berlin's Third Sex* appear on pp. 9, 13, 14, 15, 16–18, 19.

93 **"fugitive city":** Frizsche, "Fugitive City."

94 **"Older gentleman":** Hirschfeld, *Berlin's Third Sex*, 71–72; subsequent quotations from *Berlin's Third Sex* appear on pp. 50, 65, 70, 72, and 76.

96 **"Ball for the Enemies":** Beachy, *Gay Berlin*, 63.

96 **"with a few fellow doctors":** Hirschfeld, *Berlin's Third Sex*, 65; subsequent quotations from *Berlin's Third Sex* appear on pp. 31, 37, 39, 40, 47–48, 64, 65–66, 67–68.

99 **"I myself know of a case":** Hirschfeld, *Homosexuality of Men and Women*, 815.

99 **"In Berlin, it is far from unheard of":** Hirschfeld, *Berlin's Third Sex*, 33; subsequent quotations from *Berlin's Third Sex* appear on pp. 34–35, 41, 43, 85–86, 89.

102 **"Liebchen":** Beachy, *Gay Berlin*, 122.

102 **"Whether that person engages":** Quoted in Beachy, *Gay Berlin*, 128.

103 **"path over corpses":** Ralf Dose, *Magnus Hirschfeld and the Origins of the Gay Liberation Movement*, trans. Edward Willis (New York: Monthly Review Press, 2014), 45.

103 **"the supposed protector":** Quoted in Beachy, *Gay Berlin*, 130.

103 **"Dr. Hirschfeld: A Public Danger":** Elena Mancini, *Magnus Hirschfeld and the Quest for Sexual Freedom: A History of the First Sexual Freedom Movement* (New York: Palgrave MacMillan, 2010), 101.

103 **"For and Against Paragraph 175":** Magnus Hirschfeld, *Annual Reports of the Scientific Humanitarian Committee (1906-1908)*, trans. Michael Lombardi-Nash (Jacksonville, FL: Urania Manuscripts, 2022), 21.

103 **"*Eulenburgue*":** Beachy, *Gay Berlin*, 139.

104 **"*Berlinese*":** Hirschfeld, *Homosexuality of Men and Women*, 53.

Chapter 7: Some Bodies

106 **"most eye-catching examples":** Magnus Hirschfeld, *Geschlechtsübergänge* [Gender Transitions], trans. by the author (Leipzig, Germany: Verlag der Monatsschrift für Harnkrankheiten und sexuelle Hygiene, 1906), 4; subsequent quotations from *Gender Transitions* appear on pp. 4, 17.

107 **"The Relativity of Simultaneity":** Albert Einstein, *Relativity: The Special and General Theory–100th Anniversary Edition*, ed. Hanoch Gutfreund and Jürgen Renn, trans. Robert W. Lawson (Princeton, NJ: Princeton University Press, 2015), 36.

108 **"events which are simultaneous":** Einstein, *Relativity: Special and General Theory*, 37.

108 **"sexual aberrations":** Sigmund Freud, *Three Essays on the Theory of Sexuality: The 1905 Edition*, ed. Philippe Van Haute and Herman Westerink, trans. Ulrike Klistner (New York: Verso, 2016), 1; subsequent quotations from *Three Essays* appear on pp. 2, 3, 5, 6, 79.

109 **"a flabby, unappetizing fellow":** Quoted in Heike Bauer, "'Race', Normativity and the History of Sexuality," *Psychology & Sexuality* 1, no. 3 (2010), 239–49.

110 **"The autobiographical information":** Freud, *Three Essays*, 91.

110 **"no reason not to believe":** Magnus Hirschfeld, *Transvestites: The Erotic Drive to Cross-Dress*, trans. Michael Lombardi-Nash (Buffalo, NY: Prometheus Books, 1991), 153.

110 **"I did not want to write":** N. O. Body, *Memoirs of a Man's Maiden Years*, trans. Deborah Simon (Philadelphia: University of Pennsylvania Press, 2006), 108; subsequent quotations from *Memoirs* appear on pp. 7, 9, 17, 18, 21, 32, 34, 63, 71, 83, 99, 100, 101, 104, 110, 124, 130, 223, 226, 227, 228, 233.

118 **"special individuals [. . .] ancient demand":** N. O. Body, *Memoirs*, 110, 111.

118 **"not man, not woman":** Hirschfeld, *Transvestites*, 253; subsequent quotations from *Transvestites* appear on pp. 264, 275, 277–78.

120 **"disorderly conduct":** Ralf Dose, *Magnus Hirschfeld and the Origins of the Gay Liberation Movement*, trans. Edward Willis (New York: Monthly Review Press, 2014), 72.

120 **"persons who are forced":** Hirschfeld, *Transvestites*, 154; subsequent quotations from *Transvestites* appear on pp. 152–53, 154.

121 **"in terms of sexual psychology":** Magnus Hirschfeld, *Von einst bis jetzt* (memoir), trans. Michael Lombardi-Nash (Jacksonville, FL: Urania Manuscripts, 2019), 262.

122 **"continues still to bear":** "The Twelve Articles of Accusation" (online resource), St. Joan Center, Albuquerque, New Mexico (accessed June 13, 2024).

122 **"disgracefully put on the clothing":** Quoted in Helen Castor, *Joan of Arc: A History* (New York: HarperCollins, 2015), 165.

122 **"a short mantle, a hood":** Quoted in Timothy Wilson-Smith, *Joan of Arc: Maid, Myth, and History* (Gloucestershire, UK: Sutton Publishing, 2006), 76–77.

123 **"blessed a fanatically cheering crowd":** Hirschfeld, *Von einst bis jetzt*, 262.

Chapter 8: War on Many Fronts

124 **"We cannot spare Dr. Hirschfeld":** Robert Beachy, *Gay Berlin: Birthplace of a Modern Identity* (New York: Random House, 2014), 118.

125 **"Homosexuality is always":** Magnus Hirschfeld, *The Homosexuality of Men and Women*, trans. Michael Lombardi-Nash (Amherst, NY: Prometheus Books, 2000), 454–55; subsequent quotations from *Homosexuality* appear on pp. 493, 504, 632, 661, 1140.

126 **"patriotic hysteria":** Amos Elon, *The Pity of It All: A Portrait of the German-Jewish Epoch, 1743–1933* (New York: Henry Holt and Co., 2002), 302.

126 **"before the leaves fall":** Quoted in Elon, *Pity of It All*, 298.

127 **"sacred spring":** Quoted in Elon, *Pity of It All*, 319.

128 **"the punctuality which characterizes":** Magnus Hirschfeld, *Why Do Nations Hate Us? A Reflection on the Psychology of War*, trans. Michael Lombardi-Nash (Jacksonville, FL: Urania Manuscripts, 2020), 28.

128 **"all peoples and tribes":** Quoted in Elon, *Pity of It All*, 309; subsequent quotations from *Pity of It All* appear on pp. 308, 309, 310.

129 **"Many went and risked":** Quoted in Laurie Marhoefer, *Sex and the Weimar Republic: German Homosexual Emancipation and the Rise of the Nazis* (Toronto: University of Toronto Press, 2015), 39.

130 **"I crave a decent mouthful":** Quoted in Laurie Marhoefer, "How WWI Sparked the Gay Rights Movement," *Smithsonian*, May 15, 2017.

130 **"He laid down his life":** Quoted in Marhoefer, *Sex and the Weimar Republic*, 40 (emphasis in original).

130 **Nearly 3 percent:** Richard J. Evans, *The Coming of the Third Reich* (New York: Penguin Press, 2004), 140–41.

131 **"a few hundred Jews":** Quoted in Elon, *Pity of It All*, 341.

132 **"more than just a lost war":** Quoted in Peter Gay, *Weimar Culture: The Outsider as Insider* (New York: W. W. Norton, 1968), 9.

132 **"We want a socialist republic":** Quoted in Charlotte Wolff, *Magnus Hirschfeld: A Portrait of a Pioneer in Sexology* (London: Quartet Books, 1986), 167–68; subsequent quotations from *Magnus Hirschfeld* appear on pp. 167, 168.

133 **"there is nothing identical":** Magnus Hirschfeld, *What Unites and Divides the Human Race*,

trans. Michael Lombardi-Nash (Jacksonville, FL: Urania Manuscripts, 2020), 6; subsequent quotations from *What Unites* appear on pp. 5, 7–8, 15.

Chapter 9: Moving Pictures

137 **"From our standpoint":** Quoted in Laurie Marhoefer, *Sex and the Weimar Republic: German Homosexual Emancipation and the Rise of the Nazis* (Toronto: University of Toronto Press, 2015), 30.

138 **"not only have the right":** Quoted in Ina Linge, "Sexology, Popular Science and Queer history in *Anders als die Andern* (*Different from the Others*)," *Gender and History* 30, no. 3 (Oct. 2018): 595–610.

138 **two hundred film companies:** Linge, "Sexology," 597.

139 **three thousand cinemas:** Linge, "Sexology," 597.

140 **In 1919 alone:** James Steakley, "Cinema and Censorship in the Weimar Republic: The Case of *Anders als die Andern*," *Film History* 11, no. 2 (1999): 181–203.

140 **"social hygiene film":** Quoted in Linge, "Sexology," 599.

140 **"a work of art":** Quoted in Norman Page, *Auden and Isherwood: The Berlin Years* (New York: St. Martin's Press, 1998), 110.

141 **"a unification of both":** Quoted in Steakley, "Cinema and Censorship," 185.

141 **working title [. . .] "famous physician":** Steakley, "Cinema and Censorship," 196, 197.

141 **"a victory over error":** Quoted in Vito Russo, *The Celluloid Closet: Homosexuality in the Movies*, rev. ed. (New York: Harper & Row, 1987), 20.

142 **"Suicide of the factory owner":** Richard Oswald, dir., *Anders als die Andern* [Different from the Others], Berlin: Richard-Oswald-Produktion, 1919, https://archive.org/details/DifferentFromTheOthers, 3:30; subsequent quotations from the film appear at 3:45, 4:05, 4:25, 44:45, 47:40, 48:05.

143 **"I would ask that my participation":** Quoted in Steakley, "Cinema and Censorship," 197.

143 **"Love for one's own sex":** Oswald, *Different from the Others*, 30:45, 31:05; subsequent quotations from the film appear at 40:20, 48:50.

145 **"priestess of depravity":** Mel Gordon, *The Seven Addictions and Five Professions of Anita Berber: Weimar Berlin's Priestess of Depravity* (Los Angeles: Feral House, 2006), iii.

145 **"physical, psychological":** "Institute for Sexual Science, 1919–1933" (online exhibition), Magnus-Hirschfeld-Gesellschaft (Berlin) (accessed Jan. 11, 2022).

145 **"Love that dare not speak":** Quoted in Matthew Sturgis, *Oscar Wilde: A Life* (New York: Alfred A. Knopf, 2021), 532.

146 **"sturdy peasant youth":** Christopher Isherwood, *Christopher and His Kind, 1929–1939* (New York: Farrar, Straus and Giroux, 1976), 25.

146 **"Papa":** Isherwood, *Christopher and His Kind*, 26.

146 **"Karlchen":** Laurie Marhoefer, *Racism and the Making of Gay Rights: A Sexologist, His Student, and the Empire of Queer Love* (Toronto: University of Toronto Press, 2022), 154.

146 **"sex tends to polygamy":** Quoted in Charlotte Wolff, *Magnus Hirschfeld: A Portrait of a Pioneer in Sexology* (London: Quartet Books, 1986), 187.

146 ***"Huch nein!"*:** Sara Friedman, "Projecting Fears and Hopes: Gay Rights on the German Screen after World War I," Journal of the History of Ideas blog, May 28, 2019.

147 **"the realm of the perverse":** Pastor Martin Cornils quoted in Friedman, "Projecting Fears and Hopes."

147 **"glorifying":** Quoted in Steakley, "Cinema and Censorship," 188.

147 **"the filth flows":** Quoted in Marhoefer, *Sex and the Weimar Republic*, 34.

148 **"chiefly guilty for":** Quoted in Marhoefer, *Sex and the Weimar Republic*, 33–34.

148 **"swinish filth":** Quoted in Steakley, "Cinema and Censorship," 191.

148 **"If anyone calls this film":** Quoted in Steakley, "Cinema and Censorship," 191.

148 **"Hirschfeld is Jewish":** Johannes Ude quoted in Friedman, "Projecting Fears and Hopes."

149 **"social or philosophical slant":** Steakley, "Cinema and Censorship," 192.
149 **"I am conscious of the fact":** Quoted in Russo, *The Celluloid Closet*, 20.
149 **"Whereas the criminal code":** Quoted in Steakley, "Cinema and Censorship," 192.
150 **"Nothing has been as demoralizing":** Quoted in Marhoefer, *Sex and the Weimar Republic*, 32; subsequent information and quotations from *Sex and the Weimar Republic* appear on pp. 41, 49.

Chapter 10: Here It's Right!

154 **"two-fold [. . .] child of the revolution":** Quoted in Laurie Marhoefer, *Sex and the Weimar Republic: German Homosexual Emancipation and the Rise of the Nazis* (Toronto: University of Toronto Press, 2015), 4, 14.
154 **"facility for research":** Quoted in Michael Thomas Taylor, Annette F. Timm, and Rainer Herr, *Not Straight from Germany: Sexual Publics and Sexual Citizenship Since Magnus Hirschfeld* (Ann Arbor: University of Michigan Press, 2017), 1.
154 **"furniture was classic":** Christopher Isherwood, *Christopher and His Kind, 1929–1939* (New York: Farrar, Straus and Giroux, 1976), 15.
155 **"the urge to present":** Quoted in "Institute for Sexual Science, 1919–1933" (online exhibition), Magnus-Hirschfeld-Gesellschaft (Berlin) (accessed Jan. 11, 2022).
156 **twenty thousand volumes:** Robert Plant, *The Pink Triangle: The Nazi War Against Homosexuals* (New York: New Republic Books/Henry Holt, 1986), 43.
156 **"grandfather of gay liberation":** Vern Bullough, introduction to Karl Heinrich Ulrichs, *The Riddle of "Man-Manly" Love*, trans. Michael Lombardi-Nash (Buffalo, NY: Prometheus Books, 1994), 1:21.
156 **thirty-five thousand photographs:** Plant, *The Pink Triangle*, 43.
157 **"What is the best way to have sex":** Richard J. Evans, *The Coming of the Third Reich* (New York: Penguin Press, 2004), 128.
157 **over fourteen thousand:** Olivia Laing, *Everybody: A Book About Freedom* (New York: W. W. Norton, 2021), 77.
157 **"degenerative signs":** Charlotte Wolff, *Magnus Hirschfeld: A Portrait of a Pioneer in Sexology* (London: Quartet Books, 1986), 252.
157 **"Hirschfeld Museum":** Robert Beachy, *Gay Berlin: Birthplace of a Modern Identity* (New York: Random House, 2014), 162.
157 **"an institution absolutely unique":** William Robertson quoted in Beachy, *Gay Berlin*, 163.
158 **"Darwin of the Berlin sexual underworld":** Norman Page, *Auden and Isherwood: The Berlin Years* (New York: St. Martin's Press, 1998), 115.
158 **more than 1,600:** Evans, *Coming of the Third Reich*, 128.
159 **"I passionately enthuse":** "Institute for Sexual Science, 1919–1933" (online exhibition); subsequent references to the institute are found at the same website.
161 **featured "themes":** Michael Peppiatt, *Francis Bacon: Anatomy of an Enigma* (New York: Farrar, Straus and Giroux, 1996), 28.
161 **"I remember these streets":** Peppiatt, *Francis Bacon*, 28-29.
161 **two hundred thousand foreign tourists:** Page, *Auden and Isherwood*, 62.
161 **"Dollarika":** Mel Gordon, *The Seven Addictions and Five Professions of Anita Berber: Weimar Berlin's Priestess of Depravity* (Los Angeles: Feral House, 2006), 39.
162 **"prostitution, male and female":** Evans, *Coming of the Third Reich*, 233.
162 **"Paris had long since cornered":** Isherwood, *Christopher and His Kind*, 29.
162 **"You couldn't find anything":** Christopher Isherwood, *Down There on a Visit* (New York: Simon and Schuster, 1962), 35.
162 **"Berlin meant Boys":** Isherwood, *Christopher and His Kind*, 2 (capitalization in original).
162 **"because they knew it excited their clients":** Isherwood, *Christopher and His Kind*, 30.
162 **the number of queer establishments:** Mel Gordon, *Voluptuous Panic: The Erotic World of Weimar Berlin*, expanded ed. (Los Angeles: Feral House, 2006), 84.

162 **the size of the capital's queer population:** Gordon, *Voluptuous Panic*, 93.
163 **135 gay bars:** Page, *Auden and Isherwood*, 63.
163 **85 lesbian establishments:** Gordon, *Voluptuous Panic*, 108.
163 **"The Gentlemen's Bar":** "Institute for Sexual Science, 1919–1933" (online exhibition).
163 **"it was never possible":** Robert McAlmon quoted in Page, *Auden and Isherwood*, 89.
163 **"the Germans introduced all their vehemence":** Quoted in Peppiatt, *Francis Bacon*, 27.
163 **"Our department store":** Quoted in Page, *Auden and Isherwood*, 86.
163 **"evil alliances are more numerous":** Quoted in Page, *Auden and Isherwood*, 93.
164 **"women dance with women":** Quoted in Page, *Auden and Isherwood*, 62.
164 **"a supermarket of eroticism":** Friedrich Hollaender quoted in Evans, *Coming of the Third Reich*, 125.
164 **"what you don't see elsewhere":** Andreas Pretzel, *Vom Dorian Gray zum Eldorado* [From Dorian Gray to Eldorado] (Berlin: MANEO, 2012), 121.
164 **"for the people from the provinces":** Adolf Stein quoted in Pretzel, *Vom Dorian Gray*, 112.
164 **"people have become more tolerant":** Quoted in Marhoefer, *Sex and the Weimar Republic*, 30.
165 **"women who prefer to appear":** Quoted in Marhoefer, *Sex and the Weimar Republic*, 55.
165 **"they keep their [true] sexual nature":** Magnus Hirschfeld, foreword to *Berlins Lesbische Frauen* [Berlin's Lesbian Women], trans. Eliora Hansonbrook (Leipzig: Bruno Gebauer Verlag für Kulturprobleme, 1928), 8.
165 **"the ingrained bias":** Hirschfeld, foreword to *Berlins Lesbische Frauen*, 7.
165 **"love that is sacred":** Quoted in Gordon, *Voluptuous Panic*, 112; subsequent quotations from *Voluptuous Panic*, 103.
165 **women made up 36 percent:** Evans, *Coming of the Third Reich*, 127.
165 **queer female population [. . .] one hundred thousand:** Gordon, *Voluptuous Panic*, 109.
166 **"glamorous, elegant dance bar":** Pretzel, *Vom Dorian Gray*, 92.
166 **"treason":** Pretzel, *Vom Dorian Gray*, 94.
167 **"cheap tinsel":** Curt Moreck quoted in Pretzel, *Vom Dorian Gray*, 69.
167 **"We do it with Brazenness":** Gordon, *Voluptuous Panic*, 103.
167 **"We are different":** Roellig, *Berlins Lesbische Frauen*, trans. by author, 49.
168 **"CLOSED FOR PRIVATE PARTY":** Gordon, *Voluptuous Panic*, 243.
168 **"Frauline Katter":** Letter from Neukölln District Court to Gerd Katter, June 26, 1929, Magnus-Hirschfeld-Gesellschaft, Berlin.
169 **"Like the director":** "Institute for Sexual Science, 1919–1933" (online exhibition).
169 **"strike an It-Girl pose":** Isherwood, *Christopher and His Kind*, 25; subsequent quotations from *Christopher and His Kind* appear on pp. 15–16, 25, 26, 43.
170 **"few places of work":** "Institute for Sexual Science, 1919–1933" (online exhibition).
171 **"homosexual seduction [. . .] inborn predisposition":** Quoted in Marhoefer, *Sex and the Weimar Republic*, 15.
171 **Parties committed to democracy:** Evans, *Coming of the Third Reich*, 88.
172 **exchange rate stood:** Peter Gay, *Weimar Culture: The Outsider as Insider* (New York: W. W. Norton, 1968), 152–53.
172 **finally the trillions:** Richard J. Evans, *The Third Reich in Power* (New York: Penguin Press, 2005), 5.
172 **the paper had cost:** Evans, *Coming of the Third Reich*, 106.
173 **"Jewish November revolution":** Marhoefer, *Sex and the Weimar Republic*, 28.
173 **"'Jewish' republic":** Peter Gay, introduction to the Norton Paperback Edition," *Weimar Culture: The Outsider as Insider* (New York: W. W. Norton, 2001), vi.
173 **"died in Munich":** "Kill Dr. M. Hirschfeld," *New York Times*, Oct. 12, 1920.
174 **"has not found his well-deserved end":** Charlotte Wolff, *Magnus Hirschfeld: A Portrait of a Pioneer in Sexology* (London: Quartet Books, 1986), 198.
174 **"The Apostle of Sodomy":** Ralf Dose, *Magnus Hirschfeld and the Origins of the Gay Liberation Movement*, trans. Edward Willis (New York: Monthly Review Press, 2014), 35.
174 **"to destroy us":** Eberhard Jäckel and Axel Kuhn, eds. *Hitler: Sämtliche Aufzeichnungen, 1905–1924* [Hitler: All Records], trans. by the author (Stuttgart: Deutsche Verlags-Anstalt, 1980),

248–49, 286.

174 **"Confused by the mass":** Adolf Hitler, *Mein Kampf*, trans. E. T. S. Dugdale (Boston: Houghton Mifflin, 1933), 16.

175 **"The writers were—Jews":** Adolf Hitler, *Mein Kampf*, trans. Ralph Manheim (Boston: Houghton Mifflin, 1971), 58.

175 **"Was there any shady undertaking":** Adolf Hitler, *Mein Kampf*, trans. by James Murphy (London: Hurst and Blackett, 1939), 42.

176 **"against prostitution":** Quoted in Wolff, *Magnus Hirschfeld*, 235.

176 **"belonged to one race":** Quoted in Wolff, *Magnus Hirschfeld*, 237.

176 **headline called him a "homosexual":** "Institute for Sexual Science, 1919–1933" (online exhibition).

177 **"Finally a practical proposal":** Evans, *Coming of the Third Reich*, 224.

Chapter 11: On-the-Run Tour

178 **a vote of fifteen to thirteen:** Robert Beachy, *Gay Berlin: Birthplace of a Modern Identity* (New York: Alfred A. Knopf, 2014), 220.

179 **"We congratulate you":** Robert Plant, *The Pink Triangle: The Nazi War Against Homosexuals* (New York: New Republic Books/Henry Holt, 1986), 49.

179 **three Communist Party members:** Laurie Marhoefer, *Sex and the Weimar Republic* (Toronto: University of Toronto Press, 2015), 128; subsequent quotations from *Sex and the Weimar Republic* appear on pp. 113, 116, 121, 129, 151–52.

182 **Half of the financial institutions:** Plant, *The Pink Triangle*, 25.

182 **43 percent:** Richard J. Evans, *The Coming of the Third Reich* (New York: Penguin Press, 2004), 243.

183 **"Among the many evil instincts":** Plant, *The Pink Triangle*, 49.

184 **"turned their cameras":** Quoted in Laurie Marhoefer, *Racism and the Making of Gay Rights: A Sexologist, His Student, and the Empire of Queer Love* (Toronto: University of Toronto Press, 2022), 26.

184 **"Dr. Hirschfeld advocates birth control":** "Germany Settled All but 50 Claims," *New York Times*, Nov. 23, 1930.

184 **photograph Hirschfeld over a hundred times:** Marhoefer, *Racism and Gay Rights*, 27.

186 **"the humiliations [. . .] safety valve":** Associated Negro Press, "American Whites Dance for Sexual Gratification, Negroes for Joy of Living," reprinted in *Northwest Enterprise* (Seattle), Feb. 19, 1931.

187 **"the largest Negro city":** Magnus Hirschfeld, *Women East and West: Impressions of a Sex Expert* (London, William Heinemann, 1935), 4.

187 **"color of milk [. . .] one can barely":** Quoted in Marhoefer, *Racism and Gay Rights*, 103.

188 **"miscegenation":** Associated Negro Press, "American Whites Dance."

188 **120 gallons of ice cream:** "The Stevens Is Opened, A Hotel of Superlatives," *Chicago Tribune*, May 3, 1927.

189 **"subscribed to German homophile magazines":** Henry Gerber, "The Society for Human Rights—1925" in *Gay American History*, ed. Jonathan Katz, (New York: Thomas Y. Cromwell Co., 1976), 388.

189 **"the same name":** Gerber, in *Gay American History*, 388.

189 **"to combat the public prejudices":** Quoted in St. Sukie de la Croix, *Chicago Whispers: A History of LGBT Chicago Before Stonewall* (Madison: University of Wisconsin Press, 2012), 76.

190 **"Strange Sex Cult Exposed":** Jonathan Katz, *Gay American History*, 391.

190 **"conduct unbecoming":** John H. Bartlett quoted in St. Sukie de la Croix, *Chicago Whispers*, 83.

190 **"Berlin Youth, 22":** St. Sukie de la Croix, *Chicago Whispers*, 72.

190 **"In Defense of Homosexuality":** St. Sukie de la Croix, *Chicago Whispers*, 67.

190 **"Europe's Greatest Sex Authority":** Advertisement, Midwest MS Dill Pickle Box 1, Folder 71, Newberry Library, Chicago.

191 **"Step high [. . .] blasphemy!":** St. Sukie de la Croix, *Chicago Whispers*, 65, 66.

191 **"Our enemies are powerful":** Magnus Hirschfeld, "Through Science to Justice," *Earth* 1, no. 6 (Mar. 1931): 1–3.

191 **"Ku-Klux-Klan people":** Quoted in Marhoefer, *Racism and Gay Rights*, 108.

192 **"Wild Sex Talk":** Marhoefer, *Racism and Gay Rights*, 27.

192 **"oral copulation":** William N. Eskridge Jr., *Dishonorable Passions: Sodomy Laws in America, 1861–2003* (New York: Viking, 2008), 51.

193 **"fairies":** George Chauncey, *Gay New York: Gender, Urban Culture, and the Making of the Gay Male World, 1890–1940* (New York: Basic Books, 1994), 47.

193 **"Many were in women's clothing":** Quoted in Marhoefer, *Racism and Gay Rights*, 107.

193 **"the fabulously beautiful harbor":** Hirschfeld, *Women East and West*, 3; subsequent quotations from *Women East and West* appear on p. 4.

194 **"land of Walt Whitman [. . .] sanely ordered society":** Quoted in Marhoefer, *Racism and Gay Rights*, 8, 108.

194 **"prominent Long Beach dentist":** "Asama Docks on Way West," *Honolulu Star-Bulletin*, Mar. 10, 1931.

194 **"father, mother, and child":** " 'Einstein of Sex' Here on Way to Orient," *Honolulu Star-Bulletin*, Mar. 11, 1931.

194 **"the fetich of racial attraction":** Hirschfeld, *Women East and West*, 7.

195 **"Can you imagine":** Quoted in David Stannard, *Honor Killing: How the Infamous "Massie Case" Transformed Hawaii* (New York: Viking, 2005), 27.

195 **nearly one in four:** Jonathan Okamura, "Bridges or Barriers: Multiracial Families and Race Relations" in *Multiethnicity and Multiethnic Families: Identity, Development and Resilience*, ed. H. McCubbin et al. (Honolulu: Le'a Publications, 2010), 47.

195 **"a mongrel race":** Quoted in Stannard, *Honor Killing*, 4.

195 **"investigate impartially [. . .] current theories ":** Hirschfeld, *Women East and West*, 6.

196 **there had been 300:** Richard J. Evans, *The Third Reich in Power* (New York: Penguin Press, 2005), 6.

Chapter 12: Full Circle

198 **"shifting more and more":** Magnus Hirschfeld, *Women East and West: Impressions of a Sex Expert* (London: William Heinemann, 1935), 4; subsequent quotations from *Women East and West* appear on pp. 11, 29, 30, 31, 32, 34.

200 **"the world's foremost authority":** Laurie Marhoefer, *Racism and the Making of Gay Rights: A Sexologist, His Student, and the Empire of Queer Love* (Toronto: University of Toronto Press, 2022), 55.

201 **"deep pity":** Hirschfeld, *Women East and West*, 42; subsequent quotations from *Women East and West* appear on pp. 40, 46, 49, 58, 63, 64.

205 **"existence of foreign-controlled areas":** "Hirschfeld Hits Foreigners Idea of Superiority," *China Press* (Shanghai), June 11, 1931.

205 **"unmasks itself so nakedly":** Hirschfeld, *Women East and West*, 69; subsequent quotations from *Women East and West* appear on pp. 42, 49, 88.

207 **more than three nautical miles:** "Prohibition: The High Seas," *Time*, May 5, 1923.

207 **"equal to the greatest":** Daniel Burnham, "The Plan of Manila" in Charles Moore, *Daniel H. Burnham* (New York: Da Capo Press, 1968), 195.

207 **"little brown brothers [. . .] Catholic convent":** Stanley Karnow, *In Our Image: America's Empire in the Philippines* (New York: Random House, 1989), 9, 14.

208 **"American territory is closed":** Hirschfeld, *Women East and West*, 100; subsequent quotations from *Women East and West* appear on pp. 92, 94, 101, 107, 108.

210 **hundred-pound stone phallus:** Ralf Dose, *Magnus Hirschfeld and the Origins of the Gay Liberation Movement*, trans. Edward Willis (New York: Monthly Review Press, 2014), 62.

211 **"pent-up emotions":** Magnus Hirschfeld, *Women East and West*, 140; subsequent quotations from *Women East and West* appear on pp. 143, 144, 149, 155.

213 **"Vatsayana of the West":** Elena Mancini, *Magnus Hirschfeld and the Quest for Sexual Freedom* (New York: Palgrave Macmillan, 2010), 134.
213 **"the third natural sex":** Hirschfeld, *Women East and West*, 177; subsequent quotations from *Women East and West* appear on pp. 151, 162, 165, 166, 173, 189.
215 **"the student I have sought":** Quoted in Dose, *Magnus Hirschfeld and Gay Liberation*, 61.
215 **"my manuscripts and money":** Magnus Hirschfeld, *Testament. Heft II*, ed. Ralf Dose (Berlin: Hentrich und Hentrick, 2013), 126.
215 **"Many men were dressed":** Hirschfeld, *Women East and West*, 192; subsequent quotations from *Women East and West* appear on pp. 163, 164, 202, 205, 206, 214, 251, 261.
219 **"I'd like to see":** Quoted in Dose, *Magnus Hirschfeld and Gay Liberation*, 62.
219 **"Germany ought to return it":** Hirschfeld, *Women East and West*, 245; subsequent quotations from *Women East and West* appear on pp. 217, 221, 233.
221 **"The prohibition of undressing":** Quoted in Shayna Weiss "A Beach of Their Own: The Creation of the Gender-Segregated Beach in Tel Aviv," *Journal of Israeli History* 35, no. 1 (2016), 39–56.
221 **"swimmers of both sexes":** Quoted in Marhoefer, *Racism and Gay Rights*, 113.
221 **"loitered":** Hirschfeld, *Women East and West*, 278; subsequent quotations from *Women East and West* appear on pp. 271, 273, 283.
224 **nearly half of Berlin's doctors:** "Exclusion and Forced Displacement at the Charité: Persecuted Colleagues 1933–1945," Charité Memorial (Berlin) website (accessed July 17, 2024).
224 **most of the city's lawyers:** Topography of Terror (standing exhibition), Berlin (2023).
224 **less than 4 percent:** "Germany: Jewish Population in 1933," *Holocaust Encyclopedia*, United States Holocaust Memorial Museum website (accessed June 11, 2024).
224 **"from the director to the bootblack":** Hirschfeld, *Women East and West*, 268; subsequent quotations from *Women East and West* appear on pp. 273, 275, 277.
225 **"Zionism and the assimilation":** Magnus Hirschfeld, *Racism*, ed. and trans. Eden Paul and Cedar Paul (London: Victor Gollancz, 1938), 235.
225 **"the highest diplomacy":** Hirschfeld, *Women East and West*, 294.
225 **"sex is the basic principle":** Hirschfeld, *Women East and West*, 304.
225 **"'world citizen,' or 'all three'":** Quoted in Marhoefer, *Racism and Gay Rights*, 119.

Chapter 13: Exile

227 **"a German so-called Professor":** Panayiotis Vyras, "Magnus Hirschfeld in Greece," *Journal of Homosexuality* 34, no. 1 (1997): 17–29; subsequent information and quotations from "Magnus Hirschfeld in Greece" appear in the following paragraphs.
227 **"an entirely different opinion":** Quoted in Vyras, "Magnus Hirschfeld in Greece."
227 **"Jewish propaganda":** Vyras, "Magnus Hirschfeld in Greece."
227 **"arrived to our city":** Vyras, "Magnus Hirschfeld in Greece."
228 **"Aunt Magnesia":** Quoted in Laurie Marhoefer, *Racism and the Making of Gay Rights: A Sexologist, His Student, and the Empire of Queer Love* (Toronto: University of Toronto Press, 2022), 154.
229 **"his time has run out":** Ralf Dose, *Magnus Hirschfeld and the Origins of the Gay Liberation Movement*, trans. Edward Willis (New York: Monthly Review Press, 2014), 63.
229 **"abhorrent hypocrisy":** Laurie Marhoefer, *Sex and the Weimar Republic: German Homosexual Emancipation and the Rise of the Nazis* (Toronto: University of Toronto Press, 2015), 157.
229 **"the Germans have forgotten":** Quoted in Richard J. Evans, *The Coming of the Third Reich* (New York: Penguin Press, 2004), 183.
230 **printed three hundred thousand times:** Marhoefer, *Sex and the Weimar Republic*, 158.
230 **"the record of sexual type":** Quoted in Marhoefer, *Racism and Gay Rights*, 155.
231 **"Heil Hitler!":** Marhoefer, *Sex and the Weimar Republic*, 147.
231 **"Isidor":** Evans, *Coming of the Third Reich*, 207.
231 **"not an institute":** Richard Plant, *The Pink Triangle: The Nazi War Against Homosexuals* (New York: Henry Holt and Co., 1986), 61.
232 **"with its 13 million":** Quoted in Marhoefer, *Racism and Gay Rights*, 156.

232 **"a 'foreigner' ":** Quoted in Dose, *Magnus Hirschfeld*, 63.

232 **"homeland" (*Heimat*):** Magnus Hirschfeld, *Testament. Heft II*, ed. Ralf Dose (Berlin: Hentrich und Hentrick, 2013), 136.

232 **"extensive campaign":** Andreas Pretzel, *Vom Dorian Gray zum Eldorado* [From Dorian Gray to Eldorado] (Berlin: MANEO, 2012), 120.

233 **"embracing the world":** Veronika Fuechtner, "Indians, Jews, and Sex: Magnus Hirschfeld and Indian Sexology" in *Imagining Germany Imagining Asia: Essays in Asian-German Studies* (Rochester, NY: Camden House, 2013), 127.

233 **over a dozen of the capital's:** Robert Beachy, *Gay Berlin: Birthplace of a Modern Identity* (New York: Random House, 2014), 244.

234 **"For once, no joke":** Quoted in Evans, *Coming of the Third Reich*, 403–4.

234 **"One can't gobble":** Quoted in Evans, *Coming of the Third Reich*, 415.

235 **"the humiliation and debasement":** Quoted in Marhoefer, *Racism and Gay Rights*, 109.

235 **1.6 million Germans:** Evans, *Coming of the Third Reich*, 382.

233 **more than doubled under:** Evans, *Third Reich in Power* (New York: Penguin Press, 2005), 13–14.

235 **"patriotically-minded":** Quoted in Evans, *Third Reich in Power*, 22.

235 **"arrangement with the Nazis":** Pretzel, *Vom Dorian Gray*, 8.

236 **"For a freedom-loving person":** Quoted in Marhoefer, *Racism and Gay Rights*, 109.

236 **"raped":** Charlotte Wolff, *Magnus Hirschfeld: A Portrait of a Pioneer in Sexology* (London: Quartet Books, 1986), 377.

236 **"books of un-German spirit":** World Committee for the Victims of German Fascism, *The Brown Book of the Hitler Terror* (New York: Alfred A. Knopf, 1933), 158.

237 **"German Students March":** "Institute for Sexual Science, 1919–1933" (online exhibition), Magnus-Hirschfeld-Gesellschaft (Berlin) (accessed Jan. 11, 2022).

237 **"Dr. Magnus Hirschfeld is not home":** Quoted in Marhoefer, *Sex and the Weimar Republic*, 174.

238 **"un-German spirit":** "Institute for Sexual Science, 1919–1933" (online exhibition).

238 **seizing over ten thousand volumes:** Plant, *The Pink Triangle*, 43, 51.

238 **"about half a ton of books":** "Nazi Students Raid Institute on Sex; Seize Half a Ton of Scientific Material at Dr. Hirschfeld's Berlin Establishment," *New York Times*, May 7, 1933.

239 **"another part of it":** Quoted in World Committee for the Victims, *The Brown Book*, 161–62.

239 **"Germany's students are planning":** Quoted in Bärbel Schrader and Jürgen Schebera, *The "Golden" Twenties: Art and Literature in the Weimar Republic*, trans. Katherine Vanovitch (New Haven: Yale University Press, 1988), 238.

239 **a crowd of forty thousand:** "Book Burning," *Holocaust Encyclopedia*, United States Holocaust Memorial Museum website (accessed Aug. 8, 2022).

239 **where over ten thousand volumes:** Eden Paul and Cedar Paul in biographical introduction to Magnus Hirschfeld, *Racism*, ed. and trans. Eden Paul and Cedar Paul (London: Victor Gollancz, 1938), 26.

239 **"Burn Now, Magnus Hirschfeld!":** "Wer weiter-liest, wird erschossen" [Anyone Who Reads On Will Be Shot]: Die Bücherverbrennung in Berlin 1933. Exhibition (2023), Humboldt University Law School, Berlin (translation by Eliora Hansonbrook).

239 **thirty-four in all:** Olivia Laing, *Everybody: A Book About Freedom* (New York: W. W. Norton, 2021), 107.

240 **"the terrible fate which has struck":** Quoted in Wolff, *Magnus Hirschfeld*, 379.

240 **"The Auto-da-Fé":** Joseph Roth, *What I Saw: Reports from Berlin, 1920–1933*, trans. Michael Hoffman (New York: W. W. Norton, 2003), 207.

240 **"*pogrom* against advanced literature":** World Committee for the Victims, *The Brown Book*, 165.

240 **"pride of the book burners [. . .] Bibliocaust":** "Germany: Bibliocaust," *Time*, May 22, 1933.

241 **"corruption":** Wolff, *Magnus Hirschfeld*, 380.

241 **25,000 Germans moved:** "Paris in the Interwar Years—Capitale de Refuge," We Refugees—Digital Archive on Refugeedom, Past and Present (accessed Aug. 7, 2022).

242 **"The age of effete Jewish intellectualism":** "Undeutsches Schrifttum auf dem Scheiterhaufen" [Un-German Literature at the Stake], *Völkischer Beobachter*, May 12, 1933 (trans. by author).

242 **"the deepest psychic shock":** Quoted in Marhoefer, *Racism and Gay Rights*, 159.

242 **"racial hygiene":** "Institute for Sexual Science, 1919–1933" (online exhibition) (accessed Aug. 9, 2022).

243 **"the great cleansing":** "Paris Opens Library of Books Burnt by Nazis," *Guardian* (UK), May 10, 1934.

243 **"all writings":** *Liste des schädlichen und unerwünschten Schrifttums* [List of Harmful and Undesirable Literature], trans. by the author (Leipzig: Druck von Ernst Hedrich Nackf, 1938), 59.

245 **"It is hard to be dispassionate":** Hirschfeld, *Racism*, 35; subsequent quotations and information from *Racism* appear on pp. 61, 102, 198–99, 237, 241, 242, 251, 254, 264.

247 **one third of Jews:** Magnus Hirschfeld, *Women East and West: Impressions of a Sex Expert* (London: William Heinemann, 1935), 299.

247 **ratio was similar:** Evans, *Coming of the Third Reich*, 23.

247 **over 70 percent:** Hirschfeld, *Women East and West*, 299.

248 **"a trustworthy blood-test":** Hirschfeld, *Racism*, 62; subsequent quotations from *Racism* appear on pp. 35, 108, 201, 206–7, 213, 294, 296, 302.

251 **"an unlucky circumstance":** Quoted in Marhoefer, *Racism and Gay Rights*, 160.

251 **over two million:** Evans, *Third Reich in Power*, 14, 22.

251 **"Re-armament is too serious":** Plant, *The Pink Triangle*, 63.

252 **perhaps eighty-five in all:** Beachy, *Gay Berlin*, 245.

252 **twelve who were sitting Nazi members:** Evans, *Third Reich in Power*, 40.

252 **"fair-haired boy [. . .] catamites":** Quoted in Evans, *Third Reich in Power*, 32, 37.

252 **"I expect all SA leaders":** Quoted in Plant, *The Pink Triangle*, 67.

252 **"symptom of dying races":** Quoted in Evans, *Third Reich in Power*, 530; subsequent quotations and information from *Third Reich in Power* appear on pp. 331, 532, 533.

253 **"He introduced the oriental vice":** Quoted in Hirschfeld, *Racism*, 152.

253 **"Röhm's 'notorious sexual perversion,' ":** Hirschfeld, *Racism*, 152–53.

255 **twenty thousand "friends of the New Germany":** Tom Reiss, *The Orientalist: Solving the Mystery of a Strange and Dangerous Life* (New York: Random House, 2005), 288.

255 **"live to see this":** Quoted in Dose, *Magnus Hirschfeld*, 67.

256 **"My wishes regarding my burial:":** Quoted in Dose, *Magnus Hirschfeld*, 67.

256 **eight thousand Berlin Jews:** Memorial to the Murdered Jews of Europe (standing exhibition), Berlin (2023).

Epilogue: A Life's Work, Interrupted

259 **"anti-racists":** Magnus Hirschfeld, *Racism*, ed. and trans. Eden Cedar and Paul Cedar (London: Victor Gollancz, 1938), 292; subsequent quotations from *Racism* appear on pp. 5, 21, 23, 264, 305–6.

260 **"cultural decay":** Gerhard Ritter quoted in Laurie Marhoefer, *Sex and the Weimar Republic: German Homosexual Emancipation and the Rise of the Nazis* (Toronto: University of Toronto Press, 2015), 10.

261 **"nobody takes it":** Otto Friedrich, *Before the Deluge: A Portrait of Berlin in the 1920s* (New York: Harper & Row, 1972), 252–53, 410.

261 **"Max":** Otto Friedrich, *Before the Deluge: A Portrait of Berlin in the 1920s* (New York: HarperPerennial, 1995), 252–53, 410.

262 **"anti-racist":** Hirschfeld, *Racism*, 292; Ibram X. Kendi, *How to Be an Antiracist* (New York: One World, 2019).

262 **"race is the child of racism":** Ta-Nehisi Coates, *Between the World and Me* (New York: Spiegel & Grau, 2015), 7.

262 **"In the middle of this square":** Bebelplatz memorial (standing exhibition), Berlin (visited July 7, 2023) (trans. by the author).

ILLUSTRATION CREDITS

INDEX

Page numbers in *italic* represent illustrations.